I0793420

IMAGES
of Rail

BOSTON'S ORANGE LINE

ON THE COVER: A 1986 photograph shows an Orange Line train traveling down the old Elevated tracks on Washington Street in Roxbury, with the Hancock Center visible at far left and downtown Boston on the horizon. Elevated trains connected Everett to Roxbury and Jamaica Plain, passing through downtown and the South End, from the early 20th century until the Charlestown Elevated was demolished in 1975. This image is shown in full on page 65. (Photograph by and courtesy of David Akiba.)

IMAGES
of Rail

BOSTON'S ORANGE LINE

Andrew Elder and Jeremy C. Fox

ARCADIA
PUBLISHING

ISBN 978-1-4671-2047-0

Published by Arcadia Publishing
Charleston, South Carolina

Printed in the United States of America

Library of Congress Control Number: 2013936165

For all general information, please contact Arcadia Publishing:
Telephone 843-853-2070
Fax 843-853-0044
E-mail sales@arcadiapublishing.com
For customer service and orders:
Toll-Free 1-888-313-2665

Visit us on the Internet at www.arcadiapublishing.com

To Marsha Kamp Elder and Wanda Jean Fox

Contents

ACKNOWLEDGMENTS

Like any work of its kind, this book is a collaboration between dozens—if not hundreds—of photographers, journalists, historians, and rail enthusiasts, many of whom are no longer with us and could not have foreseen their invaluable contributions to these pages. To all those who recorded the history of the Orange Line and its predecessor and complementary rail lines and their surroundings, we are deeply indebted.

For their patience, forbearance, and guidance, we thank our publisher, Rebekah Collinsworth, and editor, Caitrin Cunningham.

For their assistance in accessing high-quality historical images, we thank Marta Crill at the City of Boston Archives and Tom Blake and Aaron Schmidt at the Boston Public Library.

For their many contributions to this effort and their unflagging support, Andrew would like to thank Joanne Riley, Jessica Holden, Dale Freeman, Carolyn Goldstein, Daniel Ortiz, and all his colleagues in the Joseph P. Healey Library at UMass Boston and Libby Bouvier, Neal Kane, and all his friends at The History Project. He would especially like to thank his family: Harris J. Elder, Jacob and Betsey Elder, Lucas Wesley Elder, and Jean and Paul Garvey.

For their wisdom, support, and patience while he was preoccupied with the effort to complete this manuscript, Jeremy would like to thank Roy Greene, David Dahl, David Jrolf, Janet Walsh, Dean Inouye, Steve Smith, David Filipov, Anica Butler, and all the journalists at the *Boston Globe* who have taught him so much. He would also like to thank June Carolyn Erlick, Angelia Herrin, Jenifer McKim, and Charles Sennott—all talented journalists who have generously shared their wisdom at the Harvard Extension School. And he would like to thank his family: Dale and Debbie Tully, Brandon Tully, and Kirsten Tully.

Very special thanks to Leo Sullivan and Frank Cheney, who patiently reviewed the manuscript.

For allowing us to use images from their personal collections and for answering questions we had along the way, we would like to thank the following people: David Akiba, Joe Boncek, Gene and Justyna Carlson, Frank Cheney, Tom Ericson, Ann Hershfang, Janet Hunkel, Wayne Jackson and FayFoto/Boston, Paul Locke, Andrew Lynch, Nathaniel Marsh, Steve Quinn, Anthony Mitchell Sammarco, Martha Stone, Otto M. Vondrak, and Andrew Zalewski.

Introduction

In 1987, as Boston prepared for the Washington Street Elevated's closing and the opening of a new Orange Line submerged along the Southwest Corridor, Martin F. Nolan, editor of the *Boston Globe*'s editorial page, summarized the El's impact on the Washington Street corridor:

> The squeal begins on baritone, then escalates to soprano, a giant fingernail scratching a blackboard. The sound moves with a massive shadow 30 feet above the sidewalk that blots out all light, then rumbles into a thumping clickety-clack, its echo reverberating along steel girders down the track. This teeth-chattering ritual occurs every time an Orange Line train negotiates a curve around Dudley Street—336 times a day, flooding the streets below with noise, darkness, and confusion. Silence, then light, will soon rule Washington Street from Forest Hills to Chinatown as the El ends its 86-year reign.

The Orange Line is now part of the Massachusetts Bay Transportation Authority (MBTA) and is one of five color-coded transit lines that provide an average of 1.3 million passenger trips each week. The rapid-transit line that would become today's Orange Line opened in 1901 and was then managed by the Boston Elevated Railway Company, a private enterprise established in 1894 with the support of the Massachusetts Legislature to oversee construction and management of this new electric rail service.

In 1897, the West End Railway Company, which managed Boston's electrified streetcar service, was absorbed by the Boston Elevated Railway, which would oversee the city's rail transit for the next 50 years. That same year, the first subway system in the United States opened in Boston, running beneath Tremont Street adjacent to Boston Common. Four years later, the first elevated trains began offering service from Charlestown to Roxbury.

The Main Line Elevated, the rail service that would, in 1966, become the Orange Line, opened in 1901 with its northern terminus at Sullivan Square, located at the northern edge of Boston's Charlestown neighborhood between its border with the city of Somerville and the Mystic River. From there, trains rode the Charlestown Elevated down the neighborhood's Main Street, crossed the Charlestown Bridge into downtown Boston, and entered the Tremont Street Subway, a tunnel it then shared with the streetcar line that would become the Green Line. Trains emerged from the tunnel at the Pleasant Street Incline, in the Bay Village neighborhood, and proceeded from there south down the Washington Street Elevated tracks, through the South End and Roxbury, to the southern terminus in Dudley Square.

Running a different route through downtown Boston—but connected to the Charlestown and Washington Street legs of the Elevated—was the Atlantic Avenue Elevated, which opened shortly after the Main Line. This route arced through Chinatown and the Leather District, past South Station, and along the downtown waterfront to a junction with the Charlestown Elevated at the foot of the Charlestown Bridge. The Charlestown Elevated gained an intermediate station at Thompson Square in 1902, and the Elevated saw major changes in 1908. On November 30 that year, the new Washington Street Tunnel opened, giving Main Line trains their own underground route through downtown and returning the Tremont Street Subway to streetcar use only. The Washington Street Tunnel, descending into the ground at the Canal Street Incline just north of Haymarket Square and emerging through the Ash Street Incline in the South Cove area, included four new underground stations oriented in the downtown area along Washington Street.

A year later, the southern end of the Washington Street Elevated was extended from Dudley Square to the Forest Hills area of Jamaica Plain, with an intermediate station at Egleston Square where Washington Street crosses Columbus Avenue. An additional stop was added at Green Street, between Egleston and Forest Hills, in 1912.

In 1919, the Charlestown Elevated was extended to Everett, with plans to eventually bring elevated service to Malden Center and beyond. The Charlestown El never would extend to Malden, but in 1975, the northern leg of the Orange Line was rerouted to the west, Malden Center was introduced as a stop, and the Charlestown El was dismantled.

In 1938, after years of declining ridership, accidents, and decreasing interest in and activity along Boston's waterfront caused by the Great Depression, the Atlantic Avenue El ceased operation, taking with it the last elevated railway through downtown.

The absence of elevated transportation through the city's financial center would not last long, however; in the 1950s, motor vehicles began traveling to and through Boston using the elevated John F. Fitzgerald Expressway, or Central Artery, which ran along much of the same Atlantic Avenue route previously occupied by the Elevated. The elevated Central Artery would dominate downtown Boston for nearly 50 years until its route was moved underground by the $14.6-billion Central Artery/Tunnel Project (more commonly known as the Big Dig).

In 1947, the Commonwealth of Massachusetts purchased the Boston Elevated Railway Company and, through the establishment of the Metropolitan Transportation Authority, or MTA, made rapid transit in the Boston metropolitan area a publicly owned amenity.

The MTA became the Massachusetts Bay Transportation Authority in 1964 and remained publicly operated. The MBTA quickly began making significant and lasting changes to the transit system serving Greater Boston. In 1965, it introduced the "Circle-T" emblem, or the "T," as the symbol and the transit system became popularly known.

The emblem was modeled after the graphic used for the Stockholm, Sweden, transit system, which remains in use today. At the time the new emblem was announced, there was discussion in the Boston press about how riders would interpret this new symbol of the MBTA, with some suggesting that it would become known as the "Big T."

This new emblem, part of an MBTA modernization program that eventually cost $9 million, was also an effort for the MBTA to further distance itself from its predecessor, the MTA. An MBTA spokesman at the time said: "We would appreciate your seeking clever ways to use the 'T' to identify us . . . and we hope the symbol will become a natural expression as was the 'El.'" Despite these early efforts, the authority continues to be known both as the MBTA and the T, with the terms used interchangeably.

Simultaneous with the introduction of the new emblem, the MBTA announced that the major lines of Boston's transit system would become color coded. The new designations were not implemented until 1966, when the line to East Boston became the Blue Line, the route between Ashmont and Harvard Square Stations became the Red Line (the extensions to Porter and Davis squares and Alewife would not be introduced until the mid-1980s), the trolley lines between Lechmere and points west became the Green Line, and the route between Forest Hills and Everett—the southern and northern termini for the Elevated route in 1966—became the Orange Line. A fifth, the Silver Line, opened in 2002, serving as a long-desired but sometimes maligned rapid bus route.

The Charlestown Elevated was closed and dismantled in 1975, a time when some community members could still remember the first wooden train cars that ran through Charlestown in 1901. According to Boston newspapers at the time of its dismantling, community efforts to remove the Charlestown Elevated were almost as old as the structure itself.

In 1908, just seven years after the Elevated opened, Charlestown residents unsuccessfully petitioned the Massachusetts Legislature to have the railway removed. Such early efforts would not start to pay off until the 1960s, when plans to reroute the Orange Line to the west started to take hold. The Haymarket North Extension would take the line underground at North Station, through a tunnel below the Charles River, and through Charlestown partly beneath an elevated Interstate 93.

One factor in the route change and demolition of the Elevated in Charlestown was the effort to revive the residential and commercial areas along the railway. The population of Charlestown had reached about 40,000 in 1900, just prior to the El's construction. By 1960, though, that population had been cut nearly in half. Many believed this decline was at least partly caused by the El's shadowy route down the neighborhood's Main Street.

At the same time that the state was making plans to remove an unpopular elevated railway in Charlestown at the northern end of Boston, it was planning a new superhighway network that would have cut through the southern neighborhoods of Jamaica Plain, Roxbury, and the South End. Through the 1960s and 1970s, plans were developed for the Inner Belt network of highways connecting with the elevated Central Artery that would have torn through parts of Cambridge, Milton, Canton, and much of Boston. The southwest-bound highway through downtown Boston was referred to as the Southwest Expressway and would have extended Interstate 95, after passing through Cambridge to the north, through the South End, Roxbury, and Jamaica Plain.

In 1972, after sustained community protests, Gov. Francis W. Sargent cancelled the Southwest Expressway project. Interstate 95 was instead incorporated into Route 128, an existing highway circling the Boston metro area. Soon after the expressway plans were killed, community members began working with the MBTA to determine the appropriate use of more than 100 acres of land that had been taken by eminent domain to make way for the failed expressway project. This land sat vacant for years and fell into disrepair. The idea of using it as the site of a new route for the Orange Line quickly took hold.

In 1987, the rerouting of the Orange Line from the old Washington Street Elevated to the new Southwest Corridor, created from the abandoned Southwest Expressway, resulted in the removal of the last elevated sections of the railway running through the South End, Roxbury, and Jamaica Plain—taking with them the ornate elevated stations that once served those communities.

The old elevated Orange Line blocked out the sun along Washington Street, but it also connected some of the city's poorest communities with opportunities for education, employment, and shopping in downtown Boston. The loss of that transport is still deeply felt by many it served, even after the introduction of the Silver Line, which serves communities that lost ready access to rapid transit with the dismantling of the Washington Street El.

Boston and its Orange Line have come a long way from that day in June 1901 when the first train ran on the original Elevated tracks between Dudley and Sullivan Squares. A reporter for the *Boston Globe* summed up the excitement at the time of that momentous expansion of rapid transit: "There will doubtless be a great many lame necks in Boston tonight, for not only were the first trains watched from the sidewalks, housetops, and windows of houses and stores along the line of the road, but the passengers were equally curious to see how Boston looked from the air."

One

The Boston Elevated Railway

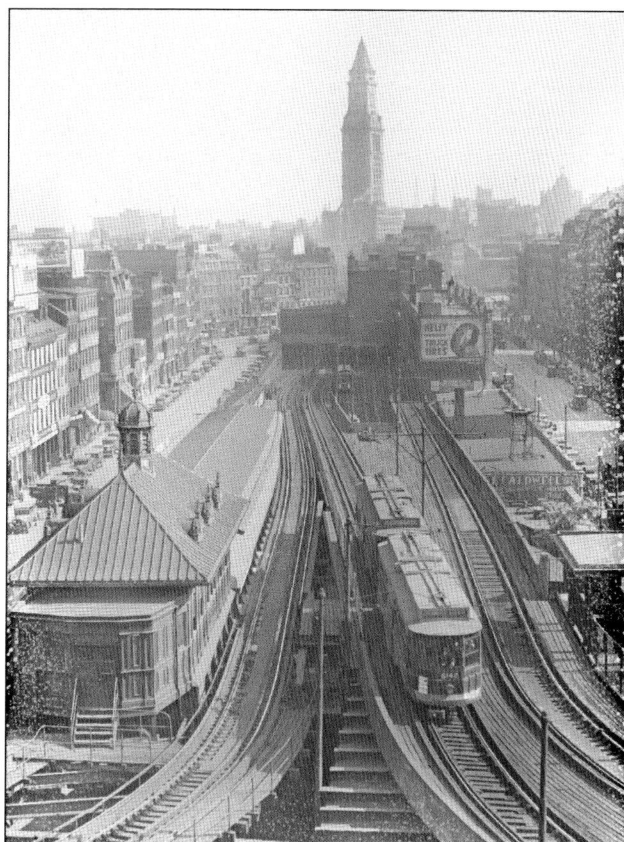

The old elevated North Station stood at the intersection of Causeway and North Washington Streets, serving the Charlestown Elevated, the Atlantic Avenue Elevated, and the Causeway Street Elevated. With the tracks at left shared by both the Charlestown and the Atlantic Avenue lines, the busy intersection required considerable attention to avoid collisions. (Courtesy of the Boston Public Library; photograph by Leslie Jones.)

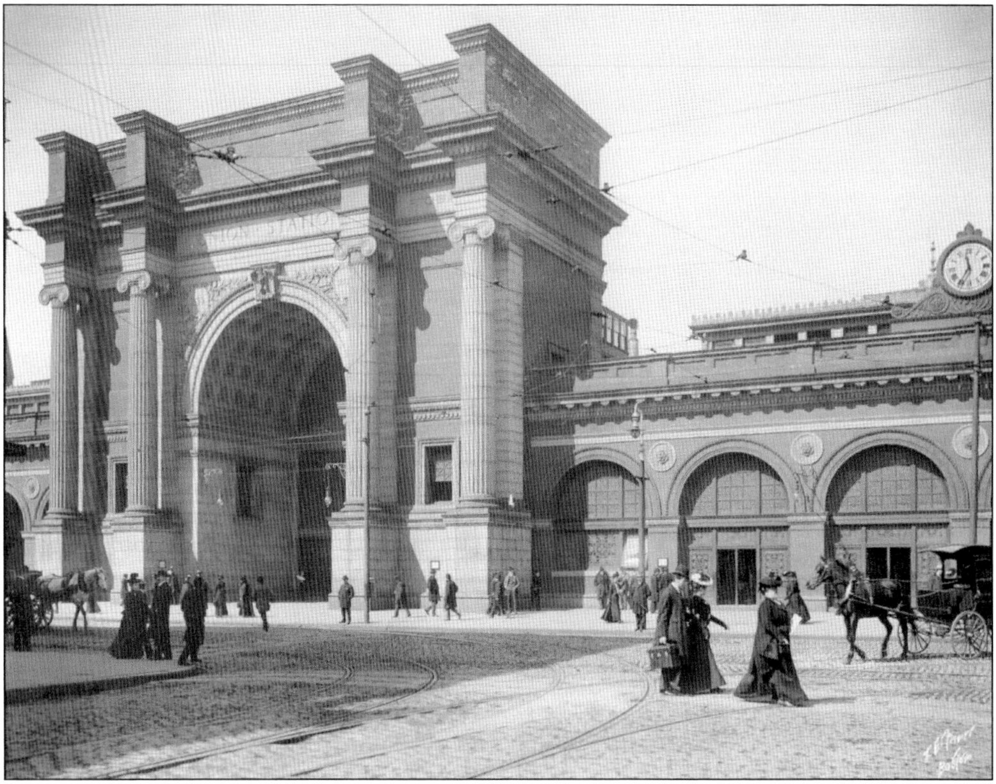

The 1890s image above, by Thomas E. Marr, is of Union Station (sometimes called North Union Station or North Station). Built in 1893 and located on Causeway Street in Boston's West End, Union Station was a major hub for trains going in and out of the city and was the largest station in the world to accommodate a single railroad. Though intended to serve as a temporary structure, the station was in use for 35 years. Union Station was demolished in 1927 and 1928 to make way for the Boston Garden (home to the Boston Bruins hockey team and to the Boston Celtics basketball team, after the Celtics were founded in 1946) and North Station. The image below, by Leslie Jones, shows the Elevated tracks, Boston Garden, and North Station in 1929. (Both, courtesy of the Boston Public Library.)

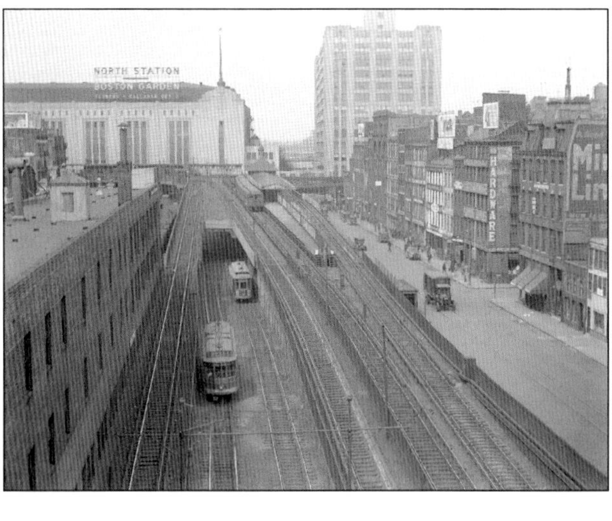

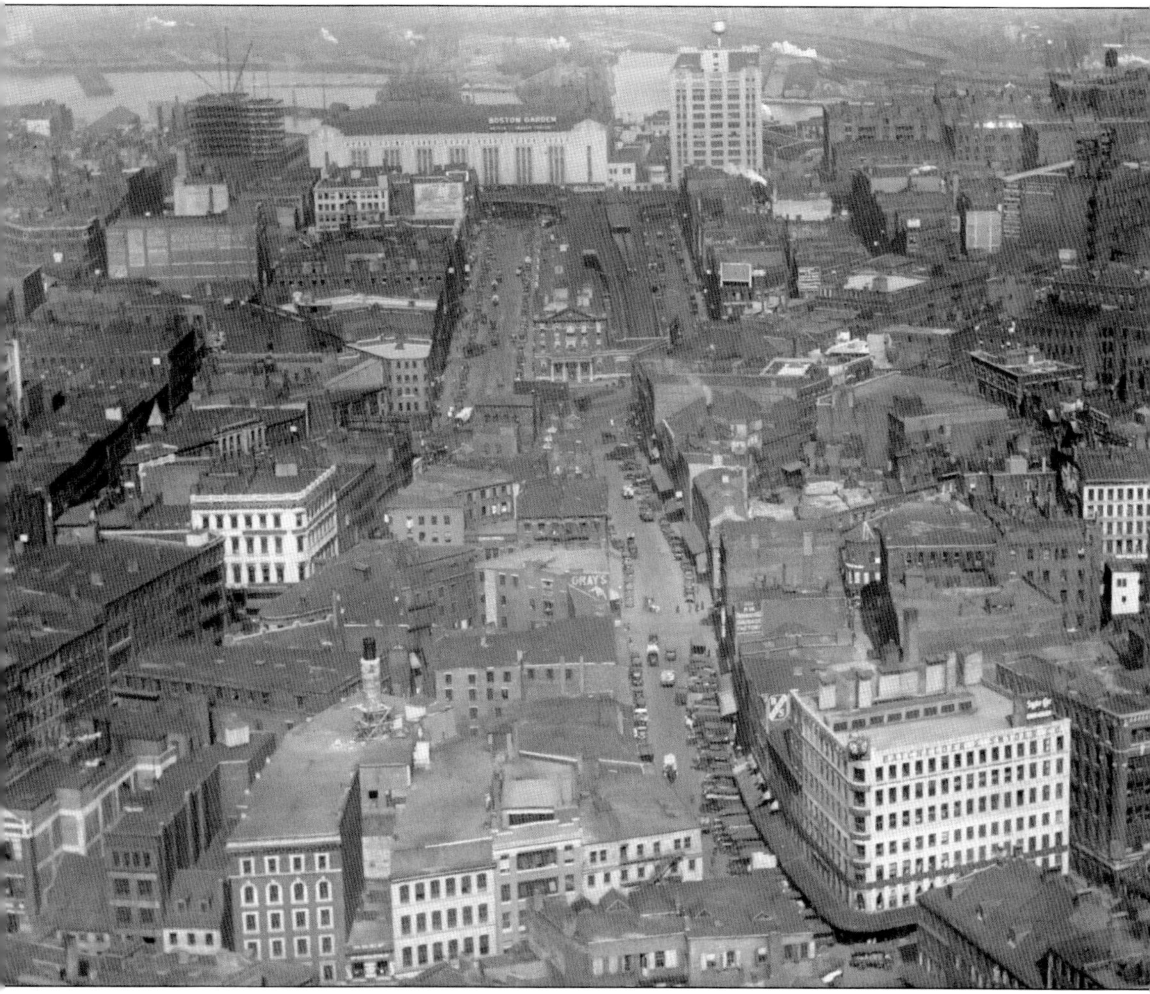

This view from 1929, looking northwest from the Custom House Tower, shows the wider context of the North Station area. The Elevated is visible at center in the upper half of the photograph, emerging from the Washington Street Tunnel between Haverhill and Canal Streets, just beyond Haymarket Square, at the point of the Bulfinch Triangle. (Courtesy of the Boston Public Library; photograph by Leslie Jones.)

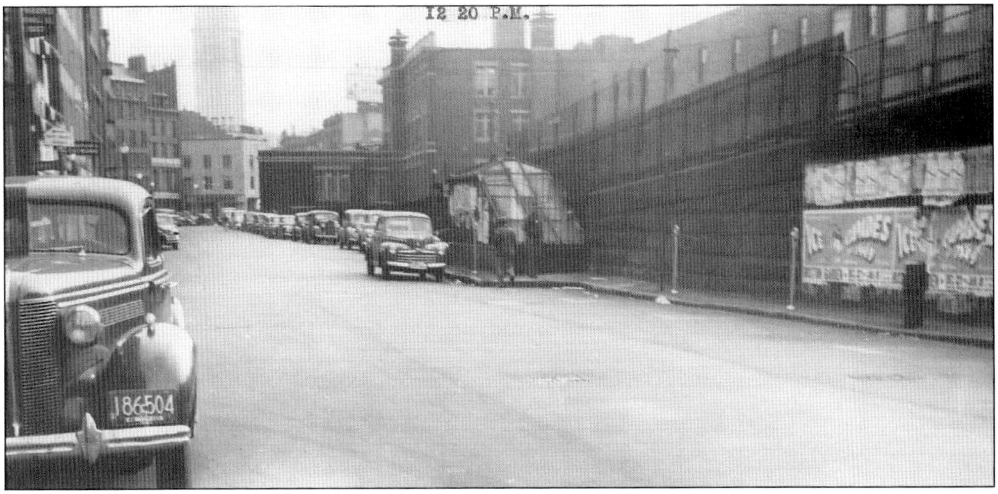

This 1948 image looks southeast down Haverhill Street toward North Washington Street, with the Canal Street Incline at right. At the incline, the Charlestown Elevated, the predecessor to the Orange Line, emerges from the Washington Street tunnel alongside the Tremont Street Subway, the predecessor to the Green Line. (Collection No. 5110.002, City of Boston Archives, Boston.)

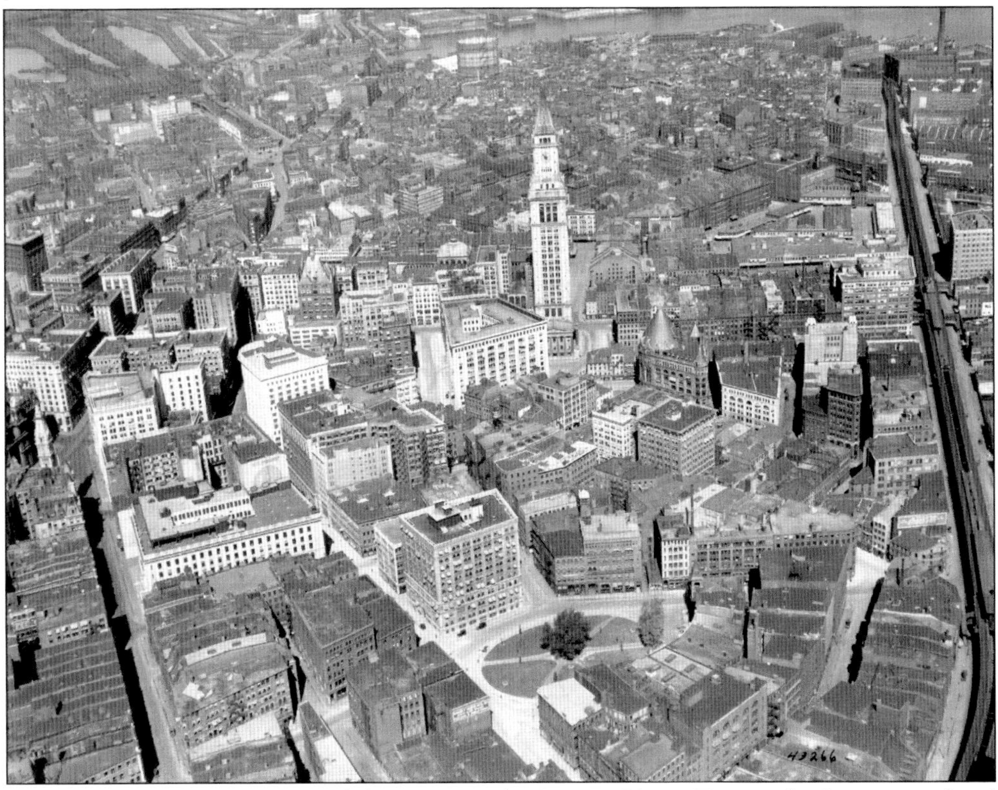

The narrow spire at the center of this image is the Custom House Tower, which was completed in 1918, seven years before this photograph was taken. The Atlantic Avenue El is at far right, cutting a line along the waterfront, and North Station is just visible in the distance at upper left. The circular park in the lower foreground was known as Fort Hill Square. (Courtesy of the Boston Public Library; photograph by Fairchild Aerial Surveys.)

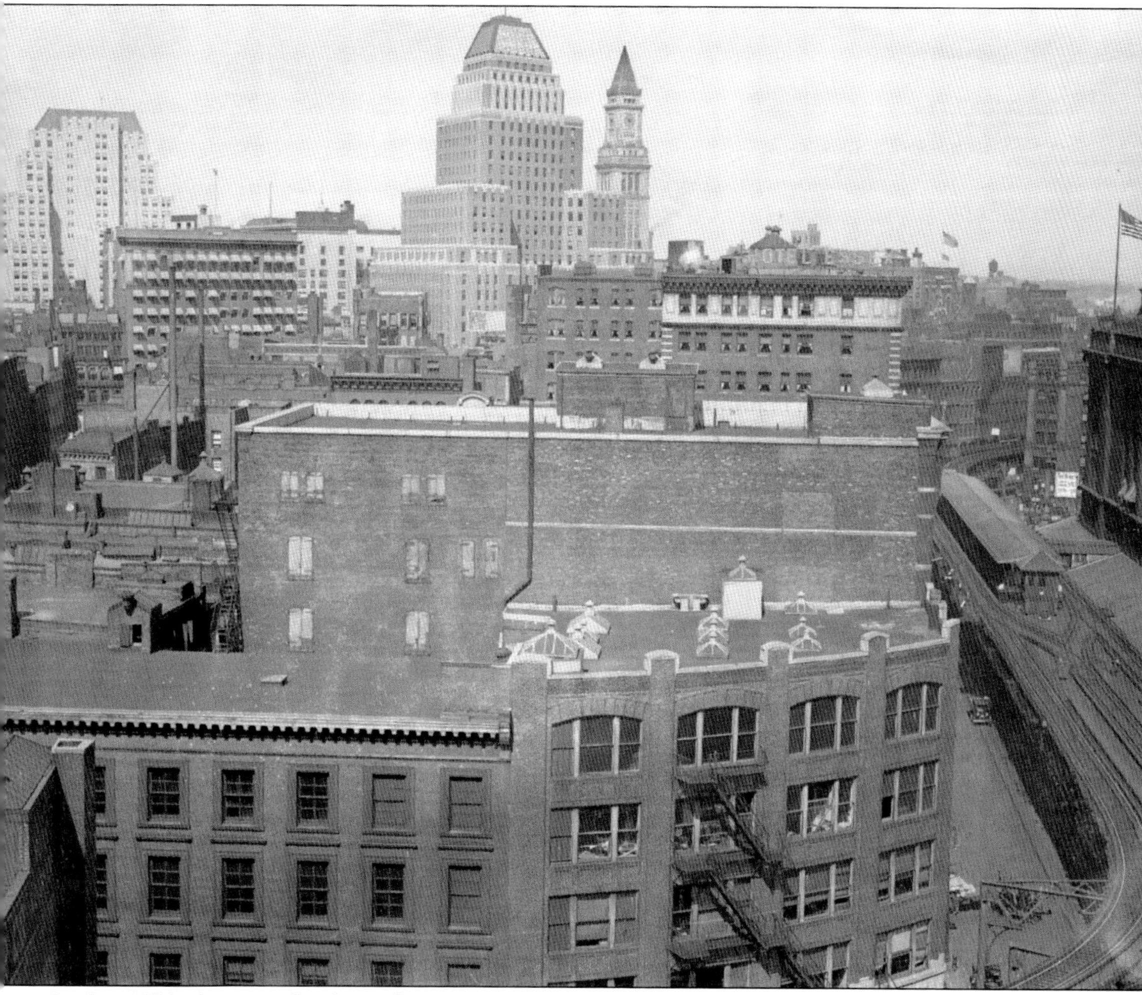

In this 1930 photograph, the Atlantic Avenue El's South Station stop is visible at right. The tallest building at the center of the image is the United Shoe Machinery Corporation Building, completed in 1929 and considered an excellent example of Art Deco architecture. Next to it is the distinctive Custom House Tower. (Courtesy of the Boston Public Library; photograph by Leslie Jones.)

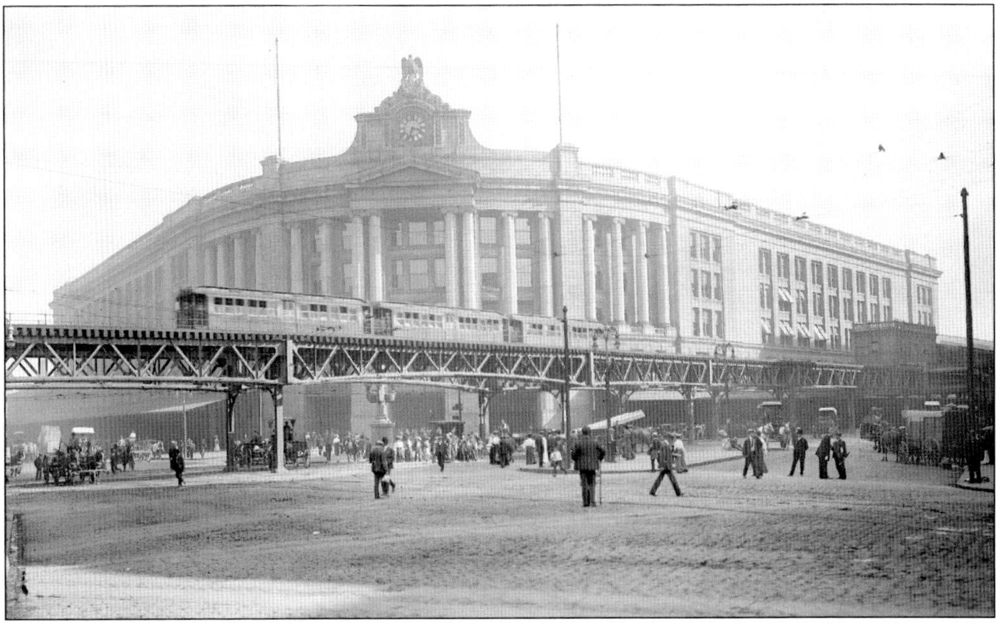

In these c. 1904 photographs, trains and commuters go about their business outside South Station, originally called South Union Station. The station opened in 1899 and quickly became the busiest train station in the United States. Designed by the architectural firm Shepley, Rutan and Coolidge, South Station was added to the National Register of Historic Places in 1975. Today, South Station provides train service to cities around the country as well as local Red Line service as part of the MBTA. As seen in these images, one of the main stops for the Atlantic Avenue Elevated was outside South Station. (Above, courtesy of the Library of Congress, photograph by Detroit Publishing Company; below, courtesy of University Archives & Special Collections, Joseph P. Healey Library, University of Massachusetts Boston: Anthony Mitchell Sammarco Collection.)

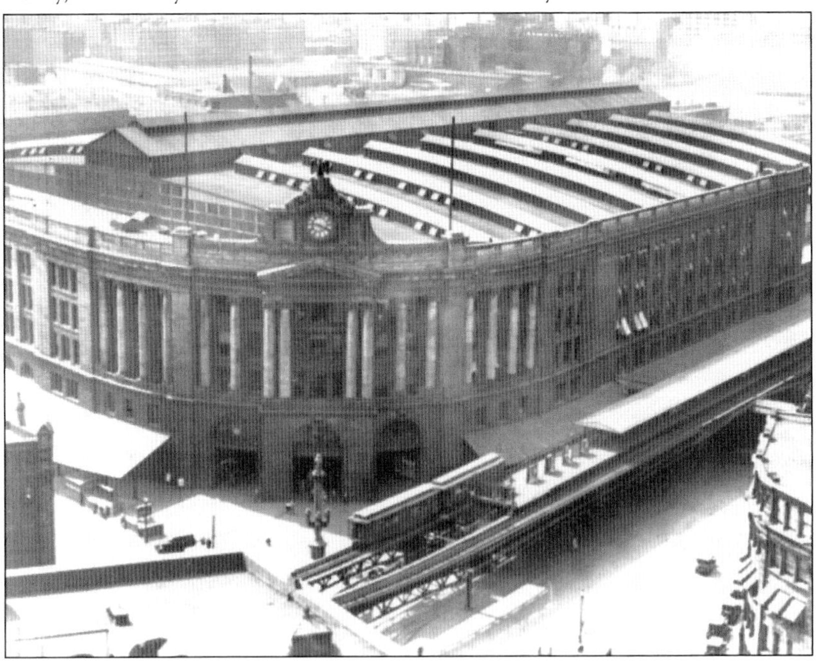

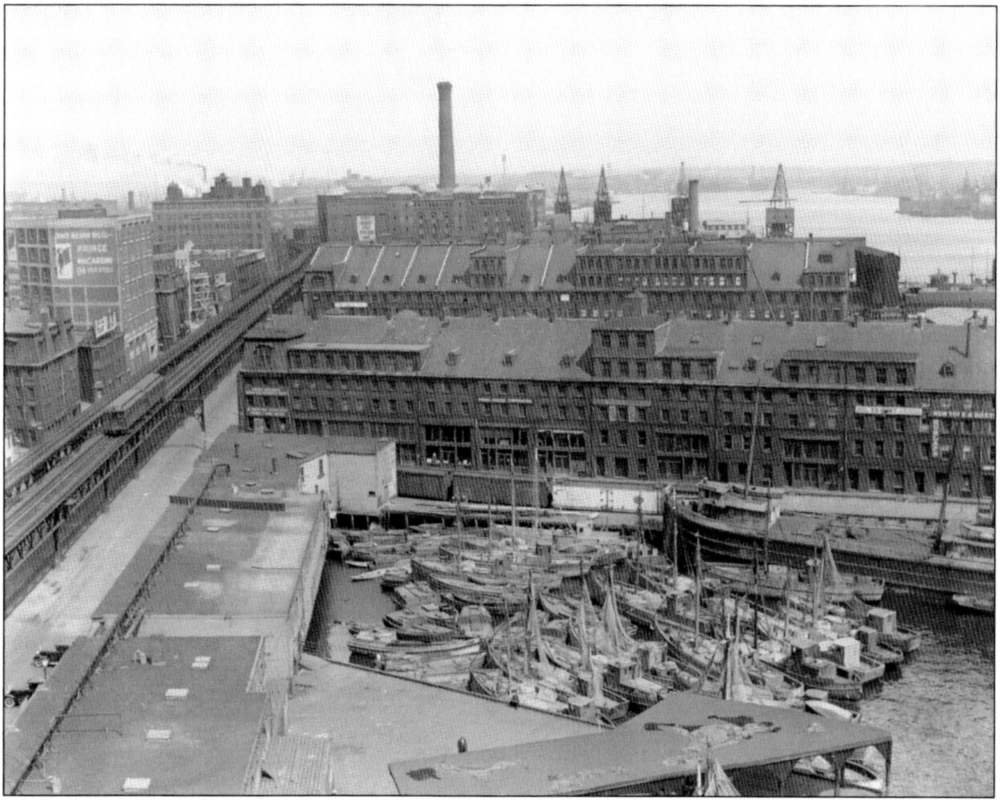

This c. 1930 image shows the Atlantic Avenue Elevated at left; note its proximity to Boston's waterfront and Commercial Wharf, which served vessels transporting cargo to and from Boston. Today, the wharf is home to leisure vessels. The two-car train traveling the tracks may be evidence of the dwindling use of the Atlantic Avenue Elevated in the 1930s. (Courtesy of the Boston Public Library; photograph by Leslie Jones.)

The building capped with a band of white windows at the center of this 1932 photograph, taken along Atlantic Avenue, is the Hotel Essex. Opened in 1899, this luxury hotel catered to travelers using South Station, which also opened in 1899. In 1983, the building was redeveloped by Hamilton Realty and Intercontinental Developers and now contains commercial and nonprofit offices. (Courtesy of the Boston Public Library; photograph by Leslie Jones.)

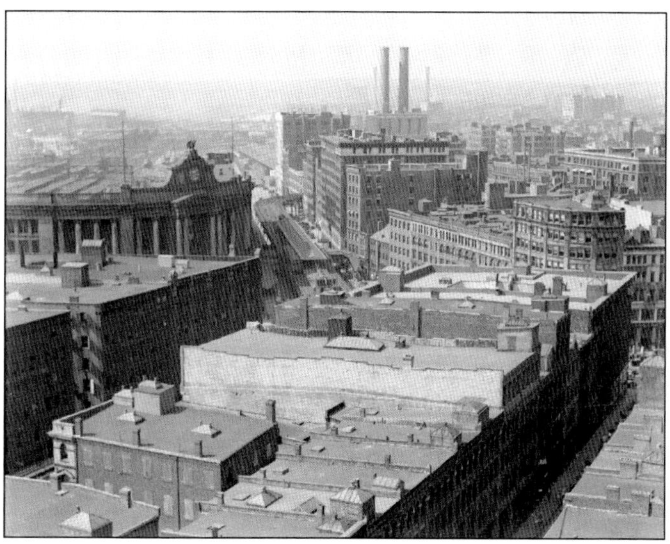

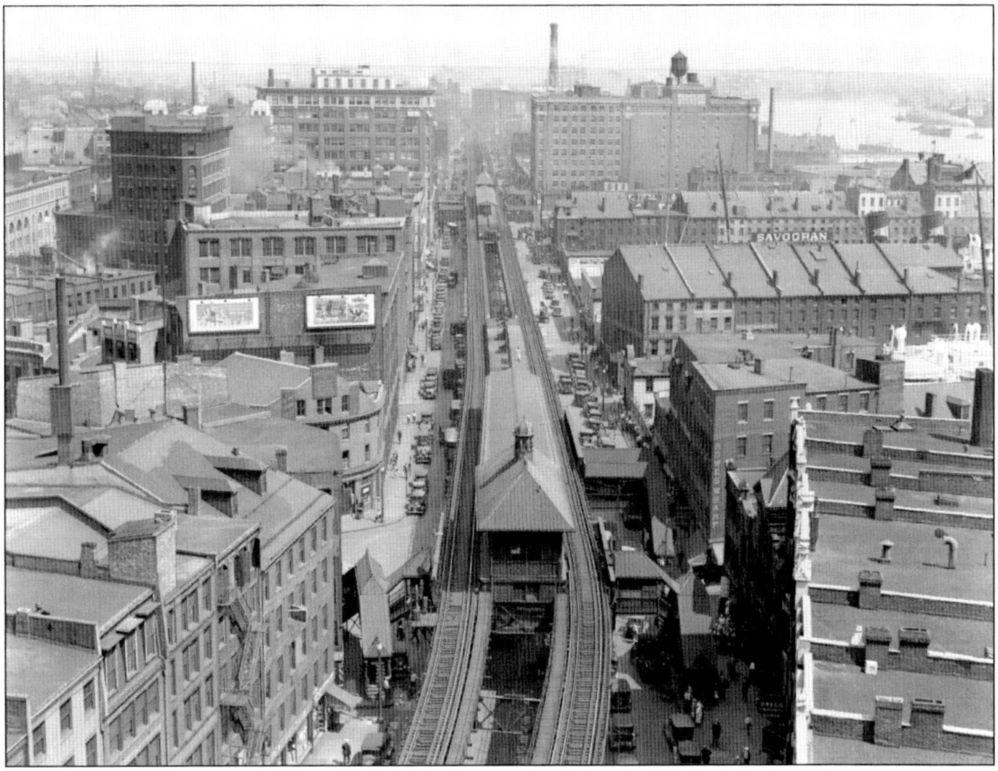

The above view along Atlantic Avenue shows the Elevated station at Rowes Wharf in 1932. In 1959, more than 20 years after the Atlantic Avenue Elevated ceased service, the elevated John F. Fitzgerald Expressway, commonly called the Central Artery, opened along much of this route, cutting a line through downtown Boston until it was moved underground as a result of the Central Artery/Tunnel Project, also known as the Big Dig. Big Dig construction began in 1991, lasted 15 years, and was the most expensive highway project in US history, with a 2006 tally estimating costs to be $14.6 billion. The image below, by Fairchild Aerial Surveys, shows the Boston Garden and North Station, just below and left of center, above the Elevated interchange at the intersection of Causeway and North Washington. (Both, courtesy of the Boston Public Library.)

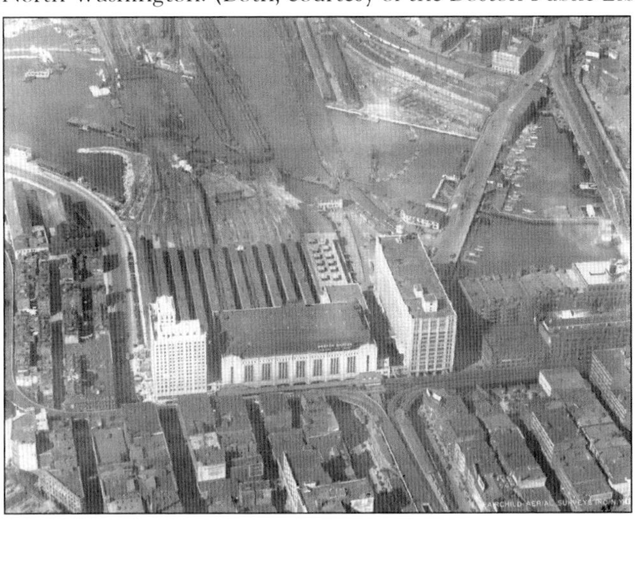

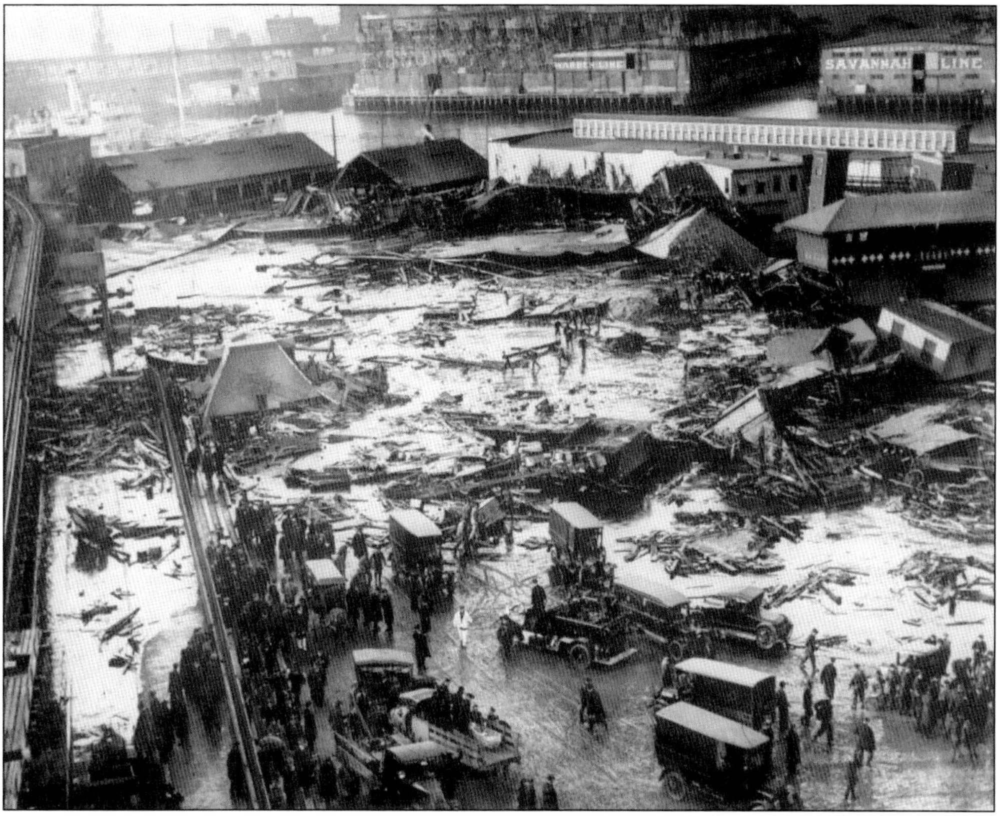

On January 15, 1919, a five-story molasses tank erupted in Boston's North End, releasing a 15-foot-tall wave of molasses that killed 21 people and engulfed everything in its path. Some still say that they can smell molasses on hot summer days in the North End, while others are skeptical that this is true or possible. (Courtesy of the Boston Public Library; photograph by the Globe Newspaper Company.)

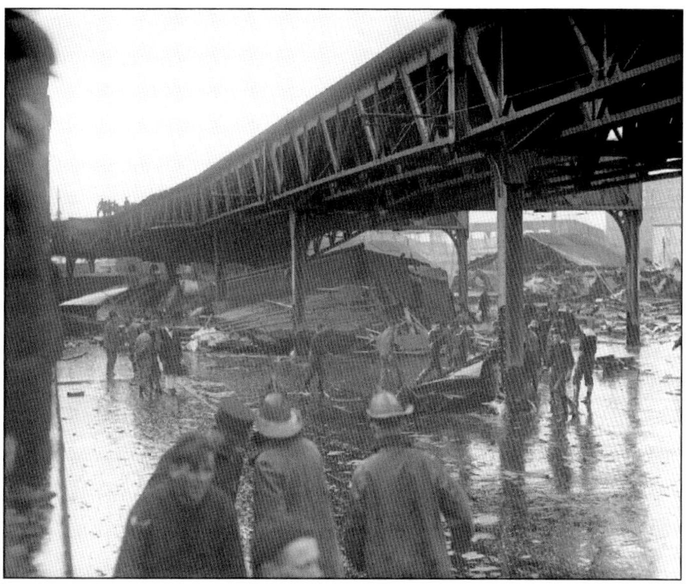

The Atlantic Avenue Elevated was badly damaged as a result of the Molasses Flood. It took more than two months for crews to repair damage to the Atlantic Avenue Elevated and for service to resume between North and South Stations. (Courtesy of the Boston Public Library; photograph by Leslie Jones.)

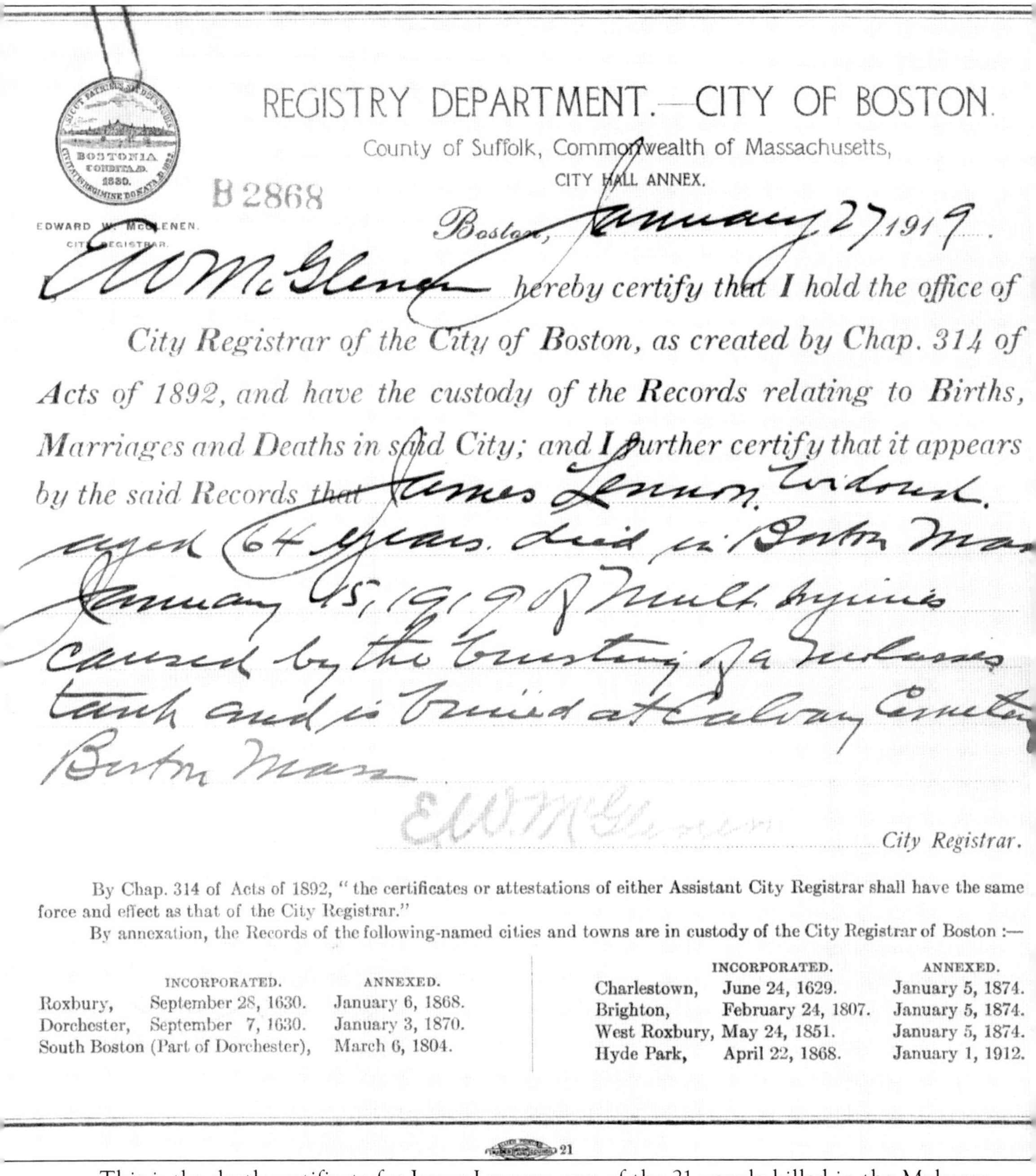

BOSTONIA CONDITA A.D. 1630. CIVITATIS REGIMINE DONATA A.D. 1822. SICUT PATRIBUS SIT DEUS NOBIS

B 2868

EDWARD W. McGLENEN, CITY REGISTRAR.

REGISTRY DEPARTMENT.—CITY OF BOSTON.

County of Suffolk, Commonwealth of Massachusetts,

CITY HALL ANNEX.

Boston, January 27, 1919.

I, E. W. McGlenen hereby certify that I hold the office of City Registrar of the City of Boston, as created by Chap. 314 of Acts of 1892, and have the custody of the Records relating to Births, Marriages and Deaths in said City; and I further certify that it appears by the said Records that James Lennon, widower, aged 64 years, died in Boston, Mass, January 15, 1919 of mult. injuries caused by the bursting of a molasses tank and is buried at Calvary Cemetery Boston Mass

E. W. McGlenen, City Registrar.

By Chap. 314 of Acts of 1892, "the certificates or attestations of either Assistant City Registrar shall have the same force and effect as that of the City Registrar."

By annexation, the Records of the following-named cities and towns are in custody of the City Registrar of Boston :—

	INCORPORATED.	ANNEXED.
Roxbury,	September 28, 1630.	January 6, 1868.
Dorchester,	September 7, 1630.	January 3, 1870.
South Boston (Part of Dorchester),		March 6, 1804.
Charlestown,	June 24, 1629.	January 5, 1874.
Brighton,	February 24, 1807.	January 5, 1874.
West Roxbury,	May 24, 1851.	January 5, 1874.
Hyde Park,	April 22, 1868.	January 1, 1912.

21

This is the death certificate for James Lennon, one of the 21 people killed in the Molasses Flood. The certificate describes Lennon's cause of death as resulting from "much injury caused by the bursting of a molasses tank." (Courtesy of University Archives & Special Collections, Joseph P. Healey Library, University of Massachusetts Boston: Massachusetts Catholic Order of Foresters Collection.)

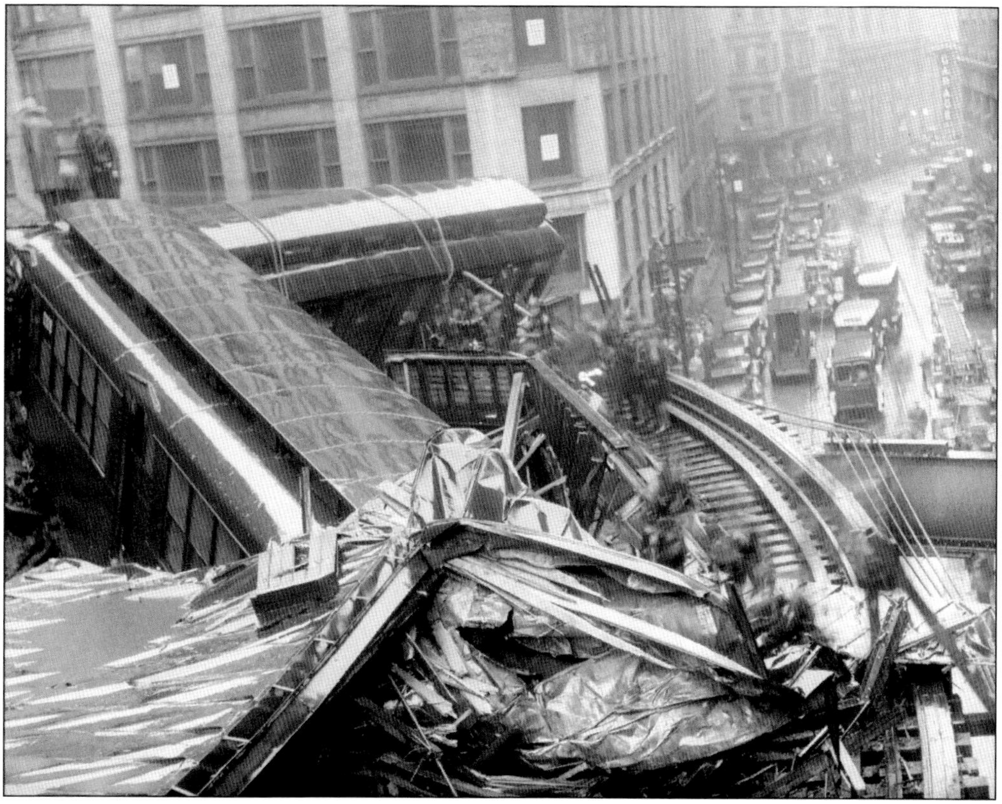

These photographs show an accident that occurred at the intersection of Harrison Avenue and Beach Street on July 22, 1928. The accident, caused by a northbound train headed for South Station, killed three passengers—George Anderson, Martin O'Connor, and Clayton Nickerson—and injured another 23. An inquest by Judge James Parmenter, of the Boston Municipal Court, found the operator of the train to be negligent. In his report, the judge wrote: "I find that the accident was caused by the culpable negligence of Bernard A. McDonald in running upon the curve at an obviously dangerous rate of speed, far in excess of that prescribed by the regulations of the railway company." In January 1929, however, a jury found McDonald not guilty. (Both, courtesy of the Boston Public Library; photograph by Leslie Jones.)

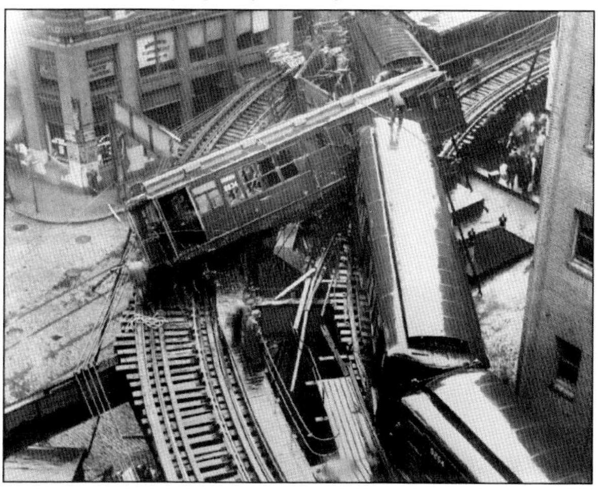

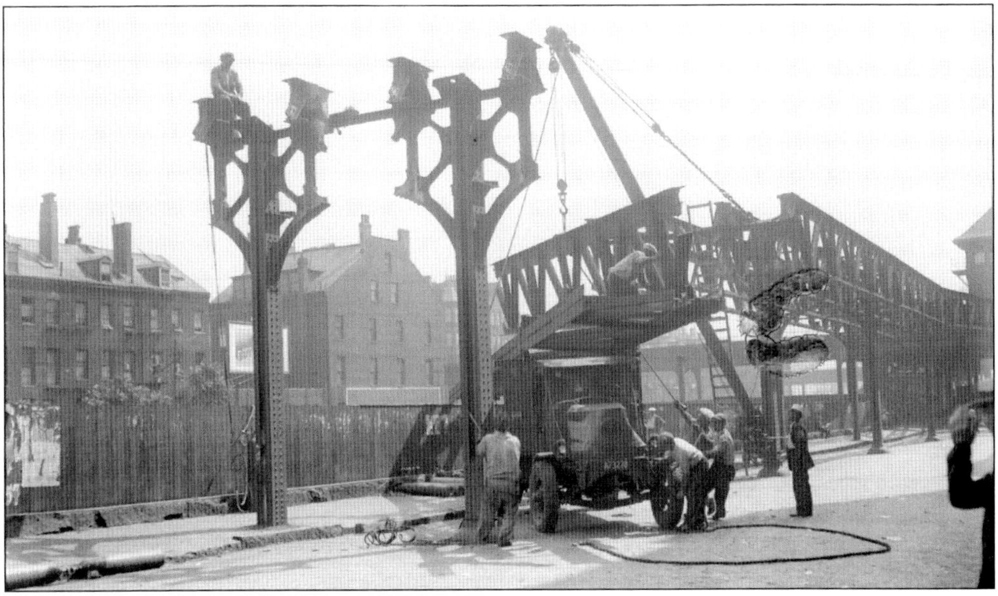

In September 1938, Edward Dana, president of the Boston Elevated Railway Company, announced that Atlantic Avenue service would end due to decreasing ridership. By then, its trains only made stops at North and South Stations from September to June, and riders found it easier to use bus lines and the subway, which had connected downtown to South Station since 1916. (Courtesy of the Boston Public Library; photograph by Leslie Jones.)

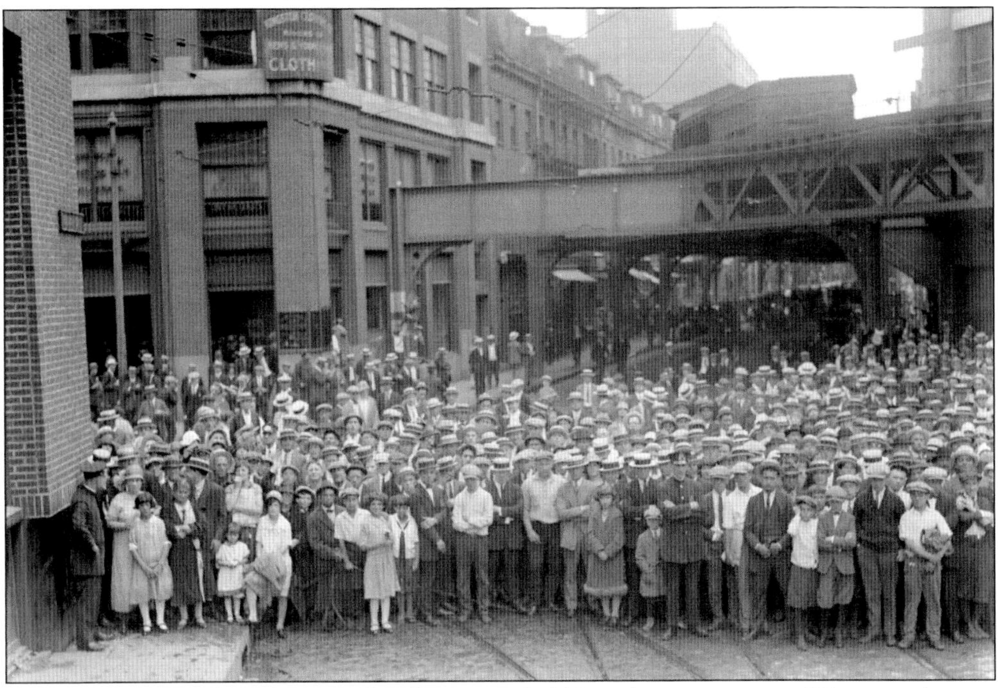

A large crowd poses for a photograph, taken around 1930, at the intersection of Harrison Avenue and Beach Street, the site of the July 1928 Elevated accident that killed three men. The building at left is the Kingston Clothing Company. The event memorialized in the photograph is unknown. (Courtesy of the Boston Public Library; photograph by Leslie Jones.)

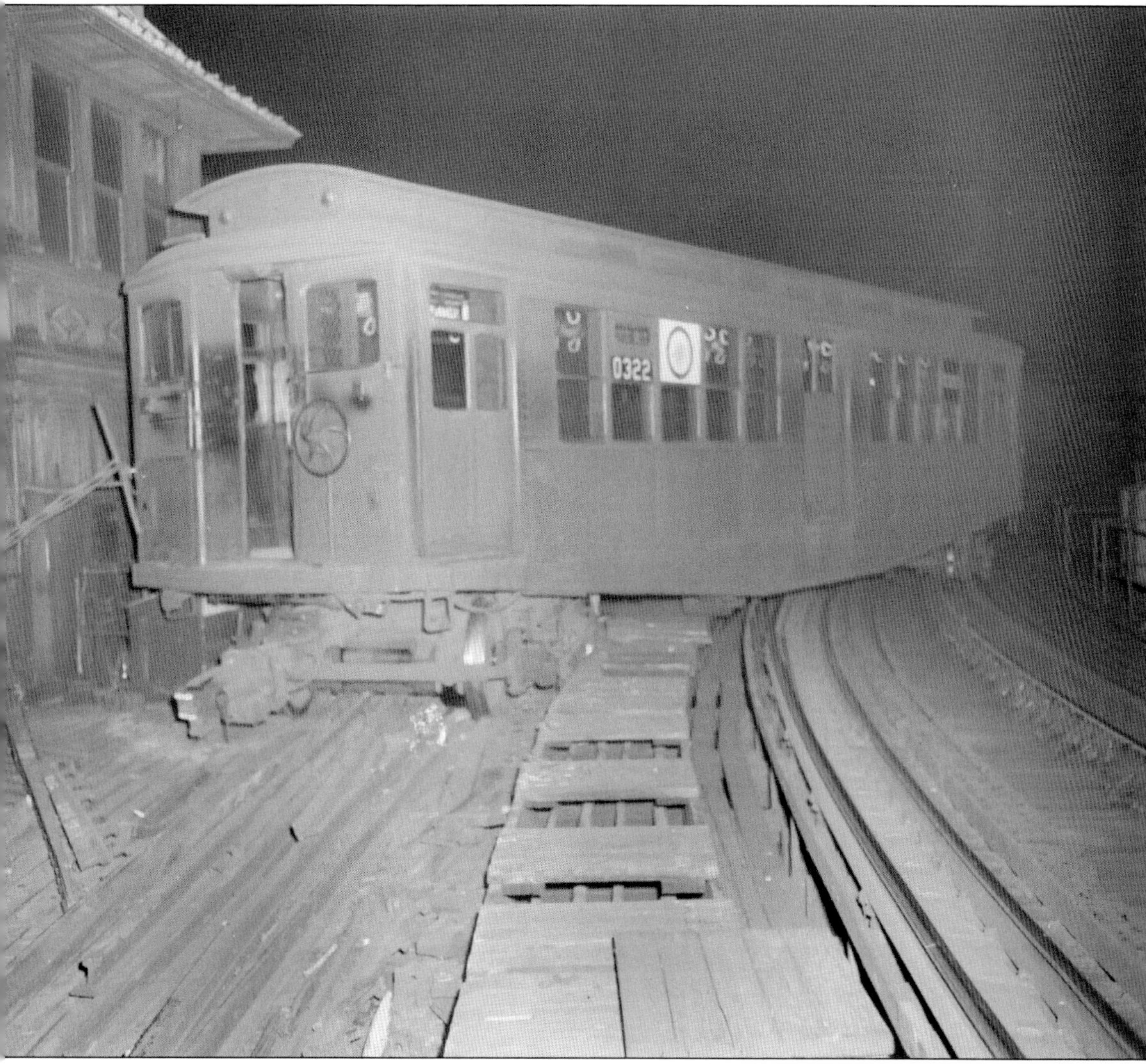

A photograph taken in 1948 or 1949, after the MTA began using its new emblem in train windows, shows a derailed Elevated train car at Sullivan Square Station in Charlestown; this is No. 0322 of the No. 8-type cars first introduced in 1921. To the left is Tower "A," one of the many control and switching towers along the Elevated route between Everett and Forest Hills. (Courtesy of the Boston Public Library; photograph by Leslie Jones.)

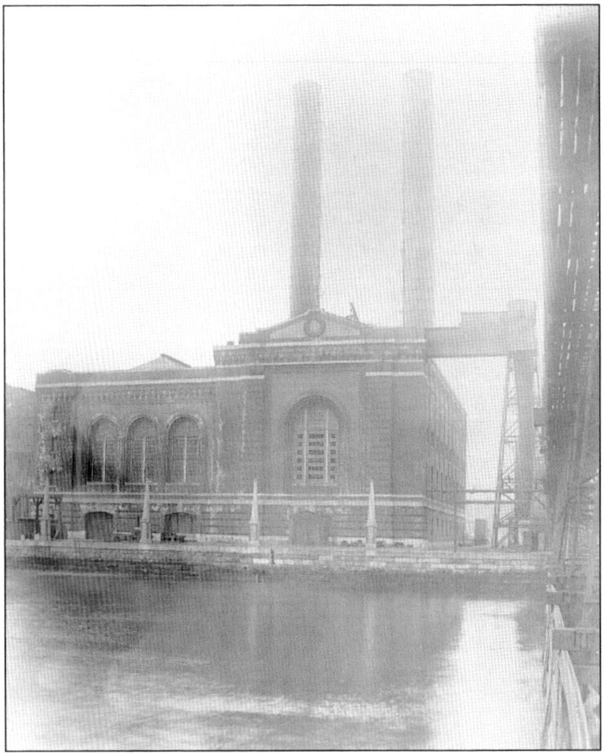

The image at left shows the power station at L and East First Streets in South Boston, just south of the Reserved Channel, which provided electricity for the Boston Elevated Railway. The image below shows a vertical Curtis turbine inside that power station, one of three 15,000-kilowatt turbines that operated in the station until 1950. Because the technology behind generating electricity was still in its infancy, the Boston Elevated Railway Company was forced to build power-generating stations along the Elevated lines to keep the trains moving. Some of these power stations have been repurposed and redeveloped over the years. (Both, courtesy of the Boston Public Library.)

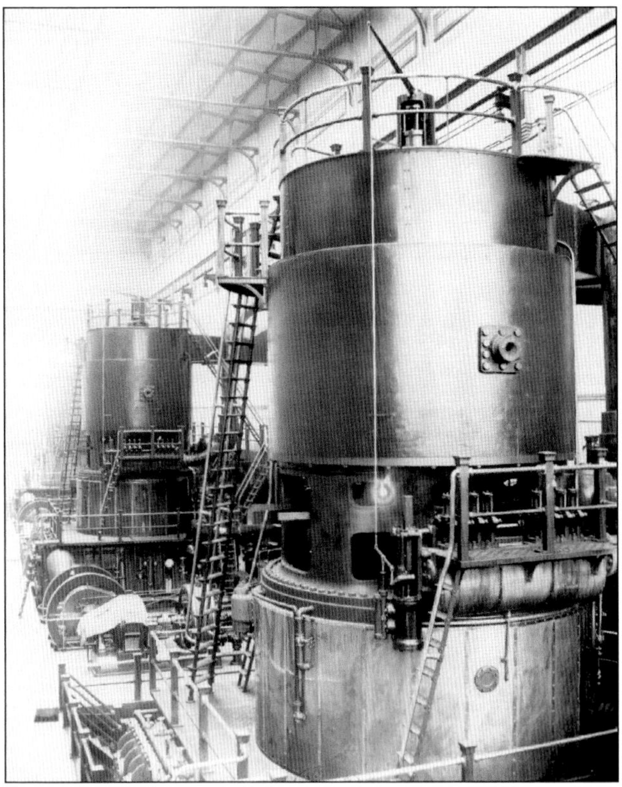

Two

The Charlestown Elevated

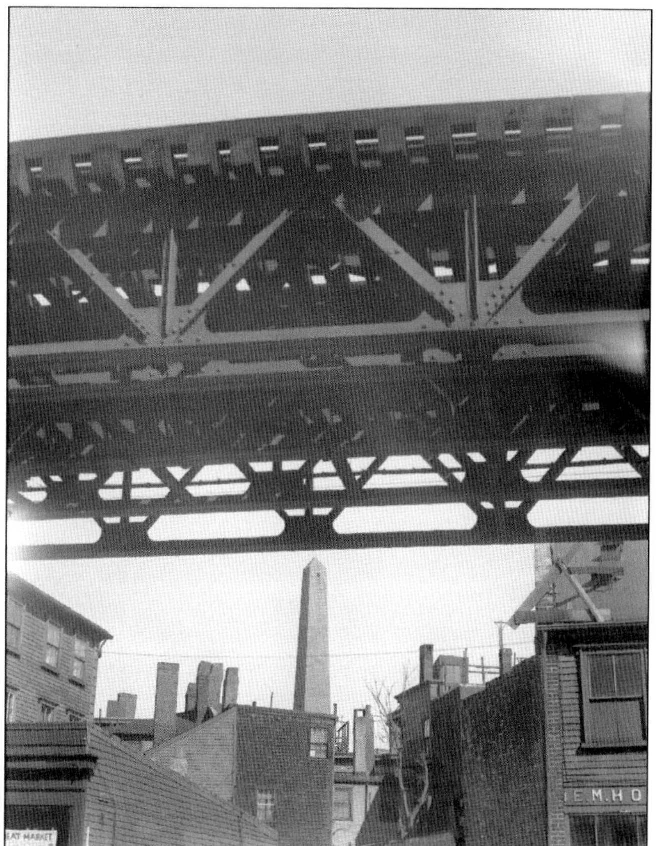

This 1938 image shows the Bunker Hill Monument from beneath the Elevated. The cornerstone of the monument, actually located on Breed's Hill (where the battle was fought), was laid on June 17, 1825, on the 50th anniversary of the Revolutionary War in a ceremony that included the Marquis de Lafayette and Daniel Webster. The monument was not completed until 1842. (Courtesy of the Boston Public Library; photograph by Leslie Jones.)

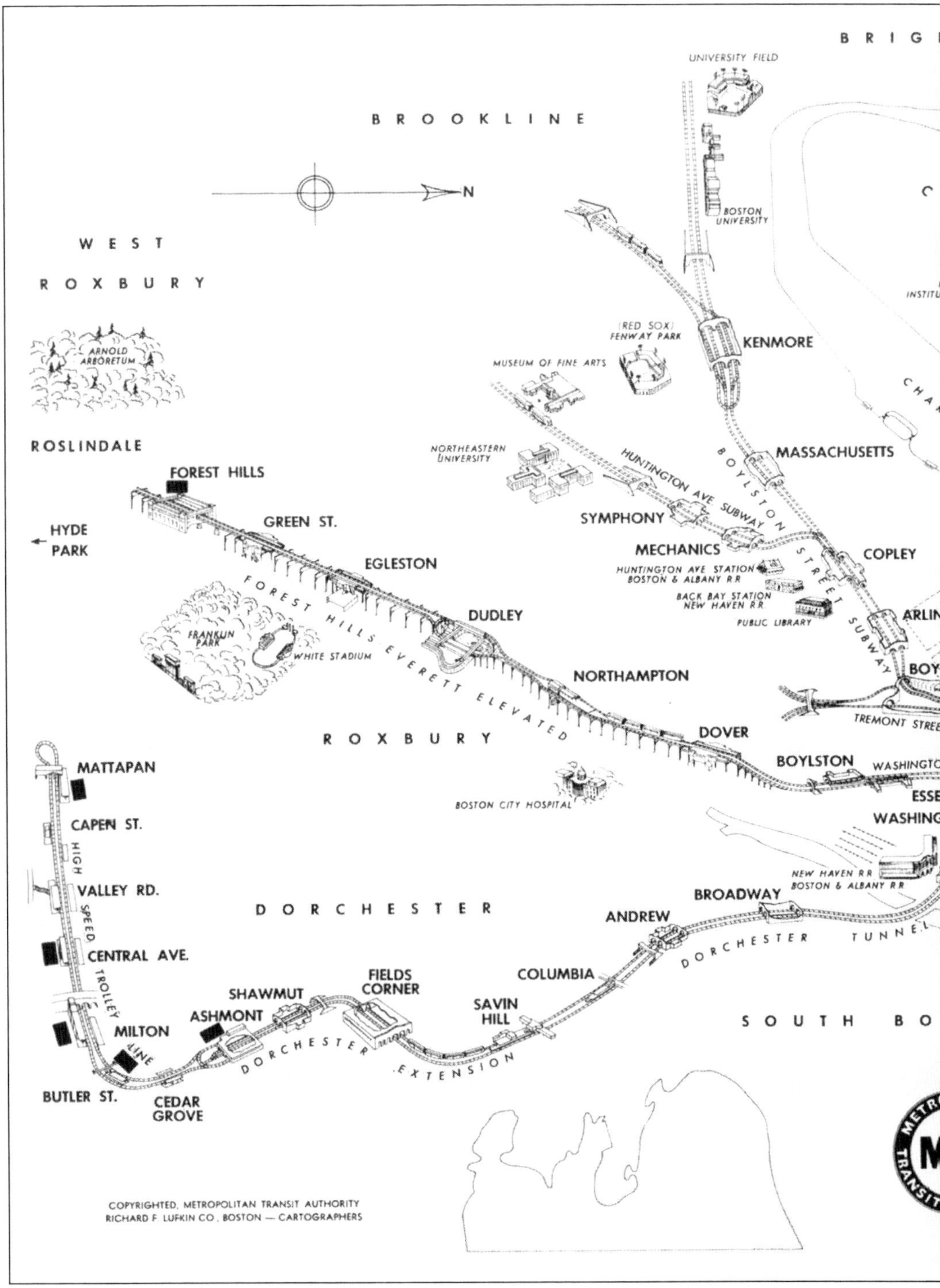

This 1954 Metropolitan Transit Authority rapid transit map shows the original alignment of the system that would later be designated as the Orange Line after the MTA became the Massachusetts Bay Transportation Authority (MBTA). The Elevated traces a path from left to right across the center of this map from Forest Hills, alongside the Arnold Arboretum, across the downtown area

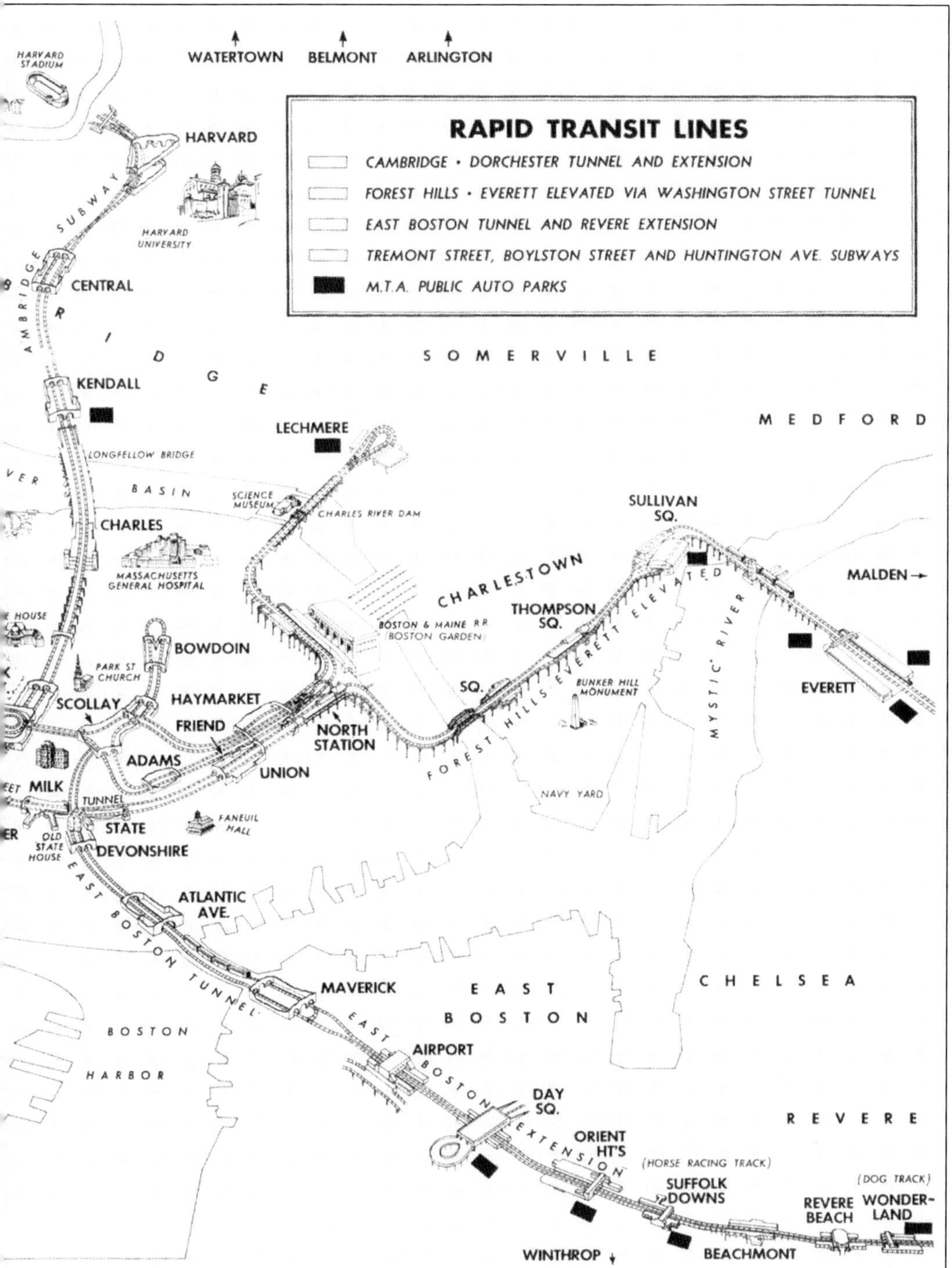

where the four lines cross, and ends at Everett at center right. The color coding of the MBTA rapid transit lines was announced in late 1965, around the time of the introduction of the new emblem, the "Circle-T," but was not implemented until later in 1966. (Courtesy of Otto M. Vondrak.)

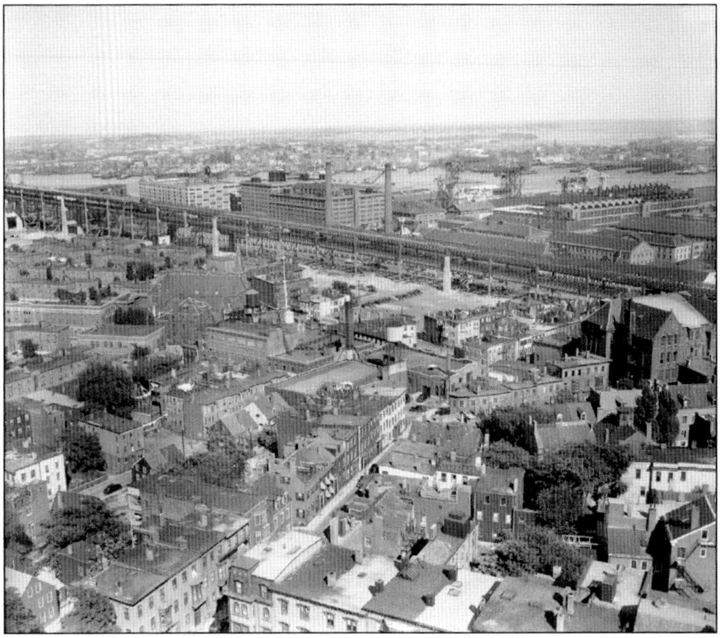

This 1950s photograph looks across Charlestown toward the Mystic River Bridge. Construction of the bridge started in 1948, it opened to traffic in 1950, and the bridge was renamed in 1963 after Maurice Tobin, former mayor of Boston. Tobin had ordered the construction of the bridge while serving as governor of Massachusetts from 1945 to 1947. (Courtesy of the Boston Public Library; photograph by Leslie Jones.)

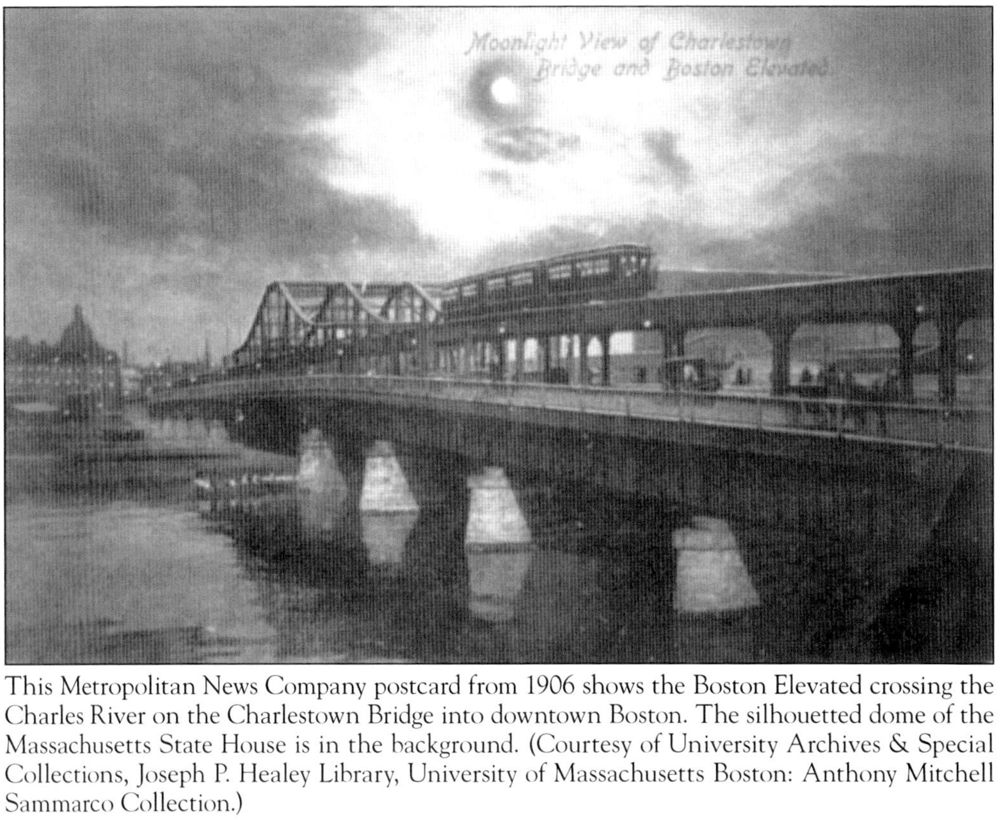

This Metropolitan News Company postcard from 1906 shows the Boston Elevated crossing the Charles River on the Charlestown Bridge into downtown Boston. The silhouetted dome of the Massachusetts State House is in the background. (Courtesy of University Archives & Special Collections, Joseph P. Healey Library, University of Massachusetts Boston: Anthony Mitchell Sammarco Collection.)

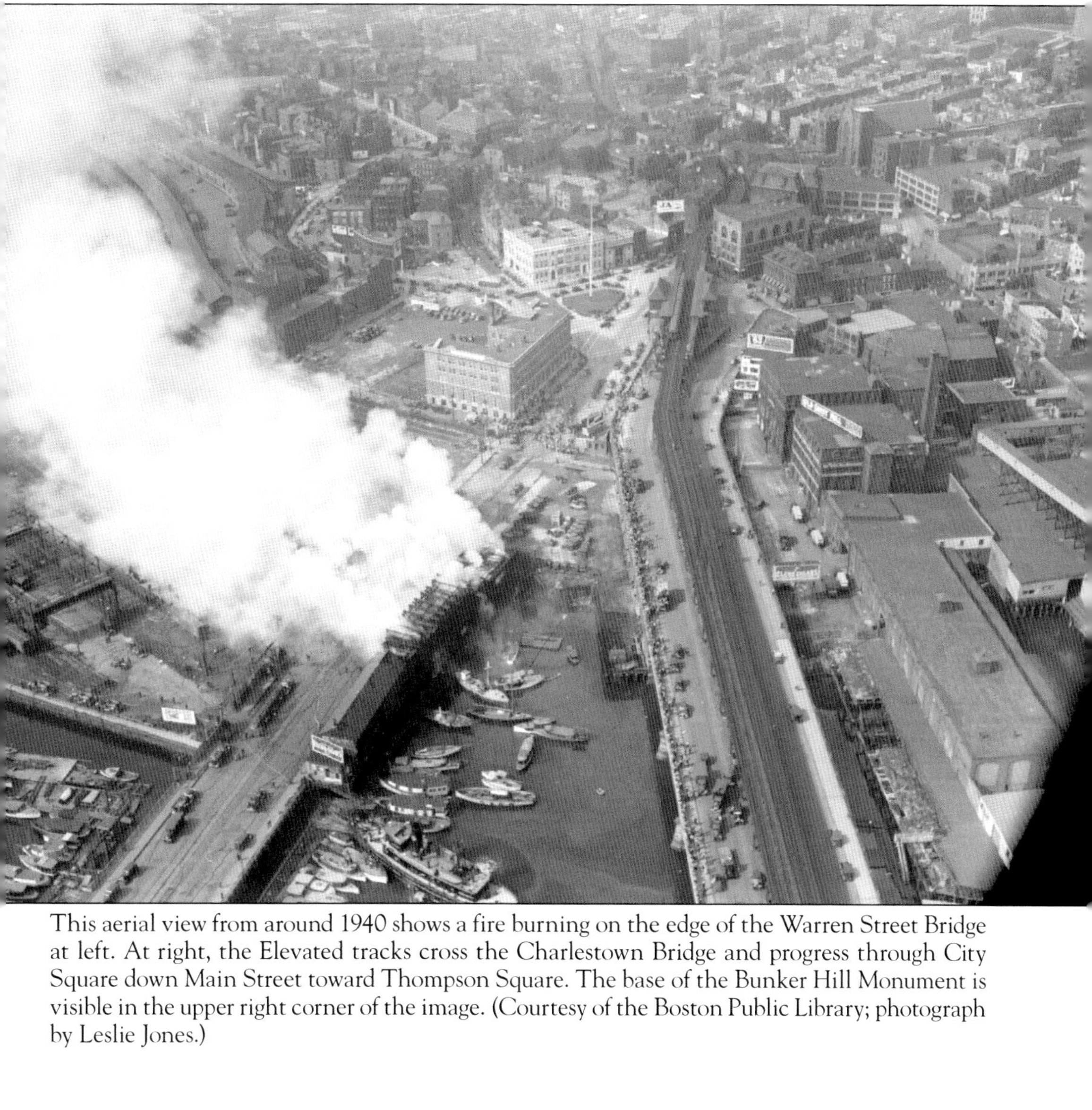

This aerial view from around 1940 shows a fire burning on the edge of the Warren Street Bridge at left. At right, the Elevated tracks cross the Charlestown Bridge and progress through City Square down Main Street toward Thompson Square. The base of the Bunker Hill Monument is visible in the upper right corner of the image. (Courtesy of the Boston Public Library; photograph by Leslie Jones.)

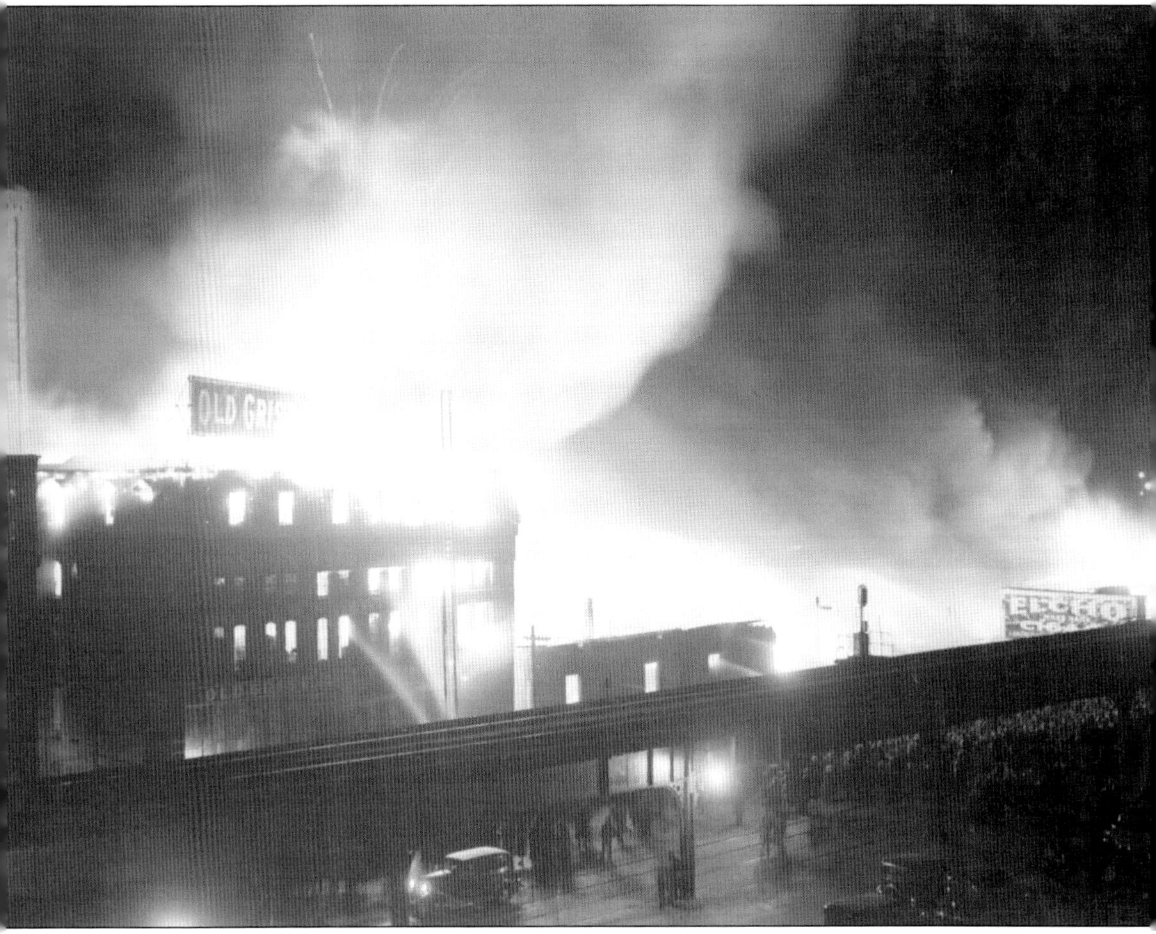

This 1936 image shows a fire near City Square that destroyed the Old Grist Mill and the *Boston Globe*'s newsprint storage house. Both buildings were owned by the Globe Newspaper Company. News coverage estimated that as many as 10,000 people watched the fire from the Charlestown Bridge. Part of the crowd is visible underneath the tracks. (Courtesy of the Boston Public Library; photograph by Leslie Jones.)

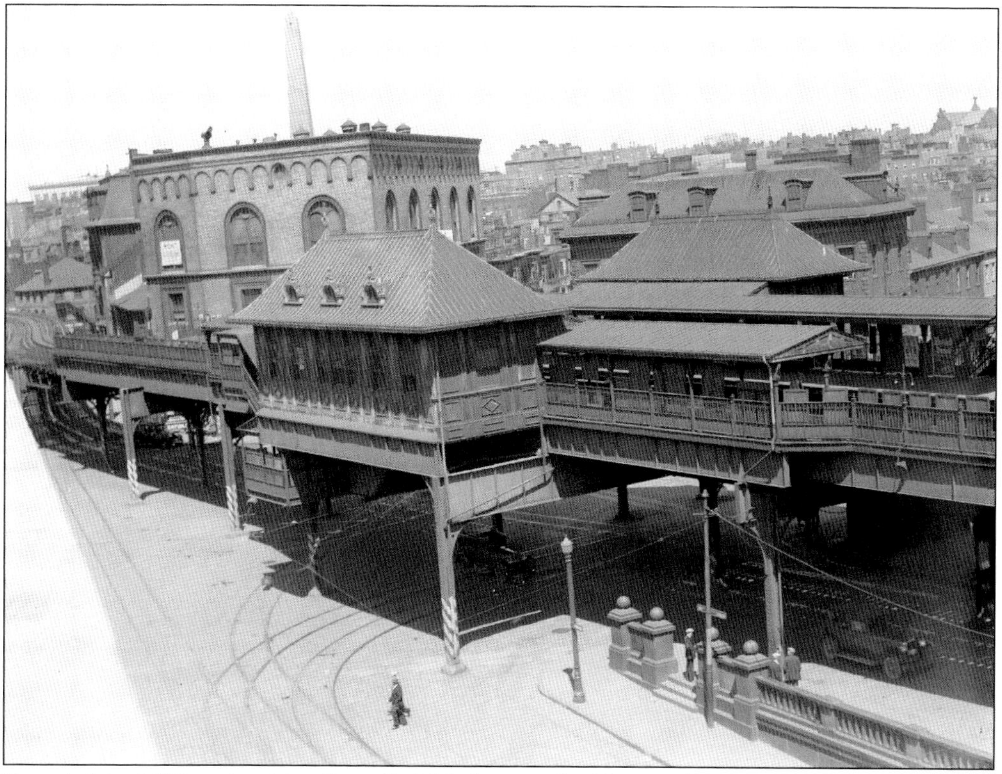

Founded in 1628 and originally called Mishawum by Native Americans, Charlestown was incorporated as a city in 1848. City Square has long been an important civic center in Charlestown. Before Charlestown was annexed to Boston in 1874, City Square was home to a variety of municipal activities ranging from government offices to libraries. The 1930 photograph above, taken by Leslie Jones, shows the City Square Station of the El and, in the left background, the Bunker Hill Monument. In the image of City Square shown below, which was published by the Metropolitan News Company, the domed building is the former Charlestown City Hall. Currently the site of the Charlestown Division of the Boston Municipal Court Department, the city hall shown in this 1901 image was completed in 1869 on the site of the former Town House, which was built in 1657. (Both, courtesy of the Boston Public Library.)

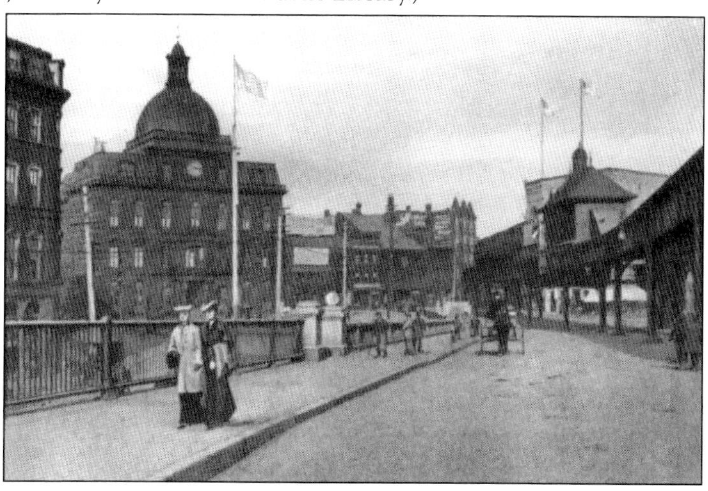

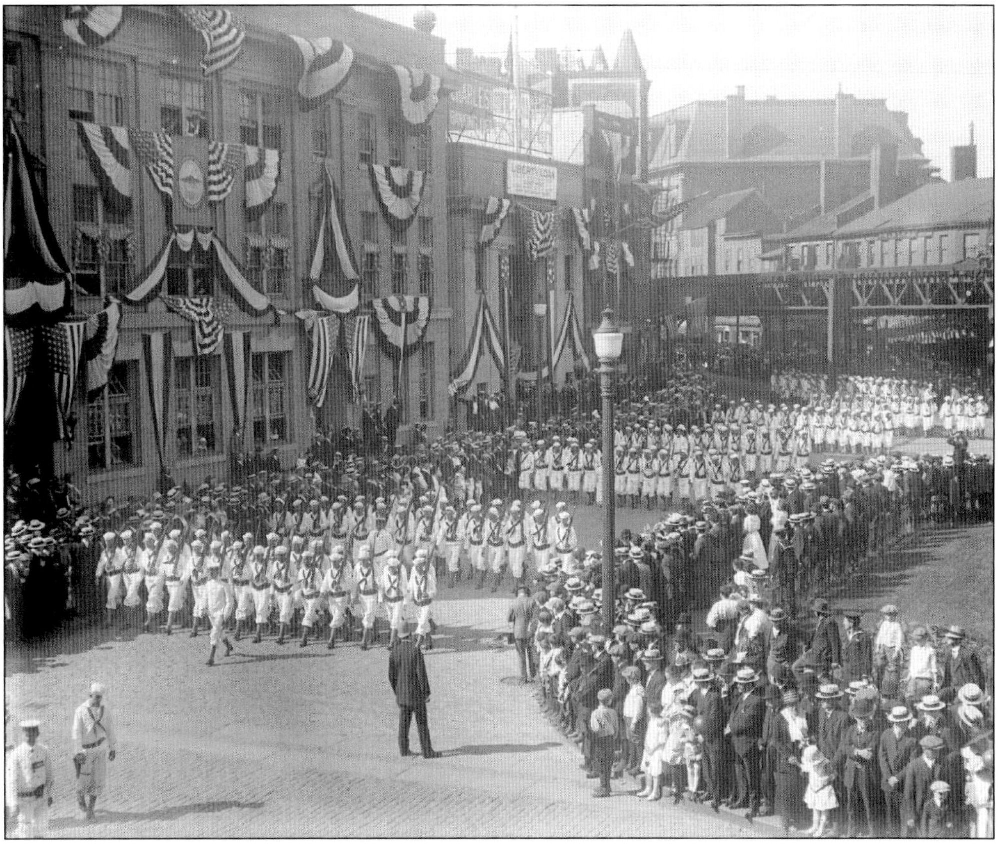

Every year since 1786, on or around June 17, a parade has taken place in Charlestown to commemorate the Battle of Bunker Hill. Fought on June 17, 1775, the Battle of Bunker Hill is considered the first major battle of the Revolutionary War. The above image, by Leslie Jones, shows sailors who were stationed in Boston marching as part of the parade. The El is visible in the background. Each year, sailors stationed to the USS *Constitution* in Charlestown lead the Bunker Hill Day Parade. The 1926 image below shows the parade as it passes through City Square and under the City Square Station of the El. (Both, courtesy of the Boston Public Library.)

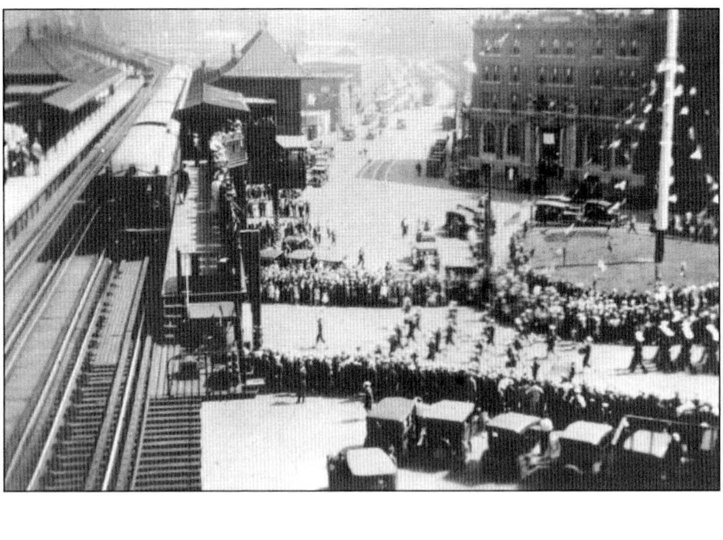

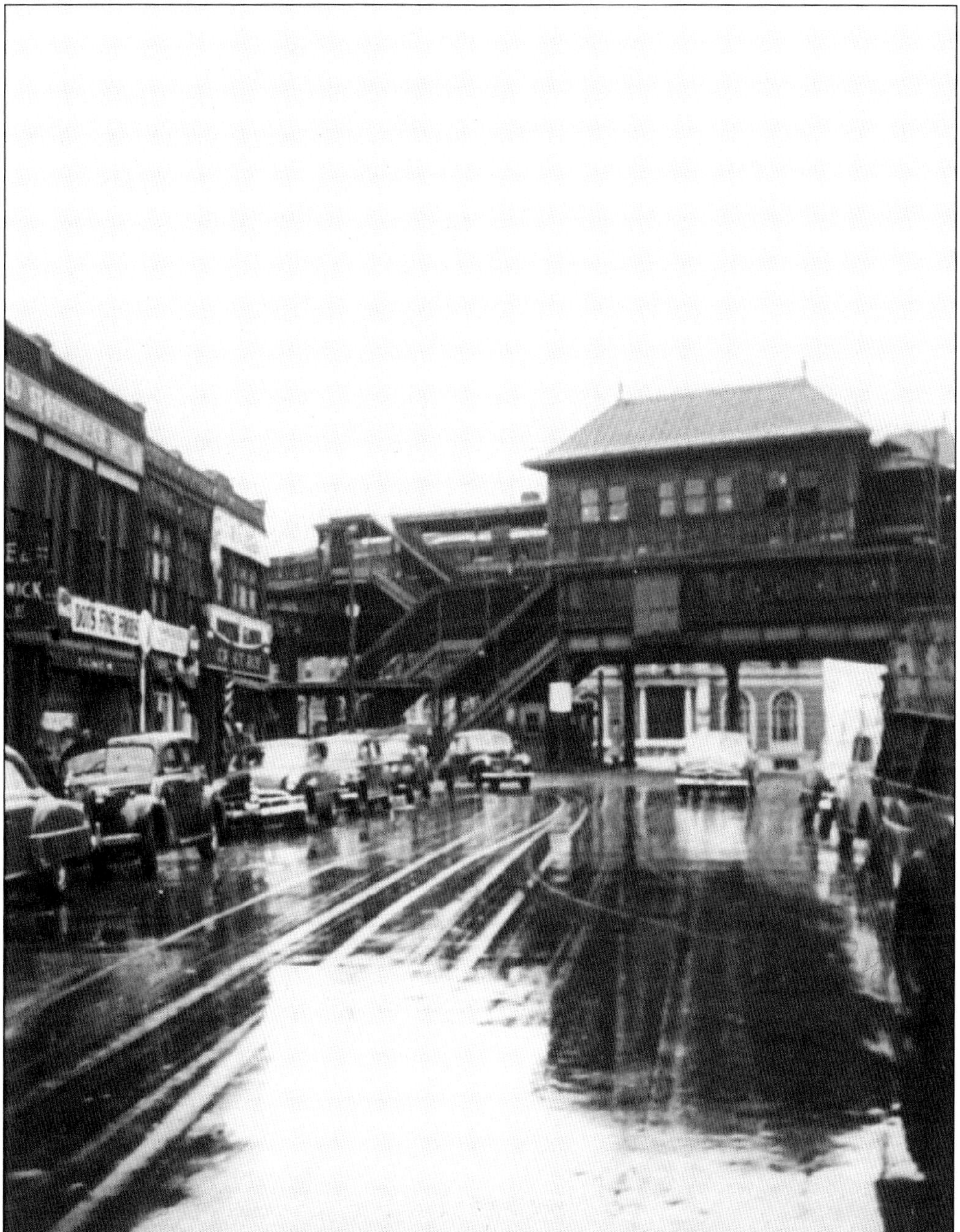

This 1950 photograph shows the elevated City Square Station looming over Chelsea Street on a rainy day. The photograph looks southwest past World Sportswear, Inc., and Dot's Fine Foods, both at left, with the first floor of the Army & Navy YMCA visible under the station. (Courtesy of Rev. Wolcott Cutler and the Boston Public Library.)

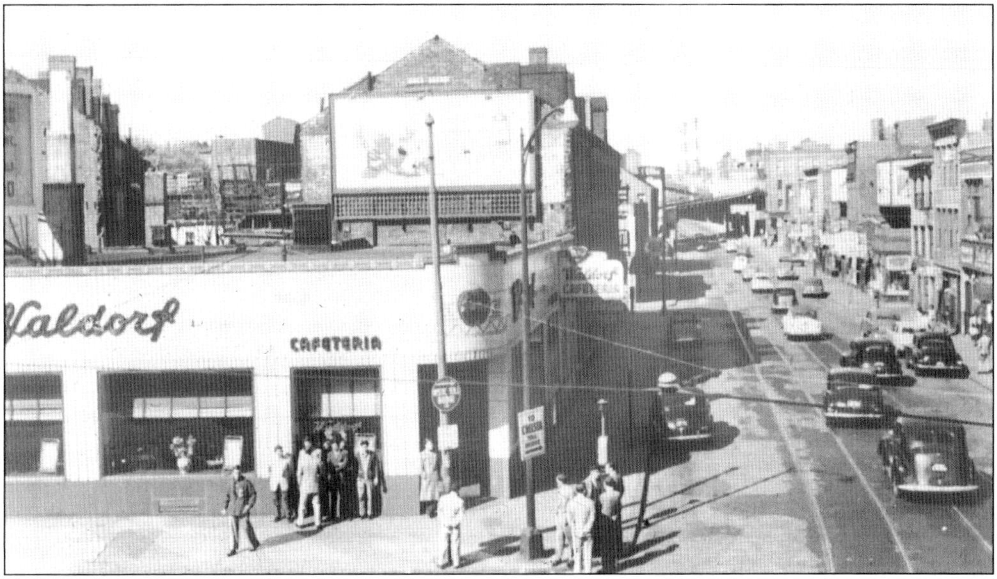

The Waldorf Cafeteria at 23 City Square, pictured here in 1950, was one of several in Boston and Cambridge in the mid-20th century, a period when several large cafeteria chains had a presence in the cities. The era was relatively short-lived, and this Waldorf location closed by 1960. (Courtesy of Rev. Wolcott Cutler and the Boston Public Library.)

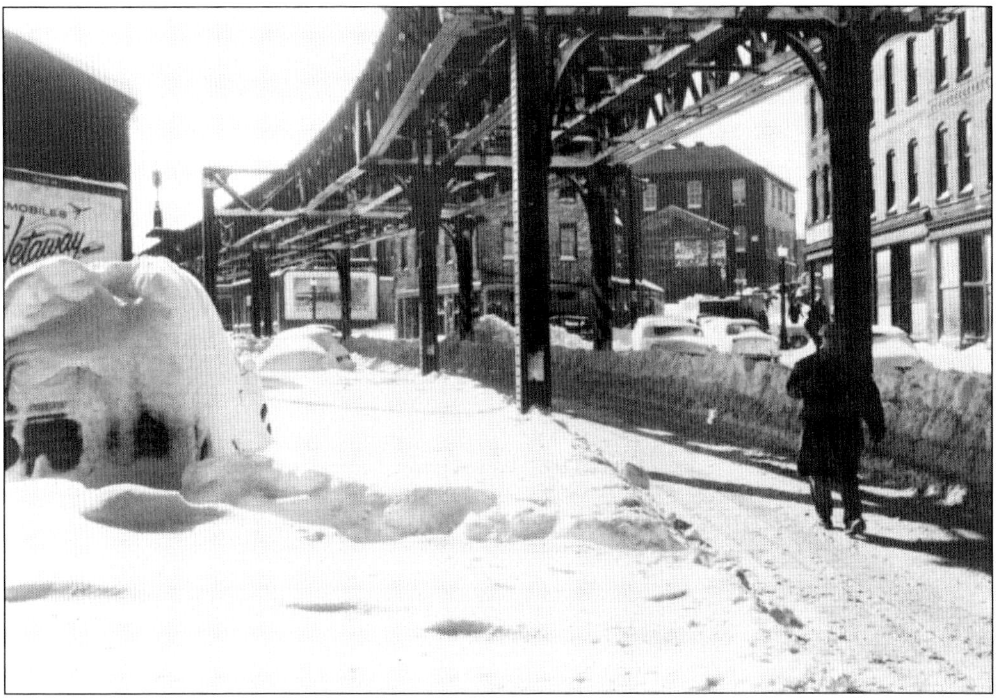

One effect of the Elevated tracks using existing roadways was an often dangerous narrowing of streets, a problem made worse by snow accumulation during winter months. This image from March 20, 1956, shows the intersection of Main Street, Harvard Street, and Devons Street just south of Thompson Square, also known as the Thompson Triangle, in Charlestown. (Courtesy of Rev. Wolcott Cutler and the Boston Public Library.)

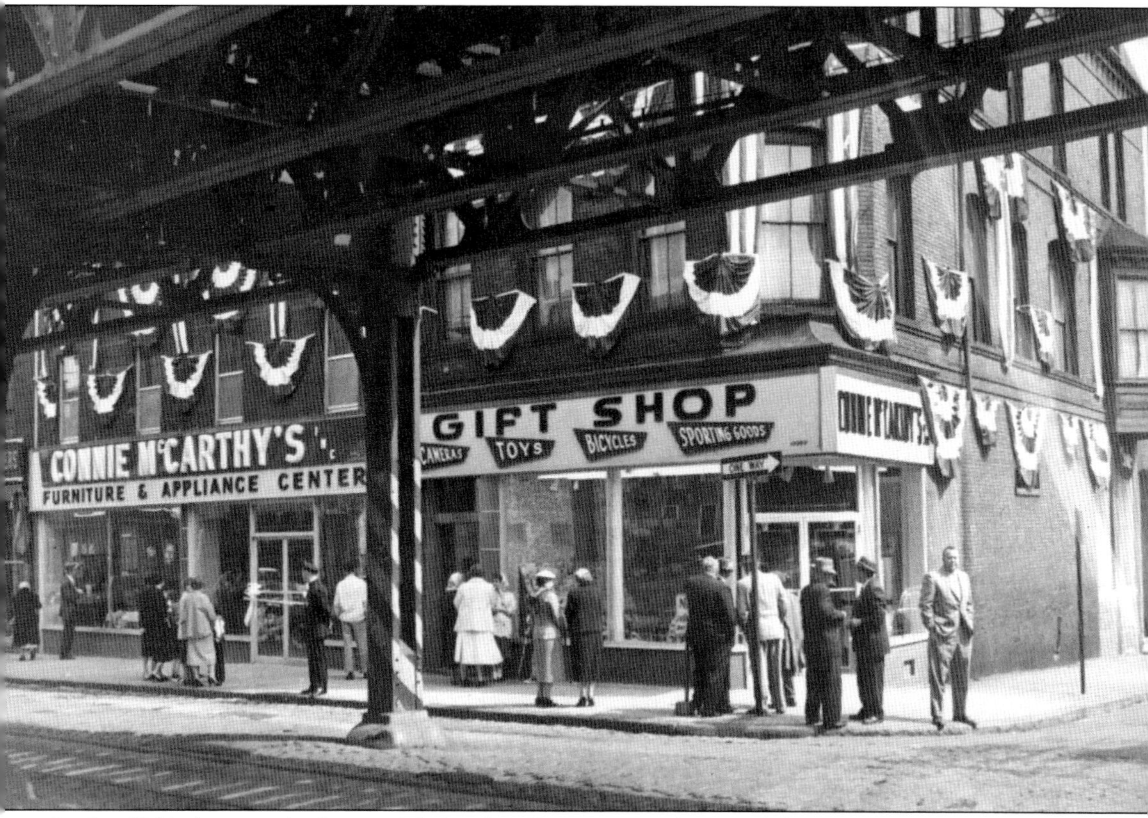

In this 1954 photograph, Connie McCarthy's Emporium is shown celebrating its opening at the intersection of Main Street and Monument Avenue, just under the El. In 2000, restaurateur Samad Naamad transformed the space into the Moroccan-themed Tangierino Restaurant, a sign of the changing face of a neighborhood once populated mostly by working class Irish Americans. (Courtesy of Rev. Wolcott Cutler and the Boston Public Library.)

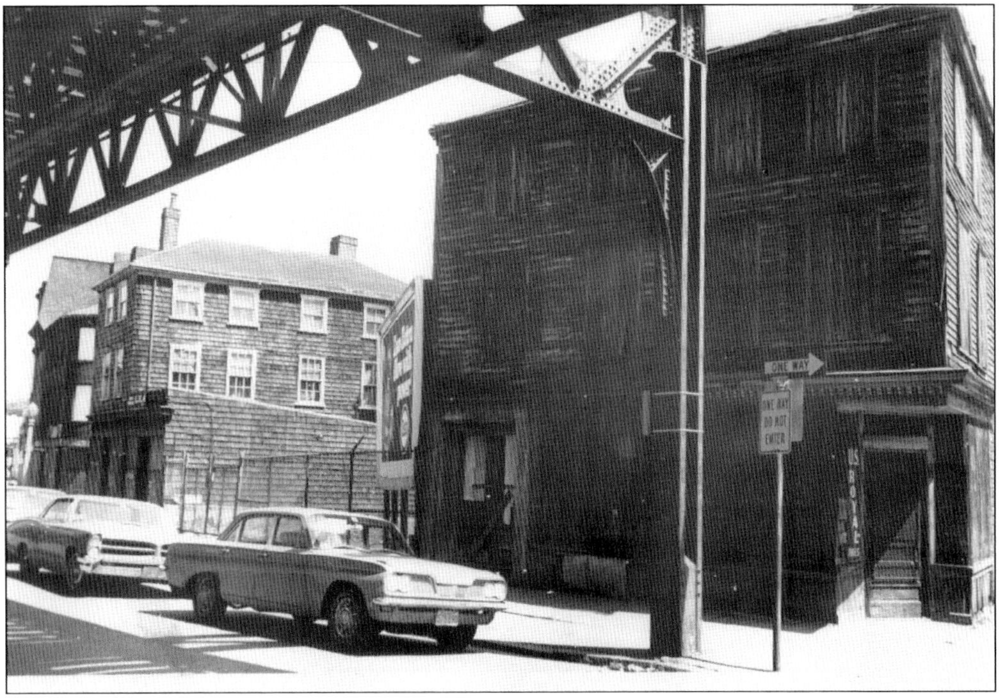

The above image shows the Warren Tavern, at Main and Pleasant Streets, cast in the shadow of the Elevated. Built around 1780, this is believed to have been one of the first houses erected after the British burned much of Charlestown in June 1775, a battle later commemorated by the nearby Bunker Hill Monument. This image from around the 1970s shows the dilapidated condition of the building at the time. The Warren Tavern had suffered, like many neighborhood businesses, from Charlestown's decreasing population, which went from 40,000 in 1900 to 14,000 in 1970. Today, the Tavern is a popular and lively neighborhood spot frequented by residents and tourists. In the image below, also from around 1970, children play in an empty lot at Main and Union Streets, just up Main Street from the Warren Tavern. (Both, Collection No. 5210.004, City of Boston Archives, Boston.)

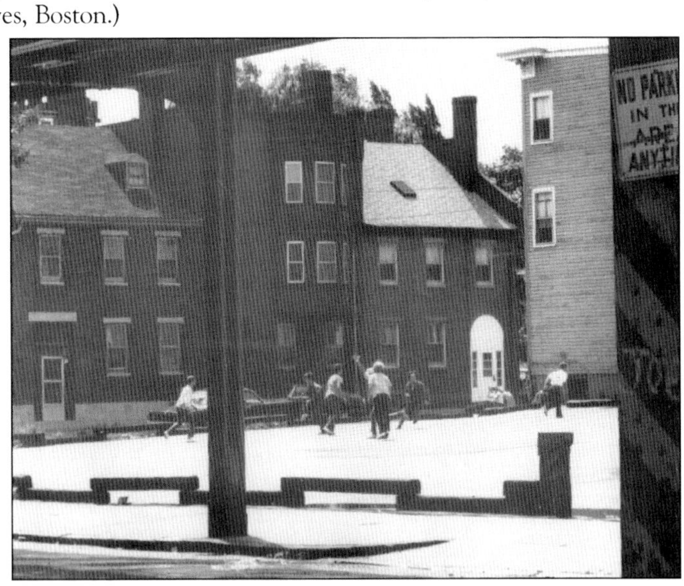

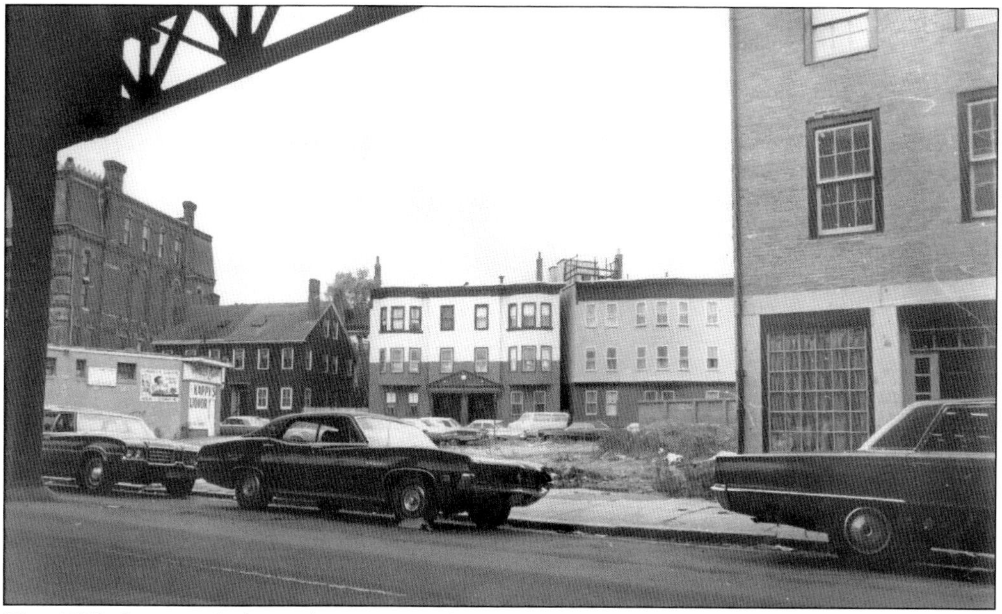

This 1972 photograph shows the meeting of Main and Warren Streets at Thompson Square. The taller structure at left in the image is the former Charlestown Saving Bank; the smaller structure in the foreground at left is a Kappy's Liquor Store, which had been located in the square at one time. (Collection No. 5210.004, City of Boston Archives, Boston.)

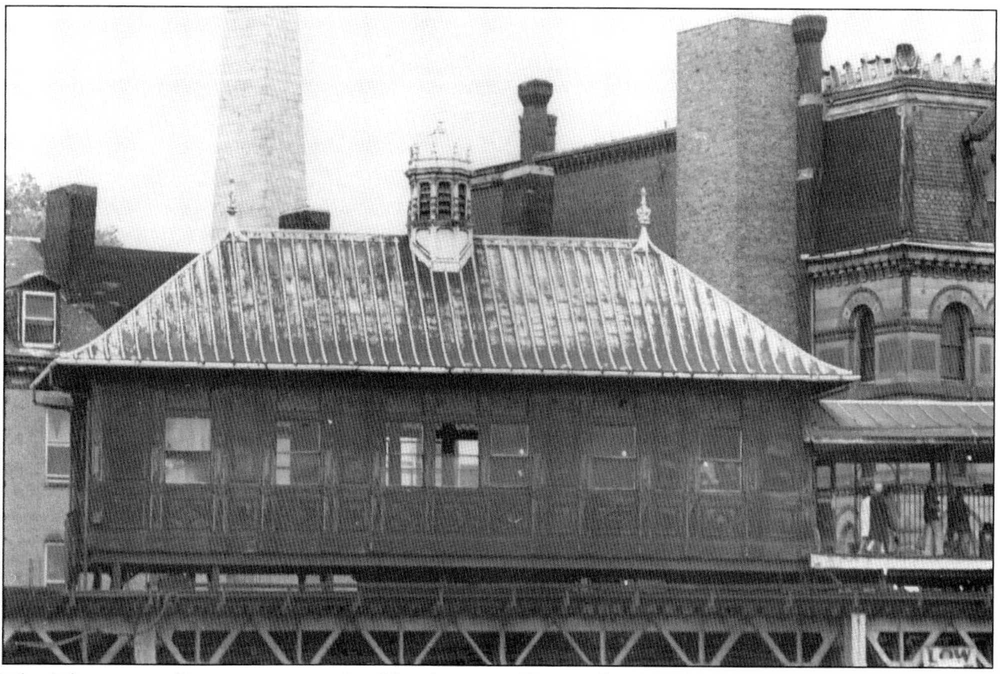

The Thompson Square stop on the Charlestown Elevated opened in the spring of 1902, almost a year after the original stops on the Charlestown line had opened for service. A section of the Bunker Hill Monument, completed in 1842, is visible in the background of this 1972 photograph. The ornate building at right is the former Charlestown Savings Bank. (Collection No. 5210.004, City of Boston Archives, Boston.)

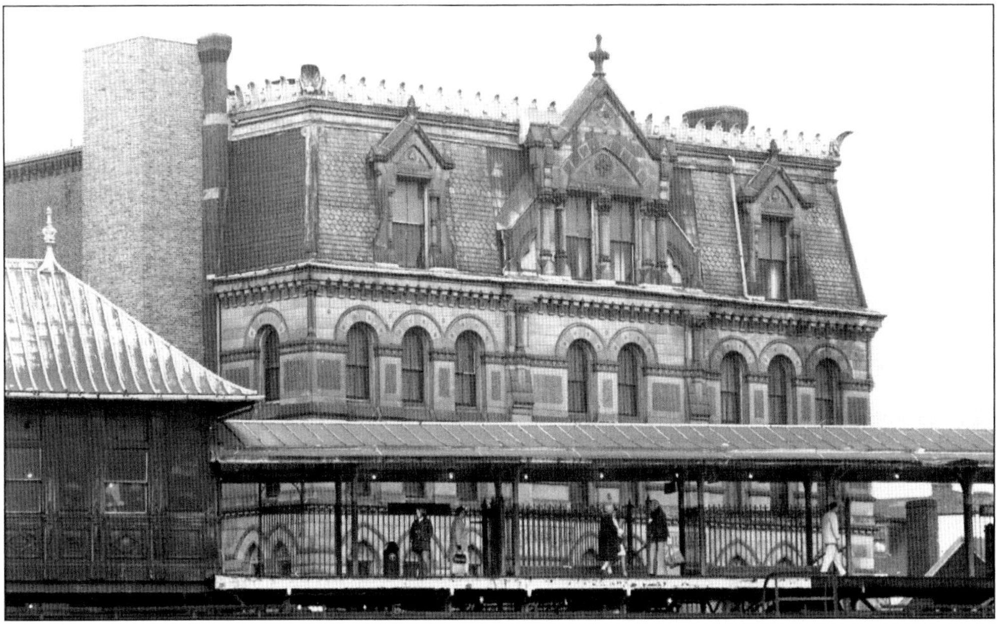

As seen above in a 1972 photograph from Thompson Square, the Elevated station sat just outside the Charlestown Savings Bank, an official Boston landmark built in 1876 in the High Victorian Gothic style with a sandstone facade broken by elaborately arched windows. Incorporated in 1854, the bank occupied the building until 1978, along with a Masonic lodge on its upper floors. The image below shows buildings along Dexter Row next to Charlestown Savings Bank. The awning marks the location of the Daniel A. Wiles Funeral Home, which operated on Dexter Row for decades. (Both, Collection No. 5210.004, City of Boston Archives, Boston.)

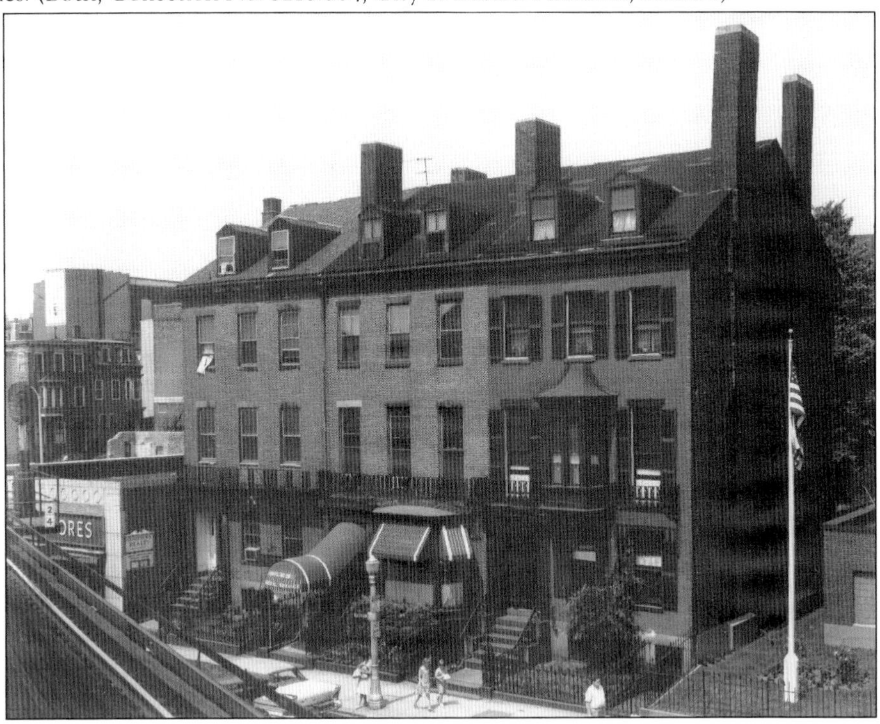

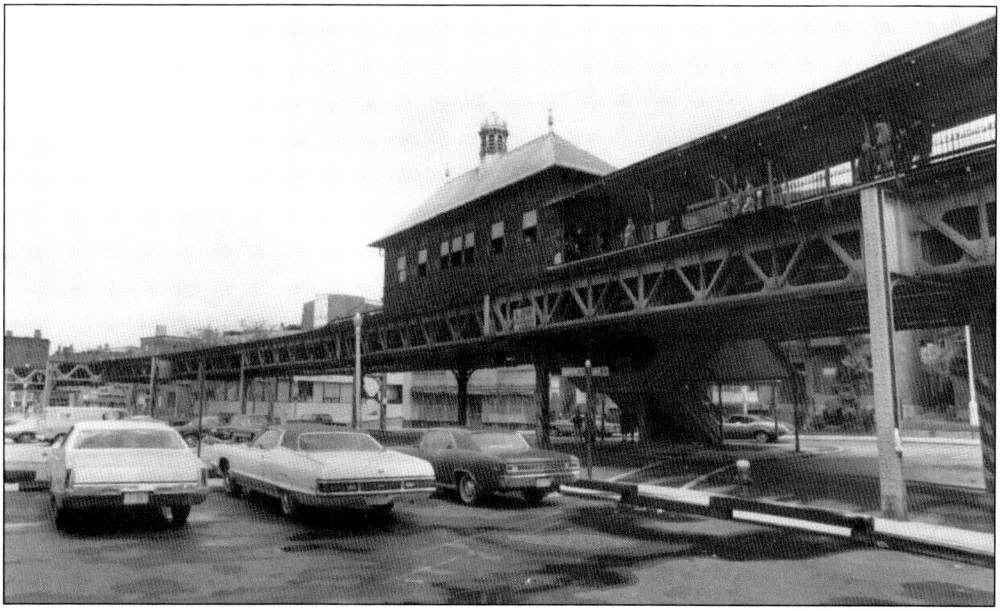

This 1970 image shows Thompson Square Station looming over a parking lot at the corner of Austin and Main Streets, just southeast of the station. The area remains a parking lot and now serves a strip mall that features a convenience store and tax preparation office. (Boston Landmarks Commission image collection, Collection 5210.004, City of Boston Archives, Boston.)

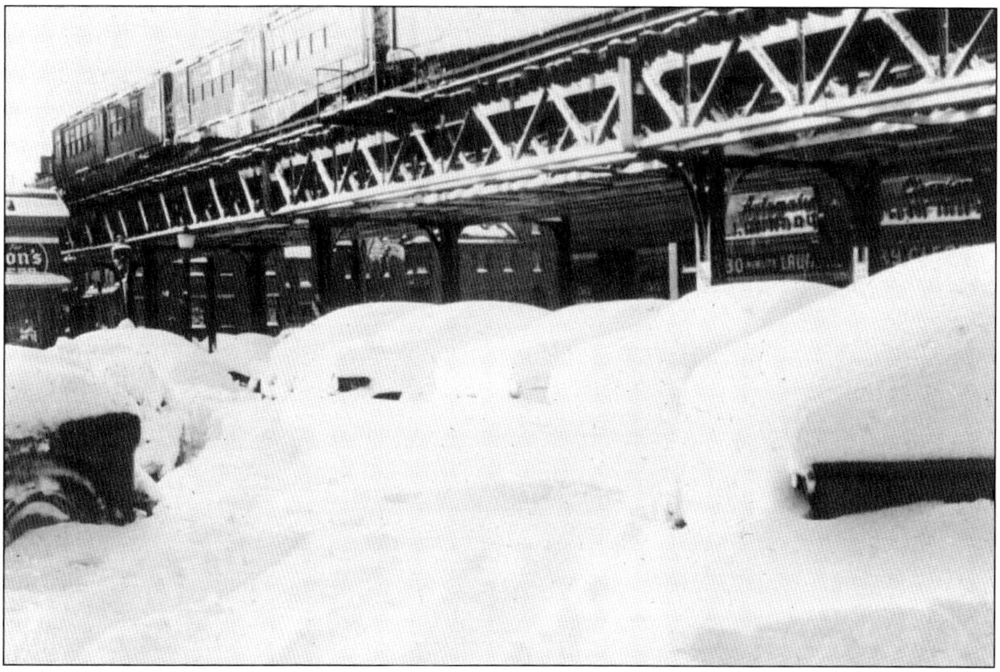

This image from March 20, 1956, shows cars in Thompson Square still buried under snow that fell four days earlier, in what *Boston Globe* weather writer Sumner Barton dubbed "the St. Patrick's Eve Blizzard of 1956." The snowstorm included winds of up to 60 miles per hour, forced thousands to abandon their vehicles, and killed 11 people. (Courtesy of Rev. Wolcott Cutler and the Boston Public Library.)

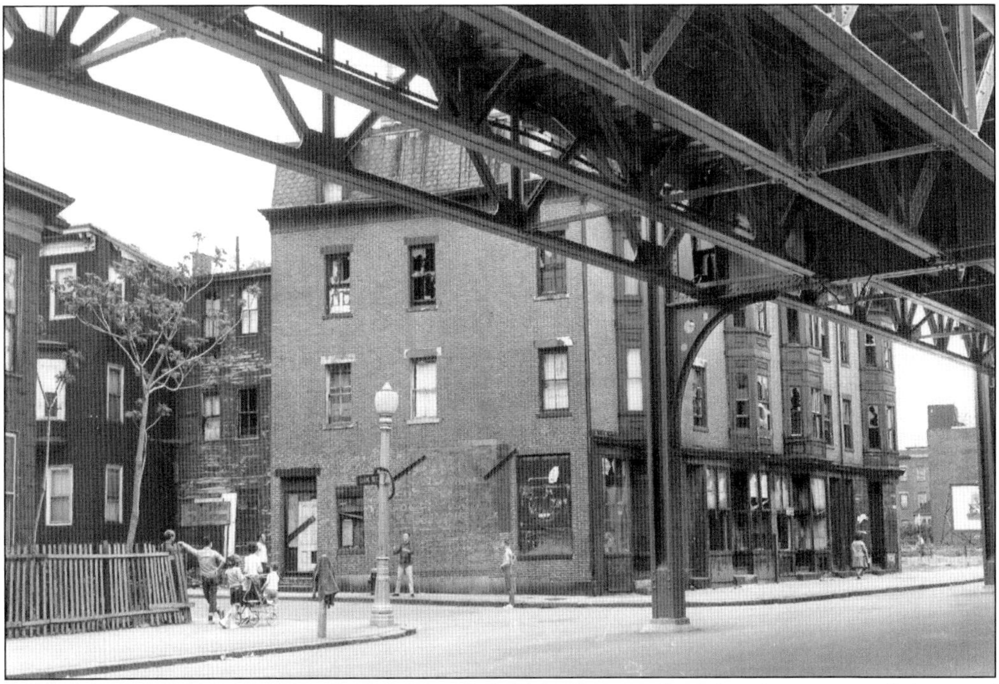

In this photograph from the 1960s, a group of children have gathered at the corner of Main and Oak Streets between Thompson and Sullivan Square Stations. The row of buildings alongside the El is badly dilapidated, with most windows broken or boarded. (Collection No. 5210.004, City of Boston Archives, Boston.)

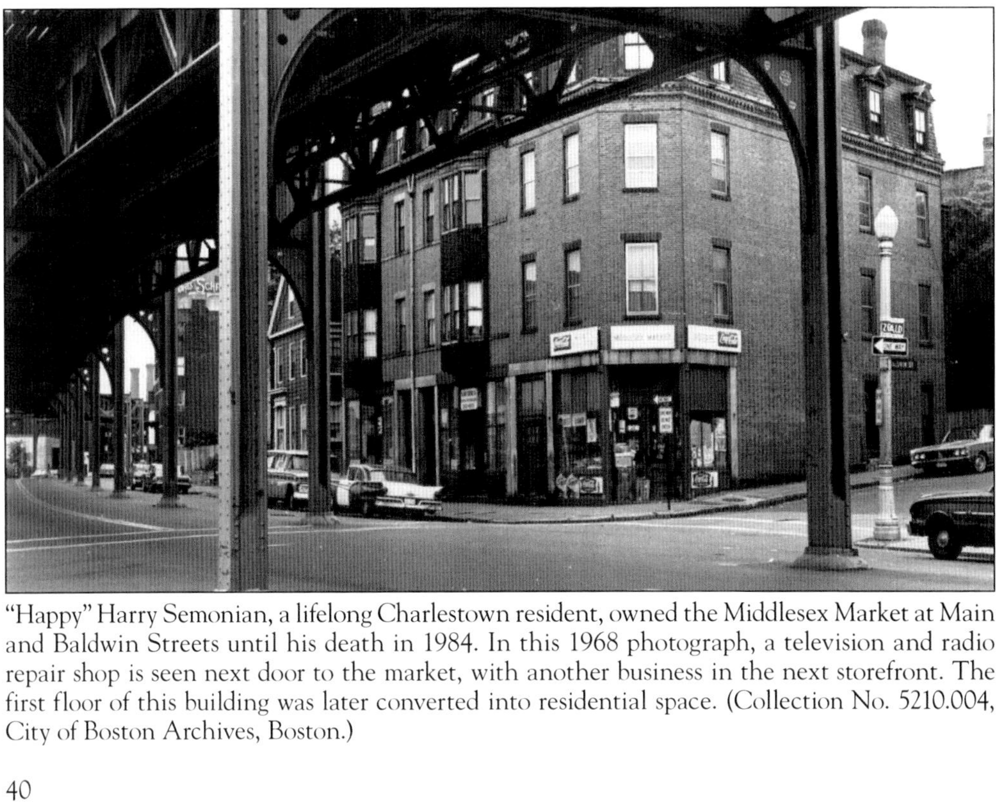

"Happy" Harry Semonian, a lifelong Charlestown resident, owned the Middlesex Market at Main and Baldwin Streets until his death in 1984. In this 1968 photograph, a television and radio repair shop is seen next door to the market, with another business in the next storefront. The first floor of this building was later converted into residential space. (Collection No. 5210.004, City of Boston Archives, Boston.)

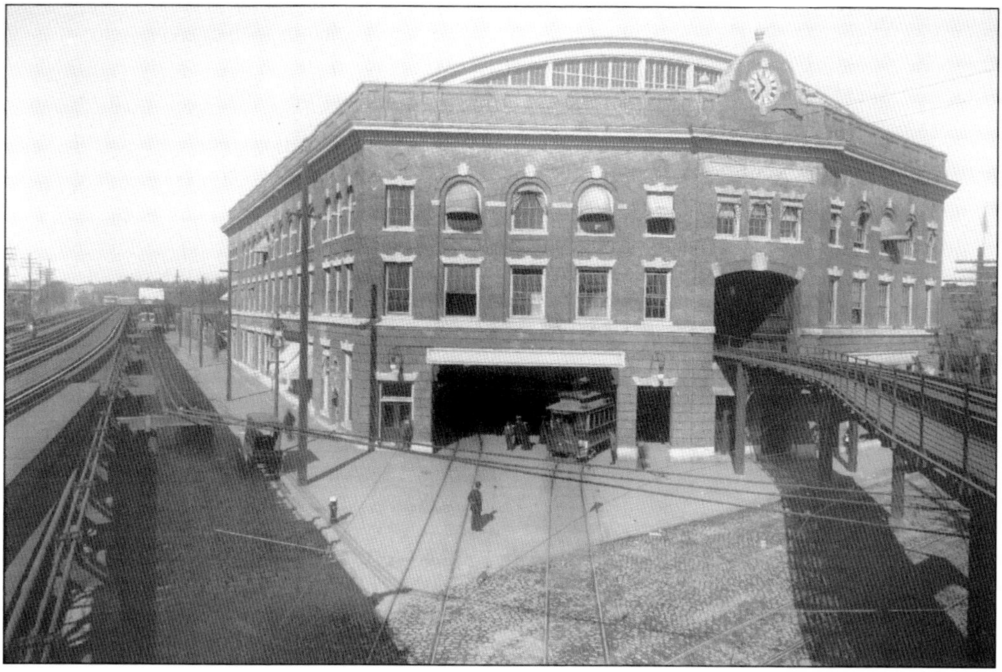

This image looks north toward Sullivan Square Station, the original terminus for the Charlestown Elevated before it was extended to Everett in 1919. Much like Dudley Street Station, the original terminus on the Washington Street Elevated, Sullivan Square Station was a major interchange on the Elevated. (Courtesy of the Boston Public Library.)

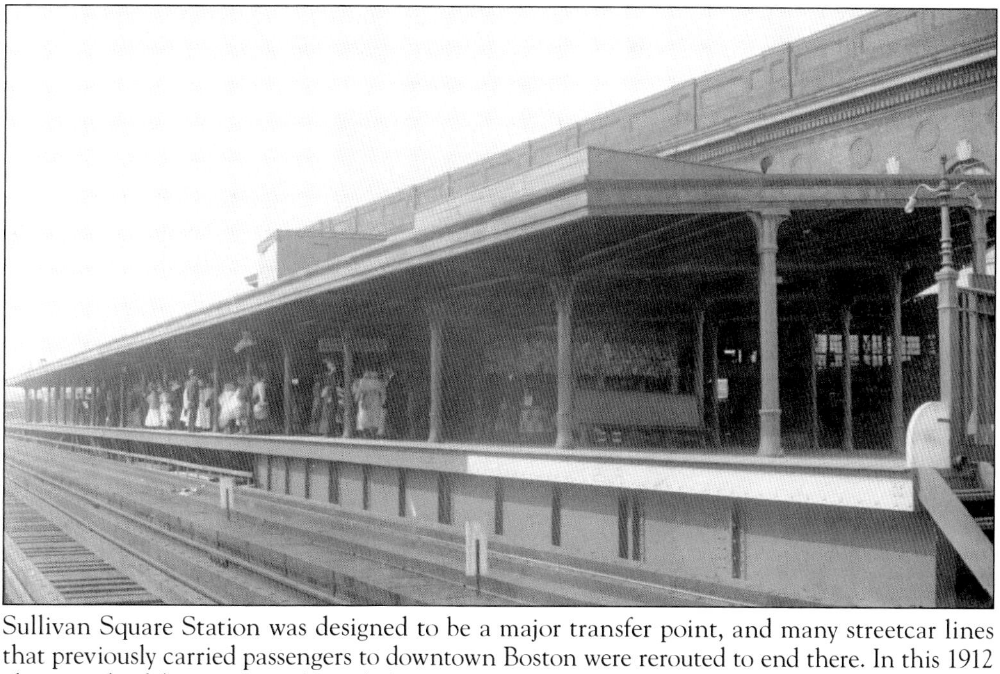

Sullivan Square Station was designed to be a major transfer point, and many streetcar lines that previously carried passengers to downtown Boston were rerouted to end there. In this 1912 photograph of the station's inbound platform, one sign above the passengers reads "Dudley Street via Tunnel," while another reads "Surface Cars to Malden and Everett." (Courtesy of the Boston Public Library.)

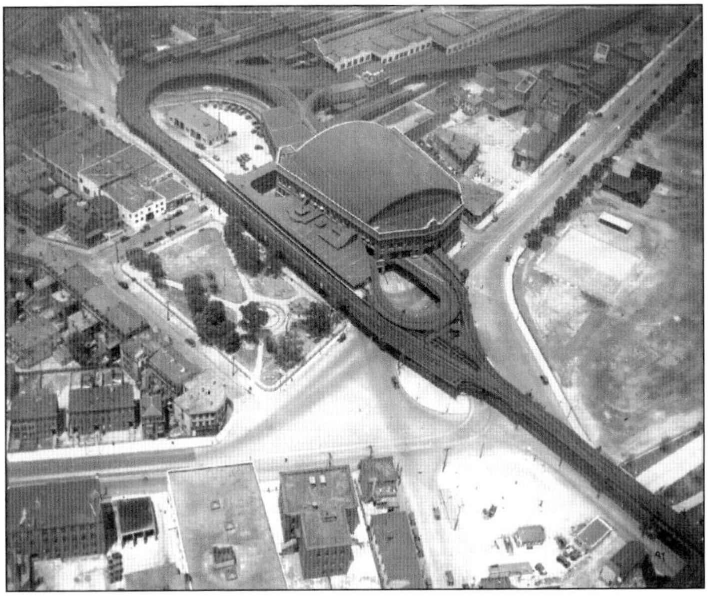

A c. 1915 aerial view shows Sullivan Square Station, near the edge of Charlestown and Somerville, with Charlestown's Main Street moving diagonally through the image from the lower left. The area surrounding the former Sullivan Square Station is now mostly parking lots and low-rise commercial space. Many of the older structures visible in this image have since been torn down. (Courtesy of the Boston Public Library.)

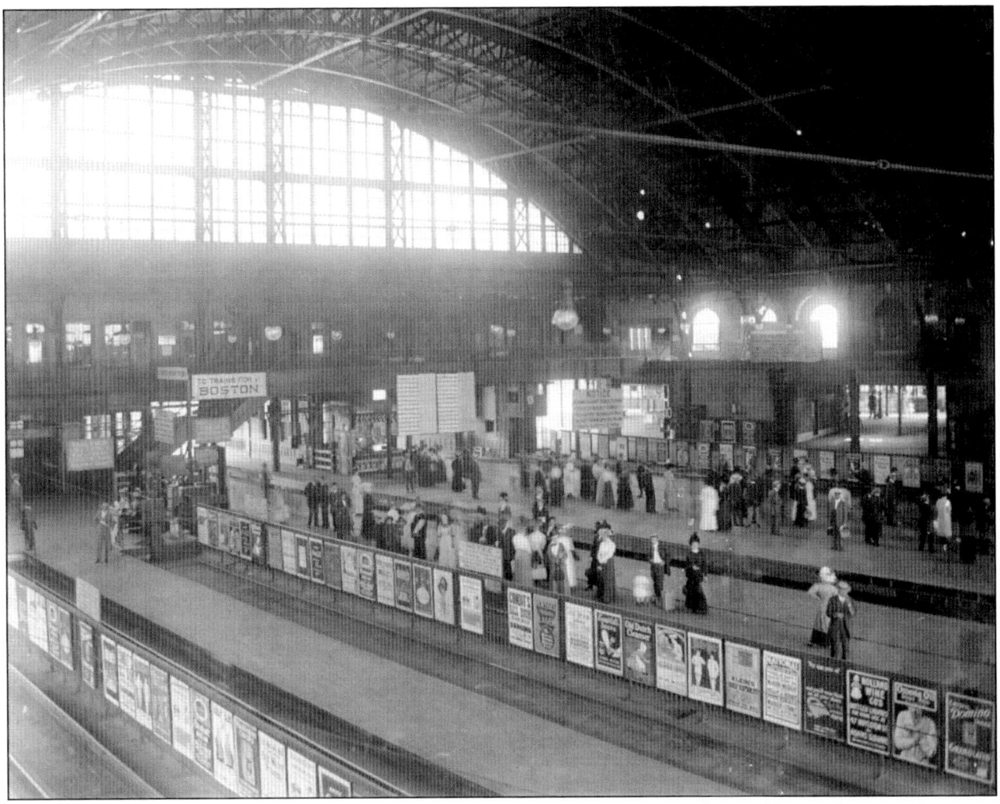

This c. 1912 photograph shows the dramatic interior platform in the Sullivan Square Station. The arched windows look south into the heart of Charlestown. A new Sullivan Square Station was built several blocks to the west in 1975 as part of a reconfiguration of the Orange Line route. The original Sullivan Square Station was damaged by fire and demolished in July 1975. (Courtesy of the Boston Public Library.)

Just east of Sullivan Square Station, Schrafft's Candy Factory looms over the Elevated in the photograph at right from June 1951. Founded by William F. Schrafft in 1861, Schrafft's was purchased in 1898 by Frank Shattuck, who expanded the company to include restaurants throughout the northeast. The Schrafft's building in Charlestown, adjacent to Sullivan Square Station, was built in 1928. Schrafft's was later purchased by Pet, Inc., and the Flatley Company purchased the building in 1984 and renovated it for use as commercial space. The 1901 image below, from the Boston Parks Department, looking west, shows the Sullivan Square playground with the Elevated tracks and station in the distance. In 1928, this area would become the site of the Schrafft's Candy Factory. (Both, courtesy of the Boston Public Library.)

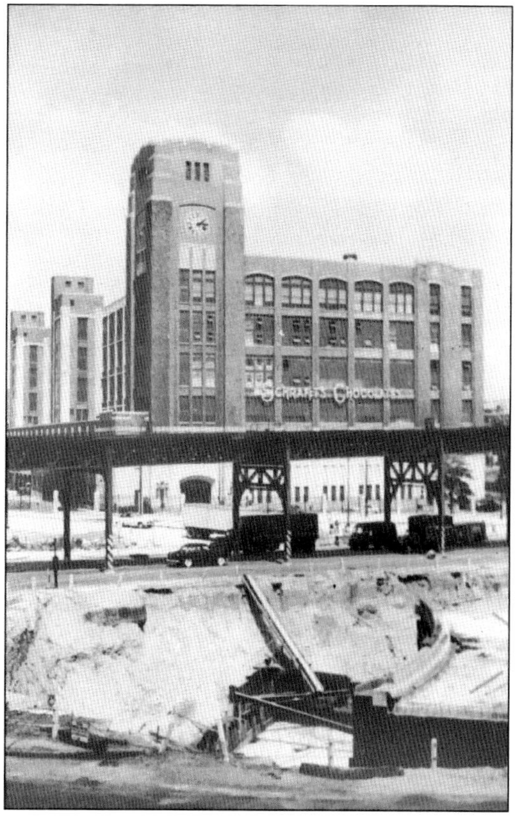

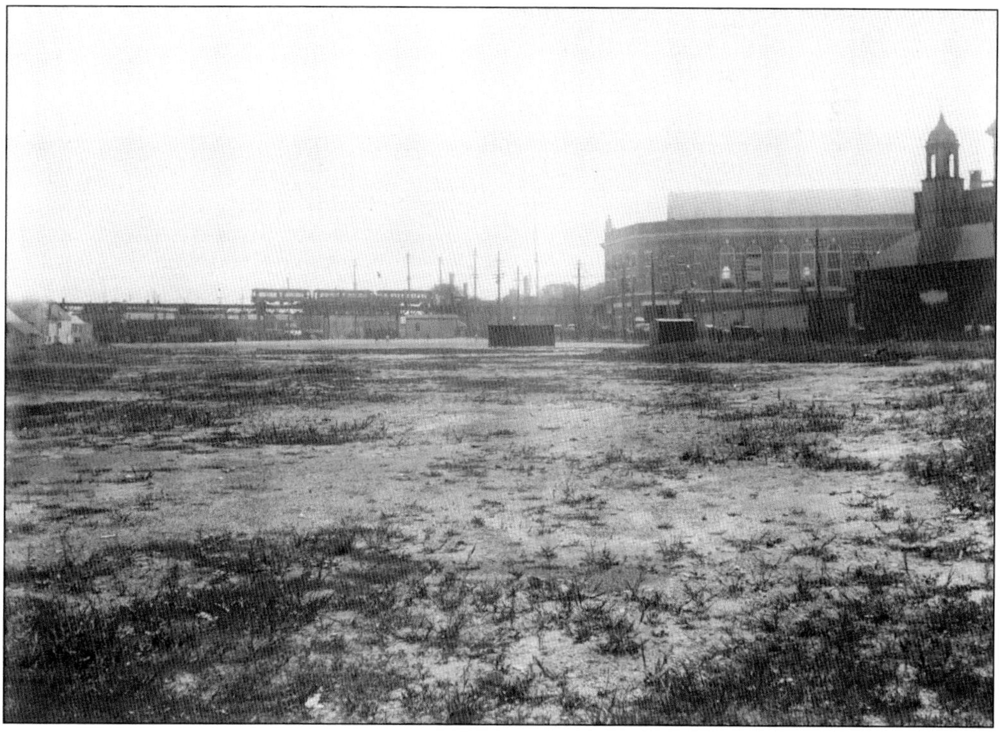

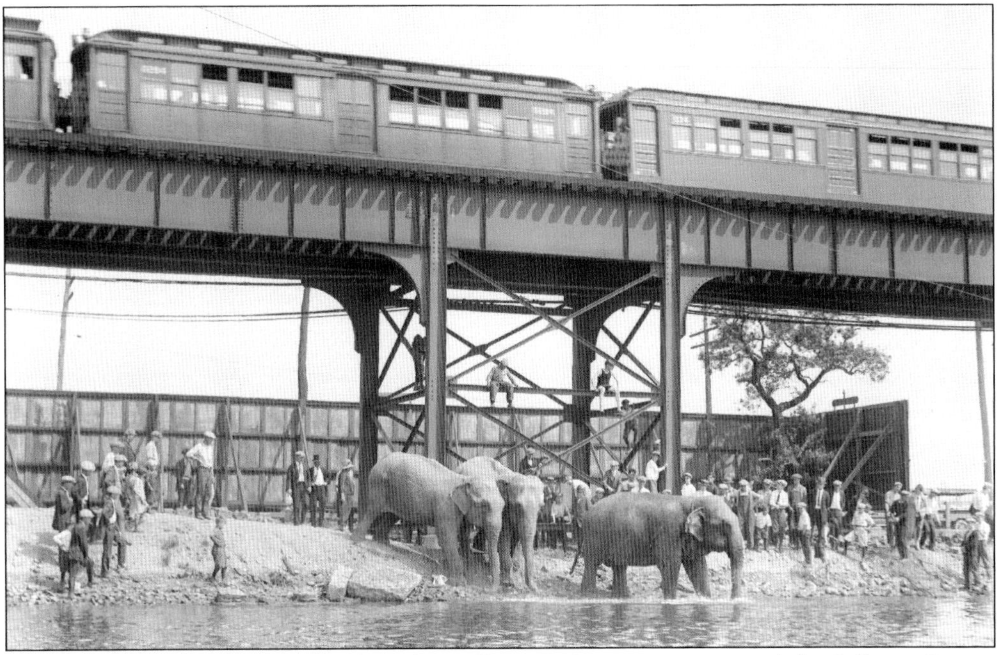

For many years, around the time of Bunker Hill Day in June, a circus visited the Sullivan Square park grounds, located between the station and the Mystic River. This photograph of elephants bathing in the Mystic River was probably taken sometime after the Elevated's extension to Everett in 1919 and before the mid-1930s, when Boston mayor Frederick Mansfield banned traveling carnivals. (Courtesy of the Boston Public Library; photograph by Leslie Jones.)

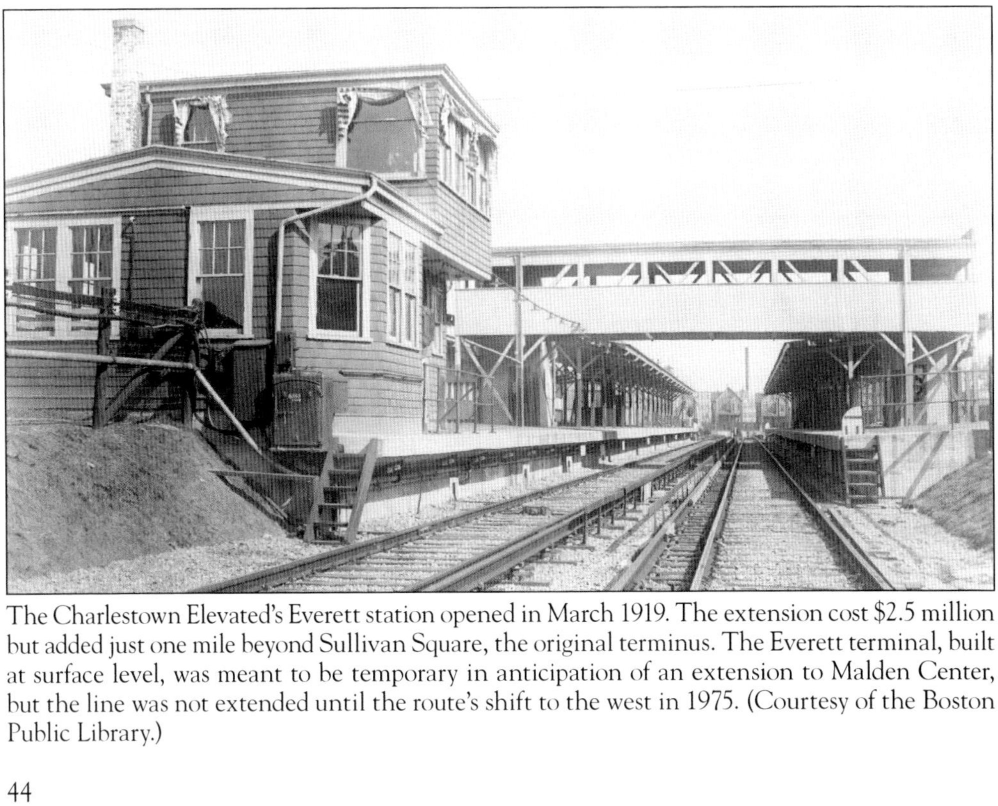

The Charlestown Elevated's Everett station opened in March 1919. The extension cost $2.5 million but added just one mile beyond Sullivan Square, the original terminus. The Everett terminal, built at surface level, was meant to be temporary in anticipation of an extension to Malden Center, but the line was not extended until the route's shift to the west in 1975. (Courtesy of the Boston Public Library.)

Three

TRAVERSING A CHANGING DOWNTOWN

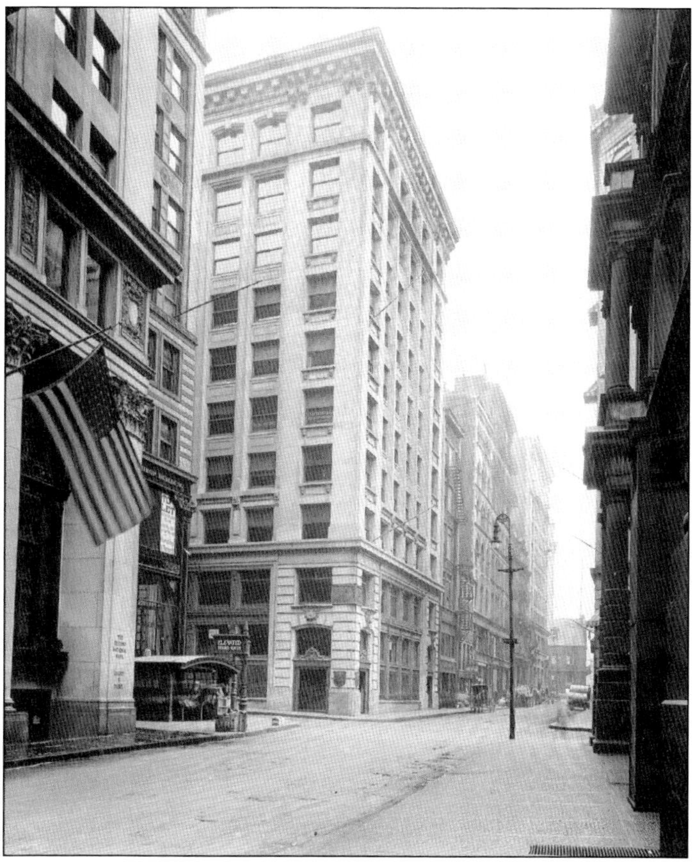

This photograph, taken before the 1930s, shows Devonshire Street at Water Street in downtown Boston. The low, arched canopy at bottom left is an entrance to the East Boston Tunnel, completed in 1904 and now part of the Blue Line, and Milk-State, now simply known as State. This entrance led to trains to East Boston but also offered connections to the Washington Street Tunnel. (Courtesy of the Boston Public Library.)

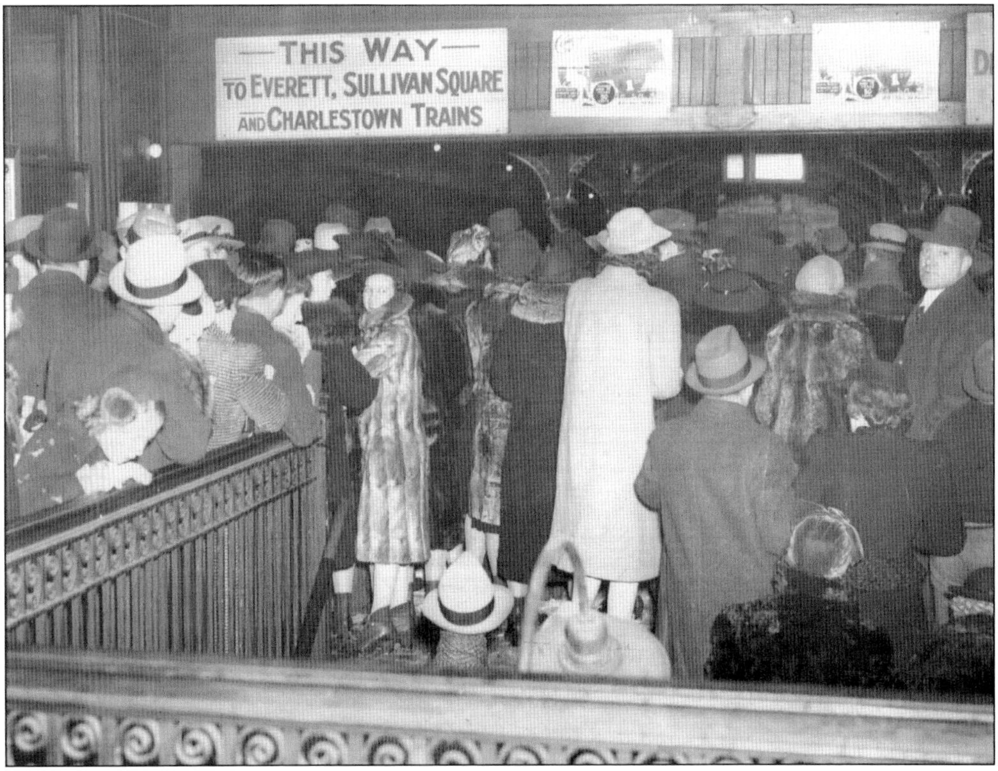

On February 14, 1940, a storm dropped 14 inches of snow on Boston and stranded thousands, including a large number of couples celebrating Valentine's Day. This image shows crowds at North Station, many of whom had just attended a Sonja Henie ice show at the Boston Garden. By the end of the show, train service throughout New England was cancelled and would not resume until the next morning. (Courtesy of the *Boston Globe*.)

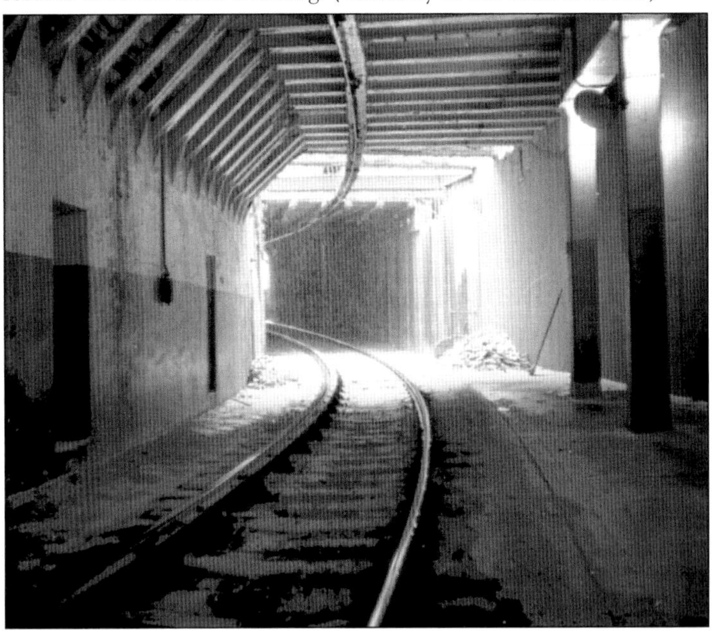

This c. 1967 photograph from the platform at Haymarket looks down the Washington Street Tunnel toward the Canal Street Incline and North Station. The Washington Street Tunnel opened on November 30, 1908. Beginning then, Main Line trains on the Elevated were rerouted from the Tremont Street Tunnel—now the central part of the Green Line—to the new tunnel. (Photograph by and courtesy of Steve Quinn.)

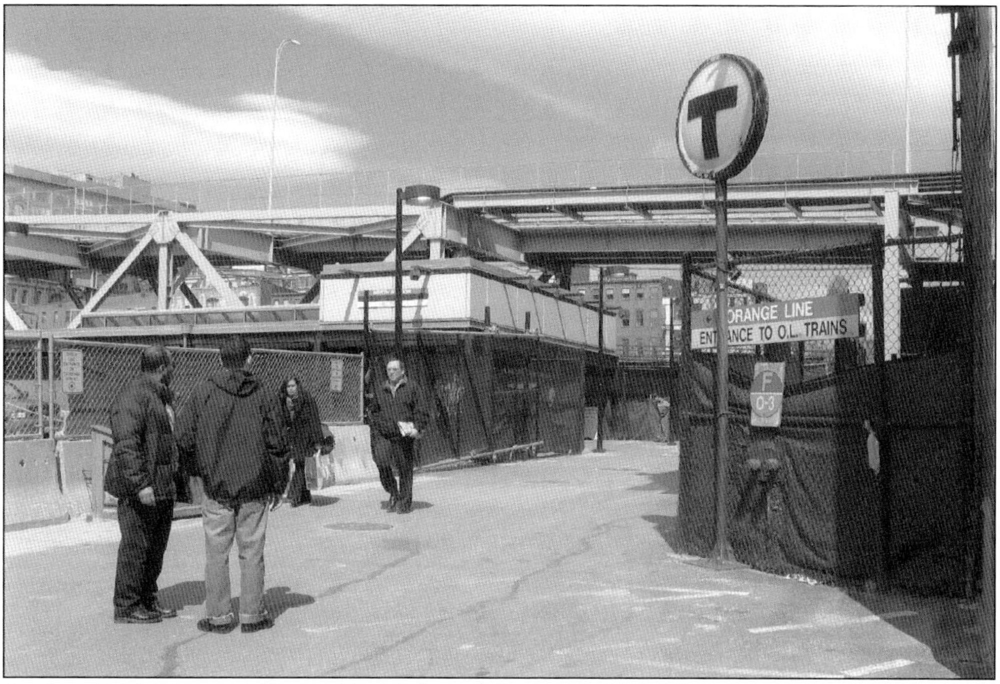

As the old Charlestown Elevated headed north, it emerged from the Washington Street Tunnel, climbed the Canal Street Incline, and stopped at an Elevated station just before the Boston Garden, which was built in 1928 and incorporated a North Station that served commuter and long-distance trains. When the Charlestown El was taken down and the line rerouted into a tunnel under the harbor and beneath Interstate 93 toward its new destination in Malden, the route included a new underground Orange Line stop at North Station. In 1995, the Boston Garden and North Station were replaced by the Fleet Center (now the TD Garden) and the current North Station. As shown in these photographs, North Station was remodeled again in 2005 to accommodate increasing ridership of the T and increasing railroad traffic. (Both, photograph by and courtesy of Andrew Lynch.)

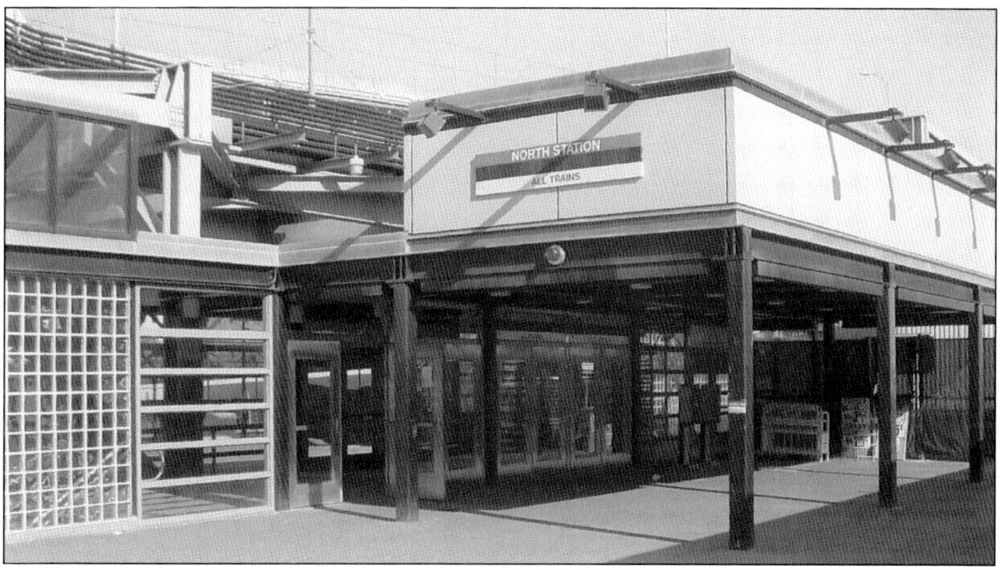

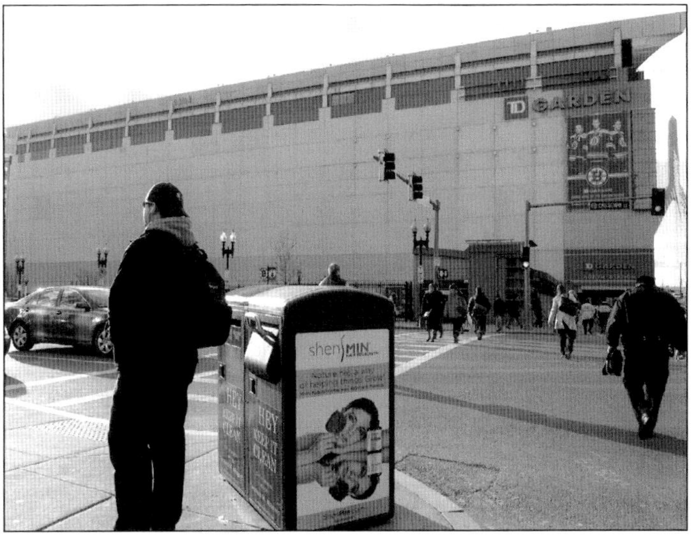

In this recent photograph, the entrance to North Station inside the TD Garden complex is visible at right, near the Leonard P. Zakim Bunker Hill Memorial Bridge, as commuters approach the station. TD Garden, home of both the Boston Celtics basketball team and the Boston Bruins hockey team, sits above the current ground-level main concourse of North Station. (Photograph by Jeremy C. Fox.)

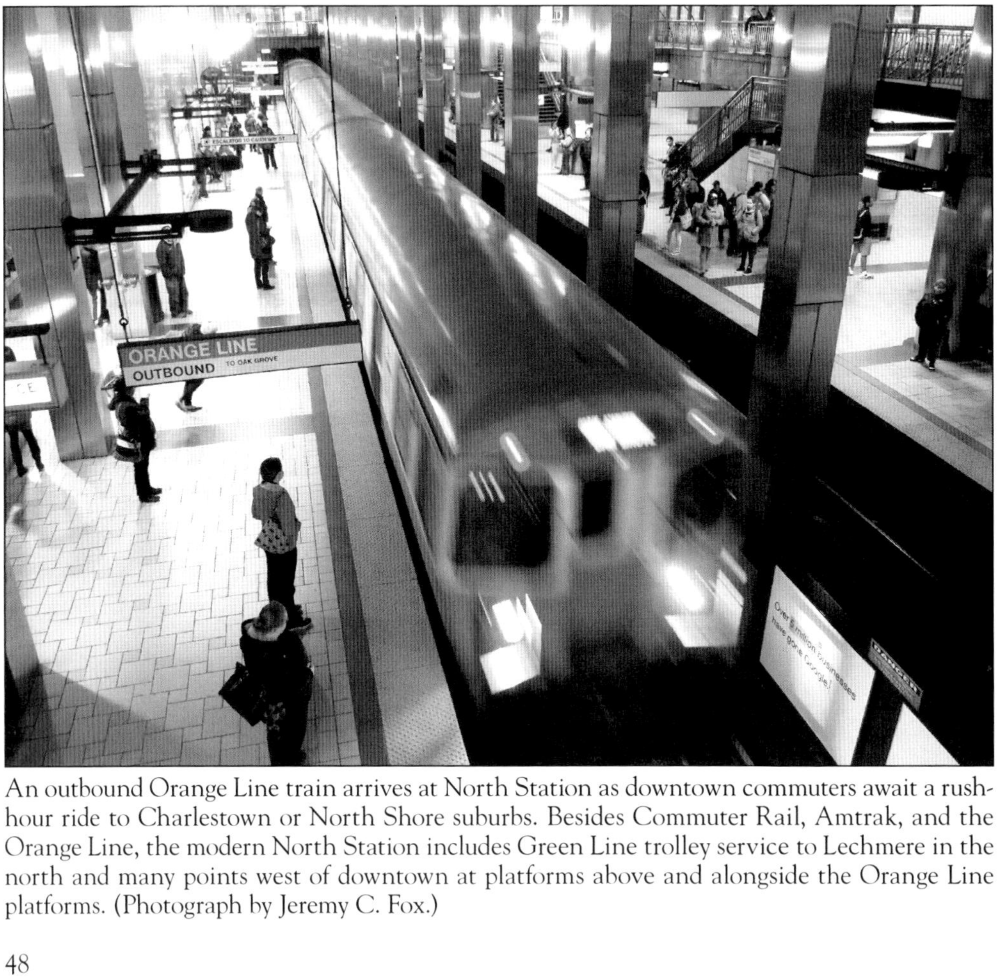

An outbound Orange Line train arrives at North Station as downtown commuters await a rush-hour ride to Charlestown or North Shore suburbs. Besides Commuter Rail, Amtrak, and the Orange Line, the modern North Station includes Green Line trolley service to Lechmere in the north and many points west of downtown at platforms above and alongside the Orange Line platforms. (Photograph by Jeremy C. Fox.)

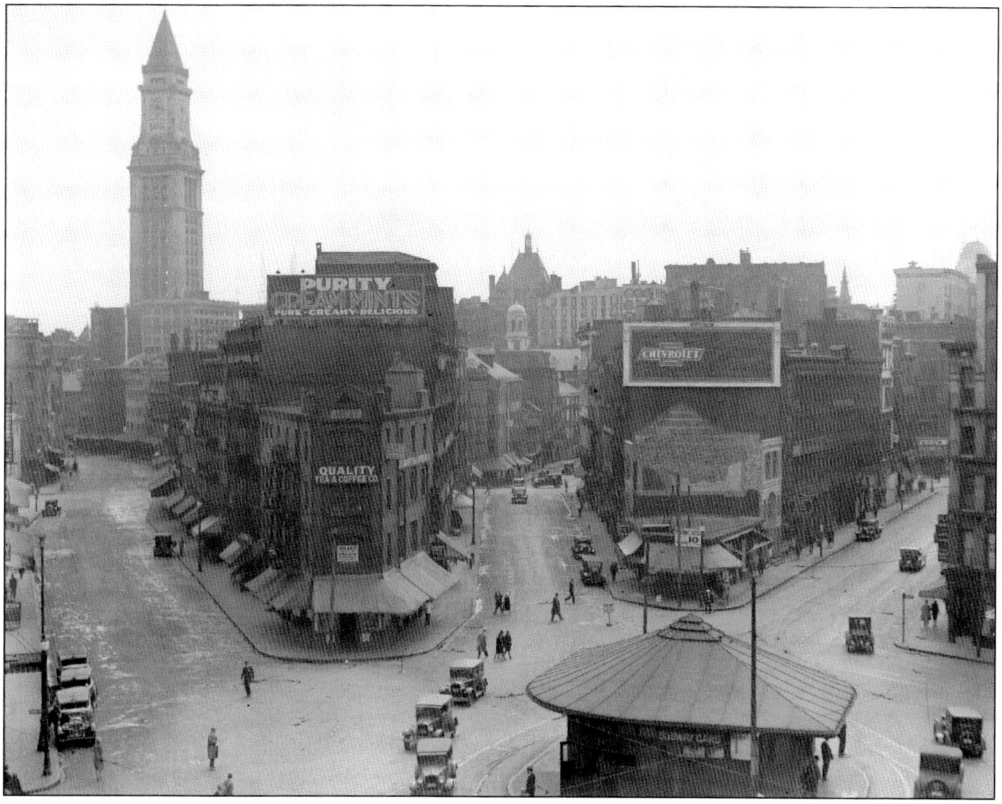

In this 1929 view looking south from the Haymarket Square Relief Hospital, the Haymarket Station headhouse is at bottom right. Blackstone Street is at left, with the Custom House Tower visible above it. Union Street runs down the center of the photograph, with the dome atop Faneuil Hall visible in the distance. At right, Washington Street leads toward Adams Square. (Courtesy of the Boston Public Library; photograph by Leslie Jones.)

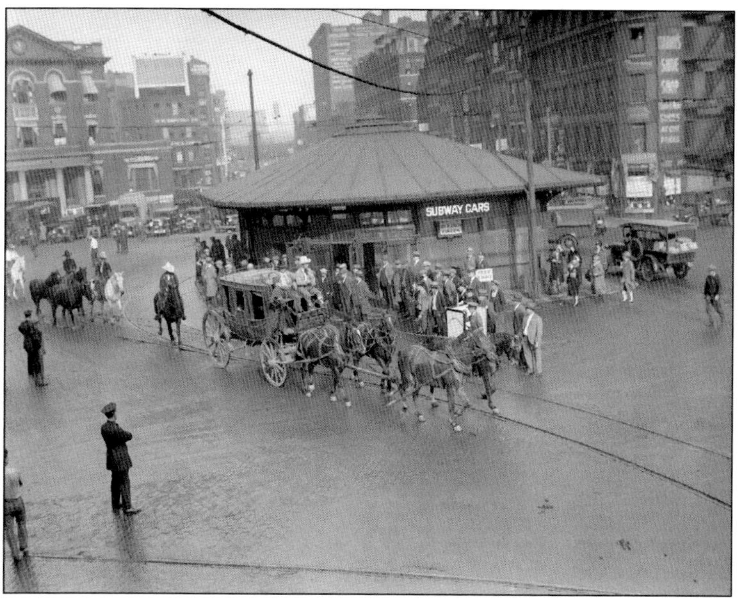

Another 1929 photograph shows Haymarket Square looking north, with the Haymarket Relief Hospital at left. Behind the hospital, Charlestown Elevated trains climbed the Canal Street Incline to North Station. The photograph captures a stagecoach passing the Haymarket Station headhouse during a rodeo parade. (Courtesy of the Boston Public Library; photograph by Leslie Jones.)

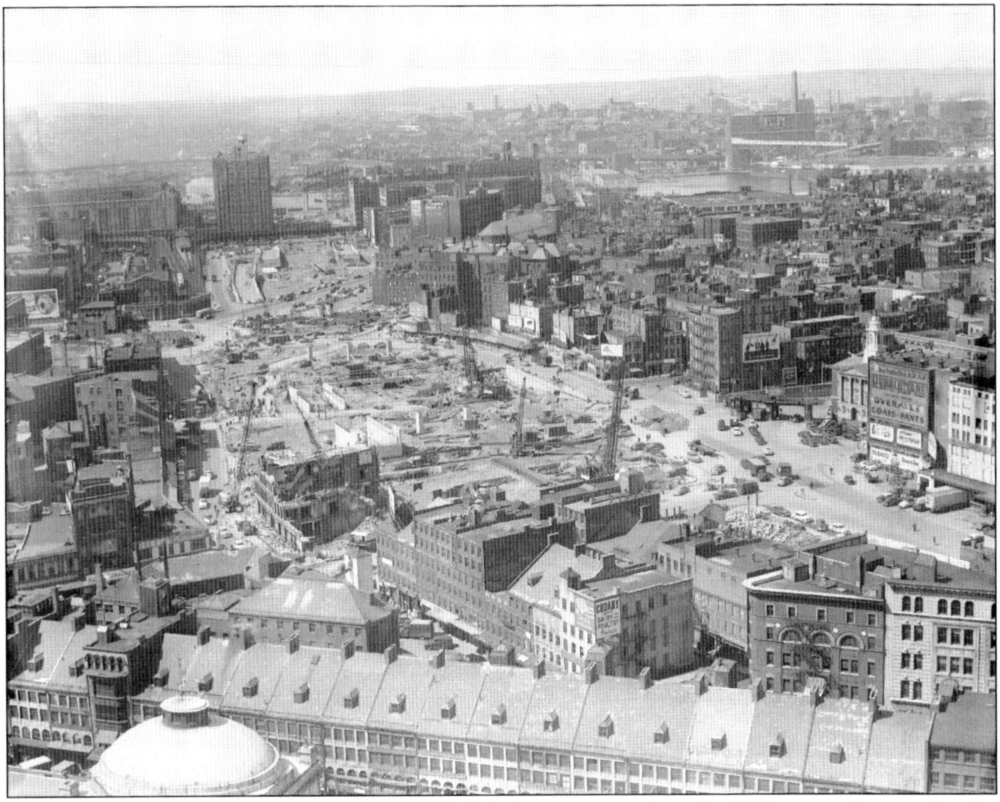

Haymarket Square was spared when adjacent blocks were razed in the 1950s to make way for the elevated Central Artery. As seen in this image looking north down Blackstone Street, demolition stopped right at the edge of the square. Haymarket Square would eventually fall to wrecking balls in the 1960s, along with the old Scollay Square, as Government Center was developed. (Courtesy of the Boston Public Library; photograph by Leslie Jones.)

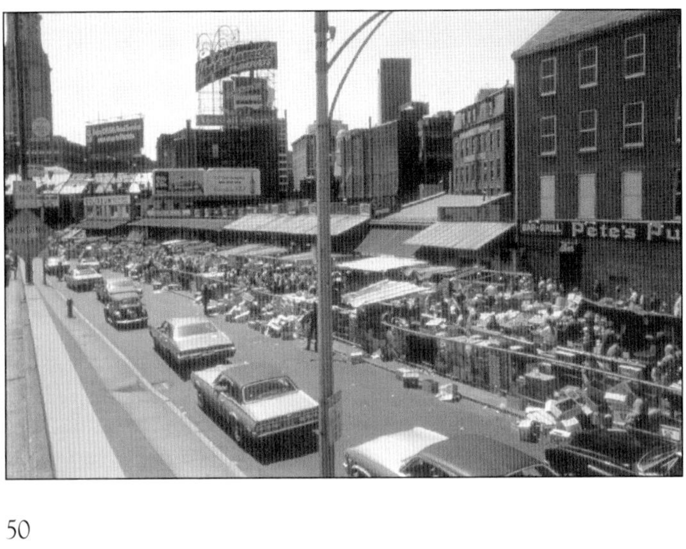

Though the old Haymarket Square was destroyed, the weekly produce market, founded in the 1830s, continued to thrive. This photograph, which looks south along Blackstone Street toward the Custom House Tower, was taken in 1973, and the market was no less lively in 2013, having outlasted the Elevated, the Central Artery, and the Big Dig. (Courtesy of the US National Archives.)

This rubble-filled 1967 photograph appears to show a disused portion of the original 1898 Haymarket Station. Built in the 1890s to serve the Tremont Street Subway, the station began serving Elevated trains between Sullivan Square and Dudley Square in 1901. Elevated trains were rerouted to the Washington Street Tunnel when it opened in 1908 but continued to use Haymarket Station. (Photograph by and courtesy of Steve Quinn.)

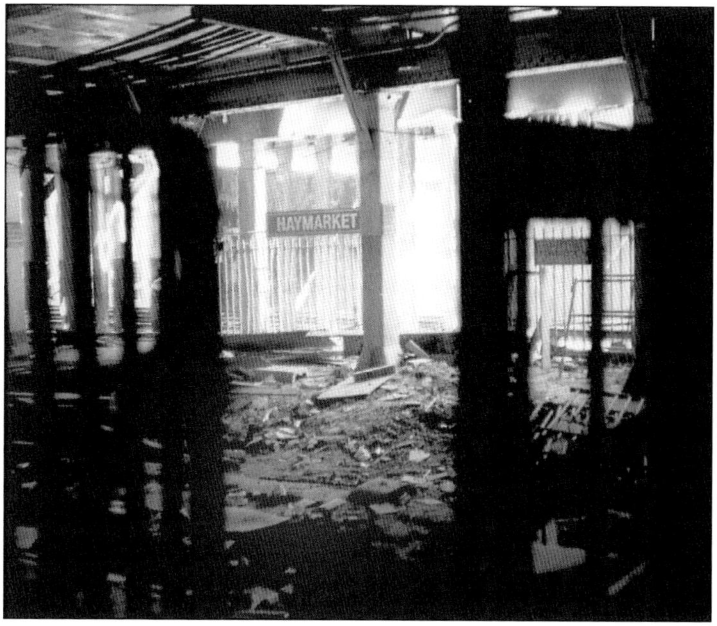

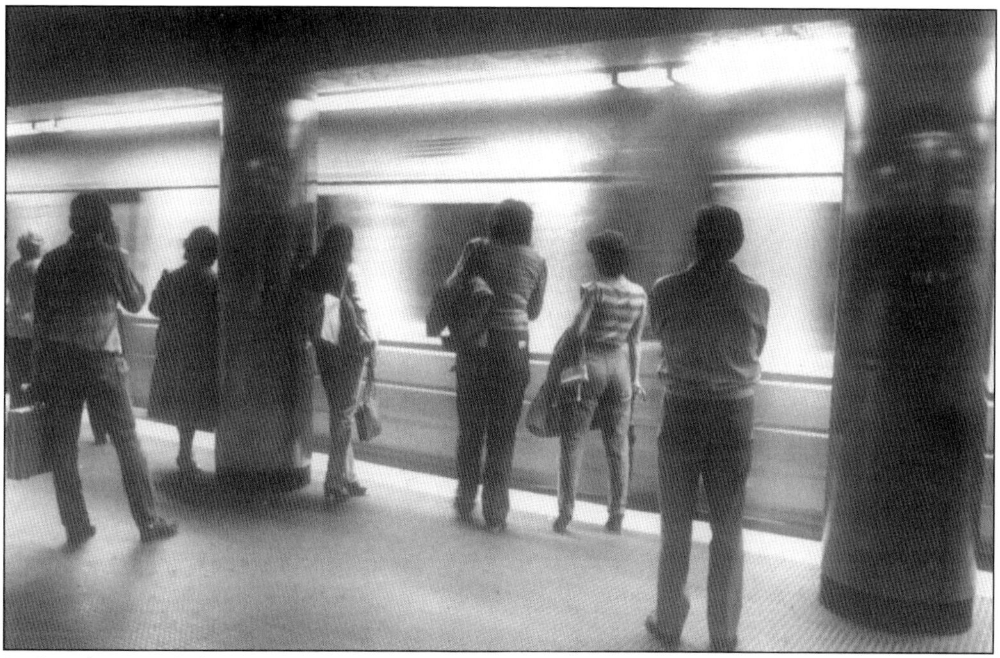

In this photograph from September 16, 1981, people wait for the Orange Line at Haymarket Station. Though still a major bus transfer center today, Haymarket Station became less significant for transfers between the Orange and Green Lines after the Green Line was also rerouted out of the Canal Street Incline and into North Station in 2004. (Courtesy of the *Boston Globe*; photograph by John Blanding.)

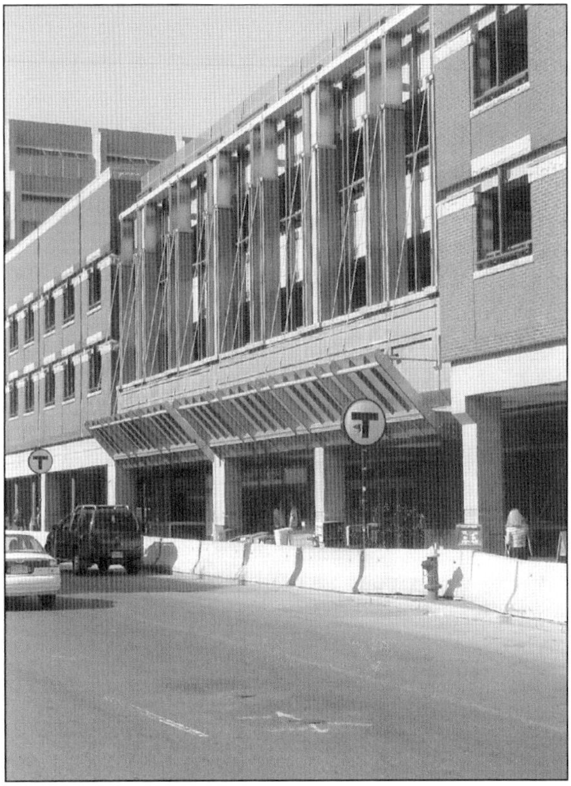

During the Big Dig, a building was constructed on a former parking lot site at Hanover and Congress Streets, southeast of the Government Center Garage, which included access to Haymarket Station below. A vent tower for the Thomas P. O'Neill Jr. Tunnel, the building also contains a parking garage and has spaces planned for the Registry of Motor Vehicles and a public market. (Photograph by and courtesy of Andrew Lynch.)

State Street Station is bookended by major historical sites. Its main entrance is a first-floor space inside the Old State House, while a second entrance (pictured) stands beside the Old South Meeting House, visible through the window at right. The station's northbound platform was known as State, while the southbound platform was called Milk (for its entrance on Milk Street). (Photograph by and courtesy of Nathaniel Marsh.)

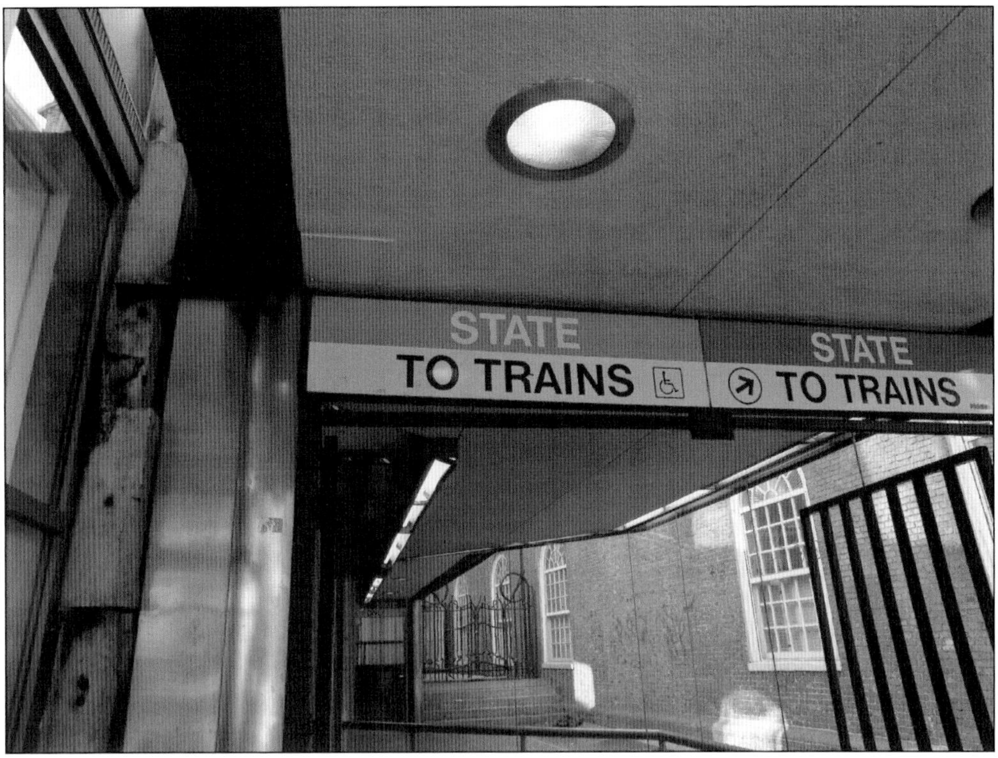

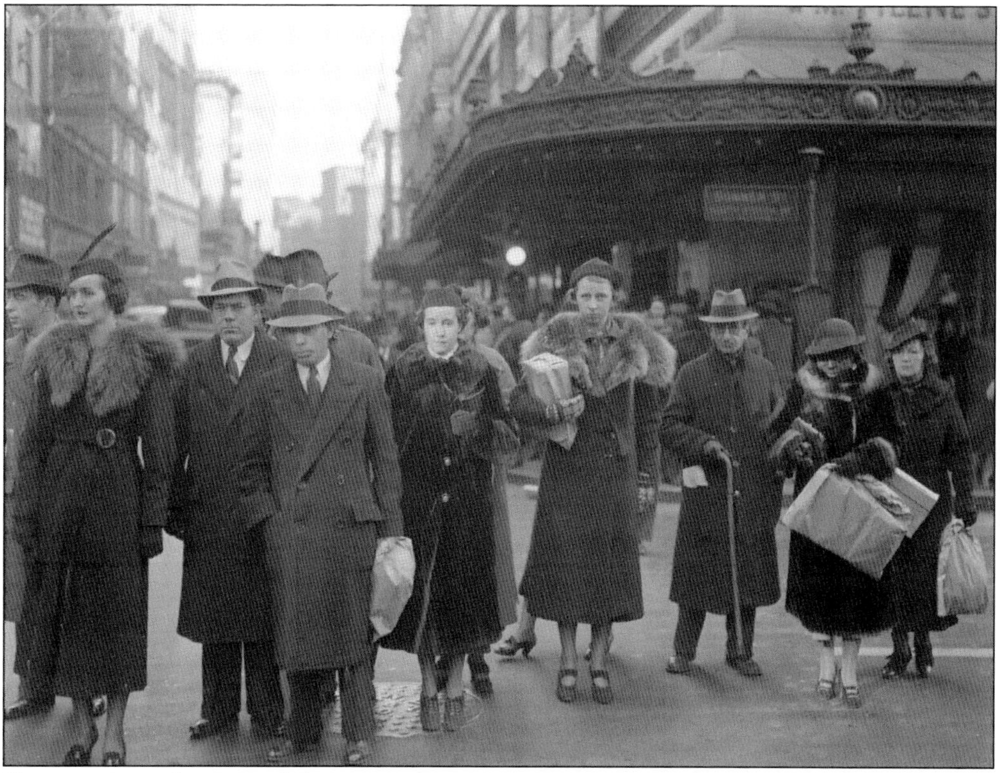

Shoppers dressed in 1940s fashions stand on Summer Street at Washington Street, near Summer Station and in front of Filene's Department Store. Opened in 1912 by Edward and Lincoln Filene, sons of founder William Filene, who began a chain of retail and clothing stores in Boston in 1881, this Filene's was the primary competitor of neighboring store Jordan Marsh. (Courtesy of the Boston Public Library; photograph by Leslie Jones.)

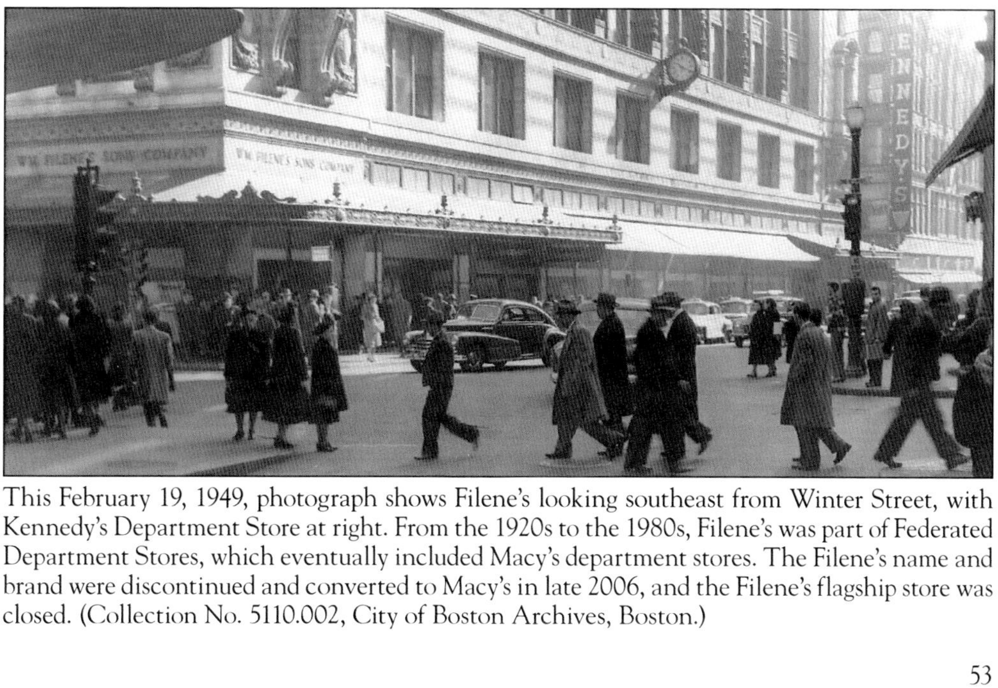

This February 19, 1949, photograph shows Filene's looking southeast from Winter Street, with Kennedy's Department Store at right. From the 1920s to the 1980s, Filene's was part of Federated Department Stores, which eventually included Macy's department stores. The Filene's name and brand were discontinued and converted to Macy's in late 2006, and the Filene's flagship store was closed. (Collection No. 5110.002, City of Boston Archives, Boston.)

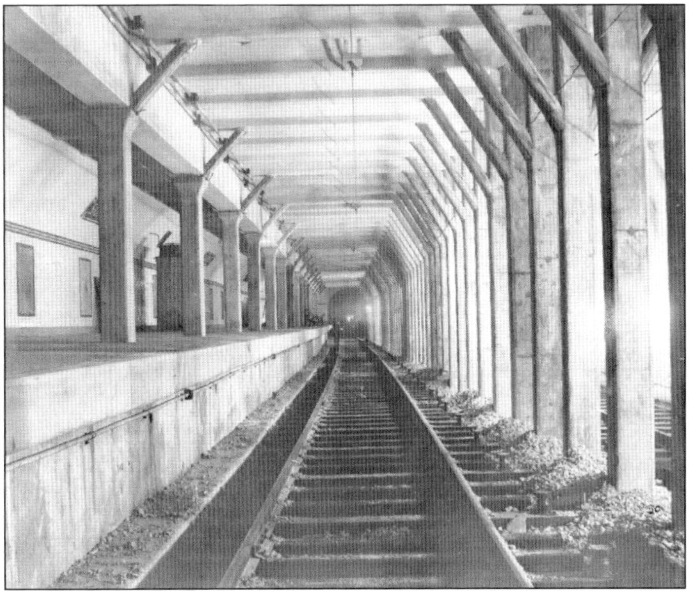

This view looks down the Washington Street Tunnel at the Summer Street platform. The northbound Summer Street platform was named for its location at the intersection of Washington and Summer Streets. The southbound Winter Street platform was so named because Washington and Summer Streets also intersected with Winter Street, a short street that runs from Washington Street to Tremont Street at the Boston Common. (Courtesy of the Boston Public Library.)

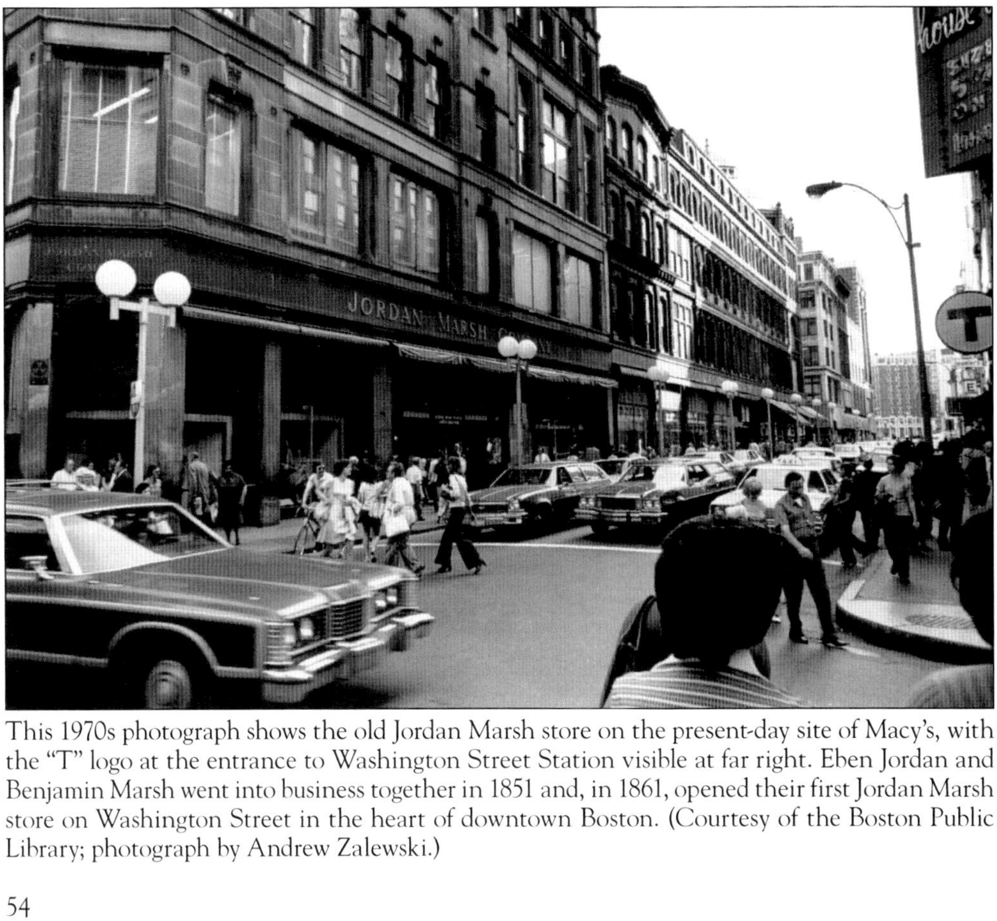

This 1970s photograph shows the old Jordan Marsh store on the present-day site of Macy's, with the "T" logo at the entrance to Washington Street Station visible at far right. Eben Jordan and Benjamin Marsh went into business together in 1851 and, in 1861, opened their first Jordan Marsh store on Washington Street in the heart of downtown Boston. (Courtesy of the Boston Public Library; photograph by Andrew Zalewski.)

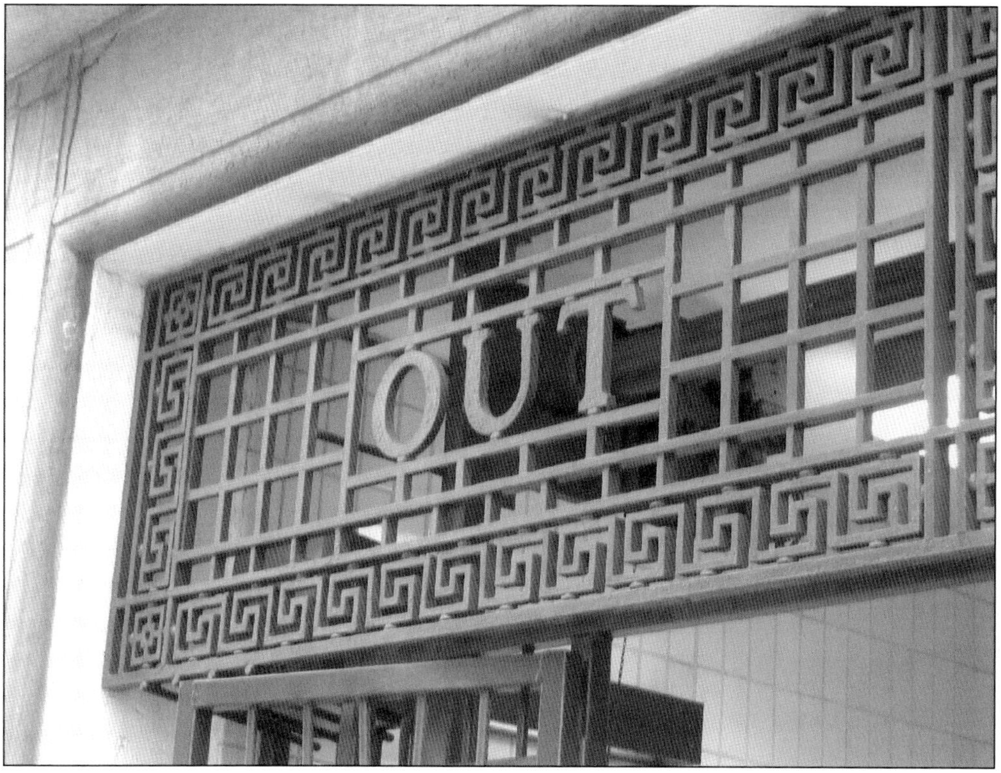

Washington Street Station was renamed Downtown Crossing on May 4, 1987, but many elements of the old station remain. These photographs from the Downtown Crossing entrance, located between 55 and 59 Temple Place, show ironwork that appears to date from its opening as Winter Station in 1908. Winter Station (the southbound platform of what is now Downtown Crossing) and Summer Station (Downtown Crossing's northbound platform) were officially united, along with the Red Line platforms beneath, under the shared name Washington Station on January 23, 1967, just over 20 years before the MBTA gave the station its current name. (Both, photograph by and courtesy of Andrew Lynch.)

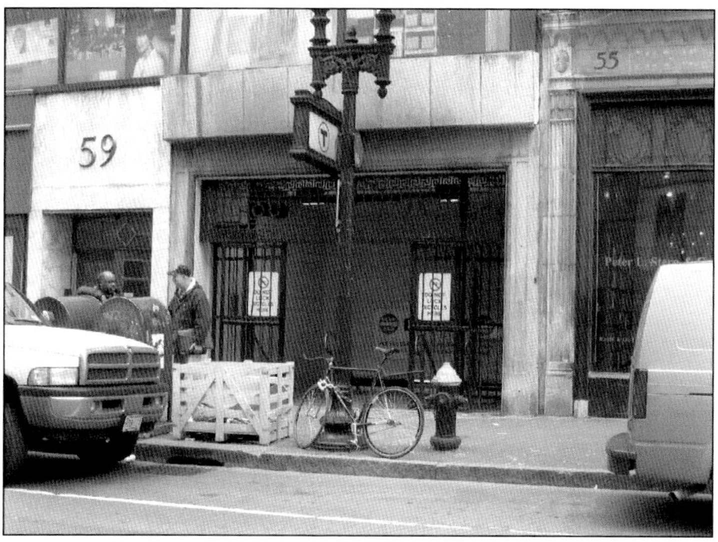

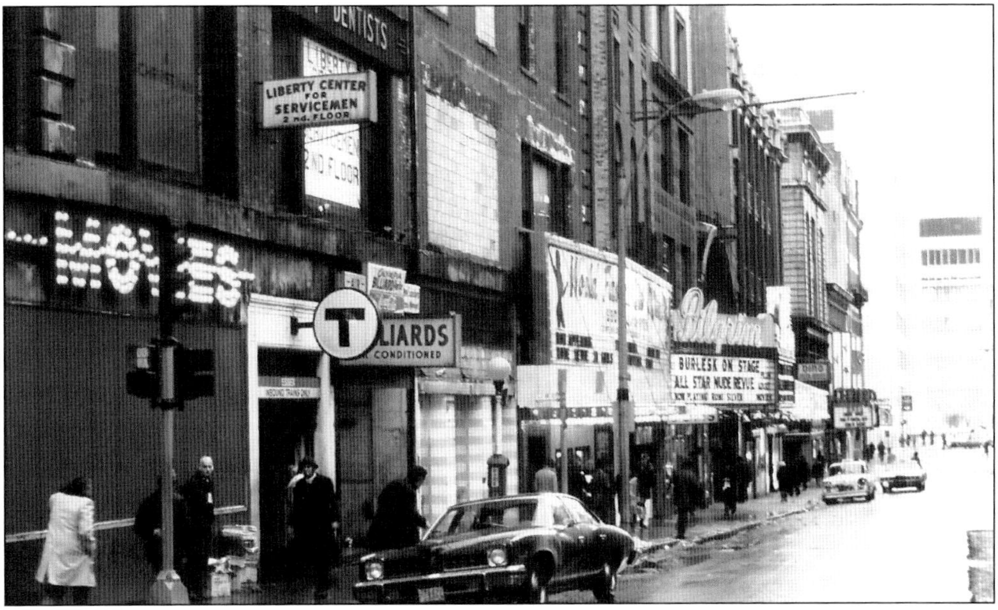

More name changes came on Lower Washington Street, where the southbound platform was first called Boylston and the northbound platform was called Essex. The entire station became Essex in 1967 and then Chinatown in 1987. This 1975 photograph shows Lower Washington Street, with Essex Station at left, when the neighborhood was known as the Combat Zone—a center of prostitution, drug dealing, and violent crime. (Photograph by and courtesy of Thomas W. Ericson.)

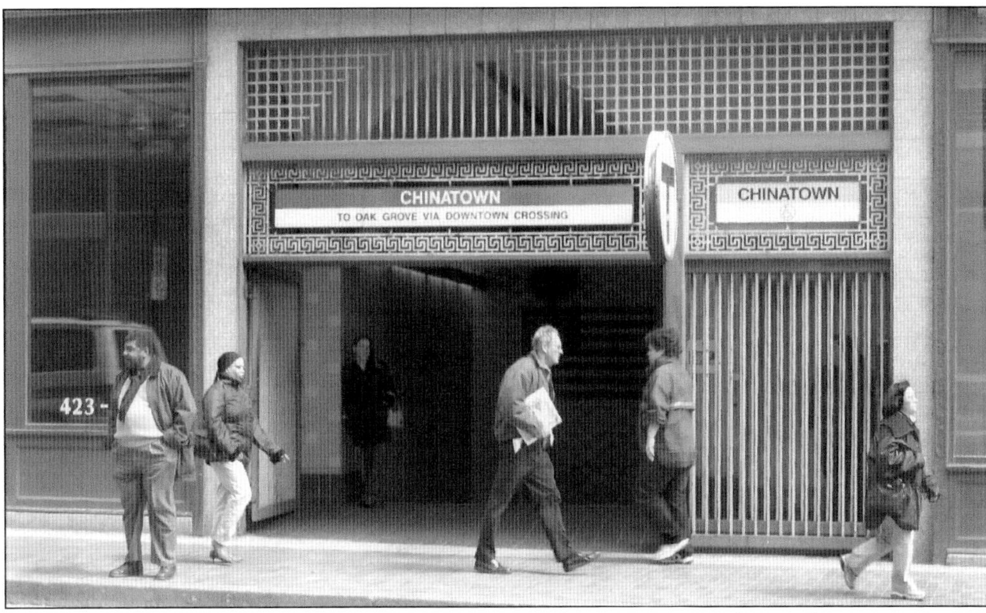

A later view of the same area, looking east across Washington Street, shows Chinatown Station after the neighborhood had been cleaned up and the Liberty Tree Building at 628–636 Washington Street (where this subway entrance stands) had been redeveloped for use by the Registry of Motor Vehicles in the late 1990s. The Boston Landmarks Commission declared the Liberty Tree Block a landmark in 1985. (Photograph by and courtesy of Andrew Lynch.)

Four

THE WASHINGTON STREET ELEVATED

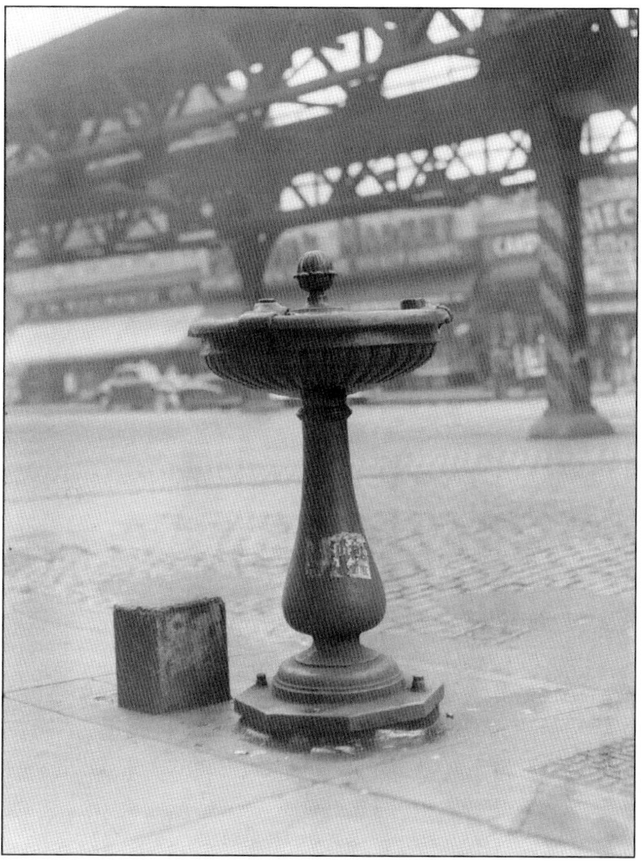

In this photograph taken sometime between the mid-1930s and mid-1950s, a water fountain stands on Washington Street in the South End of Boston, across from Folsom's Market. Folsom's Market, which billed itself as "Boston's Busiest Food Store," stood between Northampton and Lenox Streets for decades, one of many businesses that operated in the shadow of the Washington Street Elevated. (Courtesy of the Boston Public Library; photograph by Leslie Jones.)

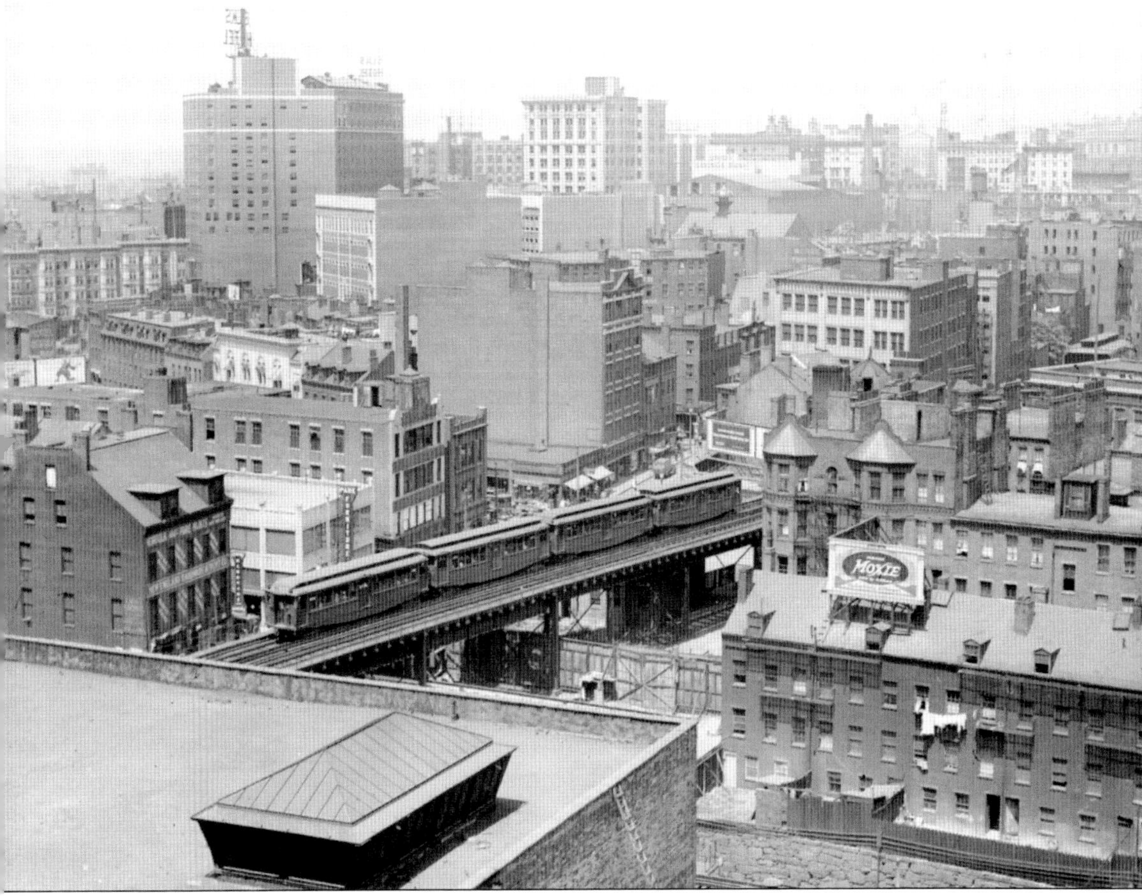

A 1929 image from a South End rooftop shows the Washington Street Elevated, with the Elks Hotel, located in the Theater District, visible at upper left. The four-car train appears to include a first and third car of the No. 1 design, used since the Elevated's 1901 opening, and a second and fourth car of the No. 7 design, introduced around 1921. (Courtesy of the Boston Public Library; photograph by Leslie Jones.)

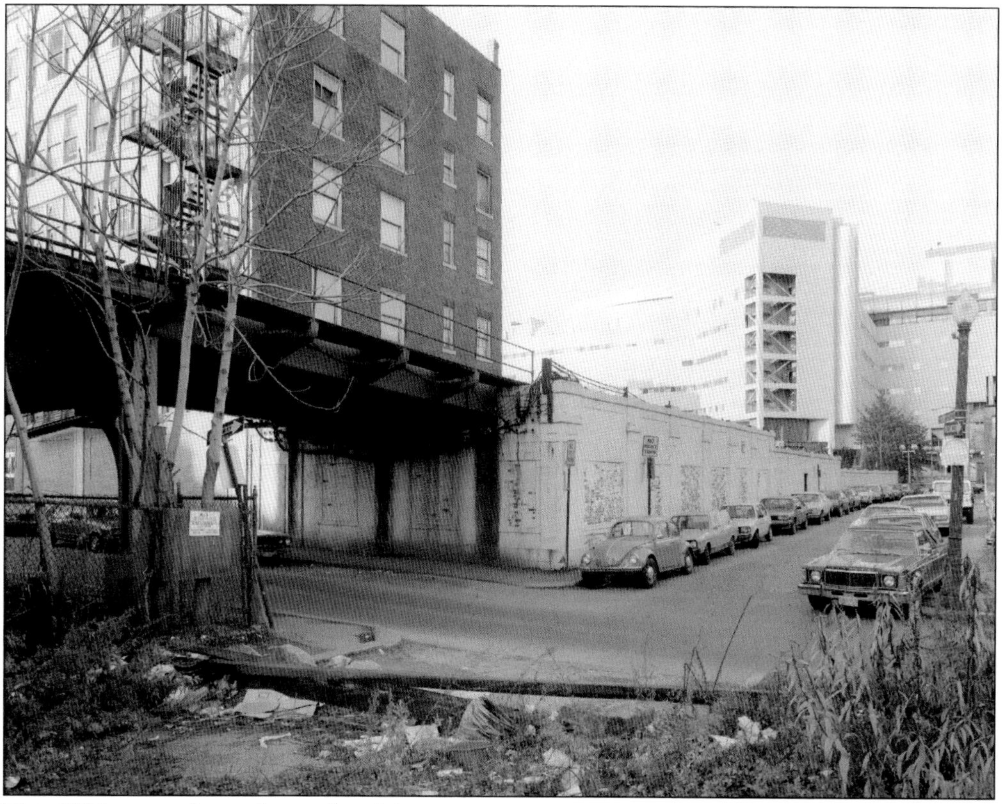

This 1982 image shows the tracks of the Elevated as they emerge from the southern end of the Washington Street Tunnel at the Ash Street Incline. The tunnel opened in 1908 and connected the Charlestown, Washington Street, and Atlantic Avenue lines. The station's underground platforms, which are still in service, originally had names based on the streets where passengers entered from aboveground. (Courtesy of the Historic American Engineering Record; photograph by Richard Cheek.)

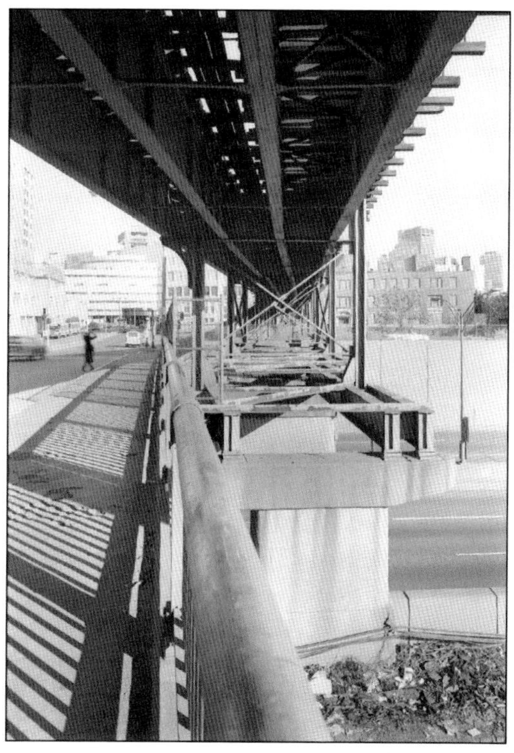

After emerging from the Washington Street Tunnel, the El crossed the Massachusetts Turnpike. The main section of the turnpike—from the New York State border to Route 128 outside of Boston—was completed in 1958. In 1964 and 1965, the Boston extension was completed, bringing the turnpike from Route 128 to the Central Artery in downtown Boston. (Courtesy of the Historic American Engineering Record; photograph by Richard Cheek.)

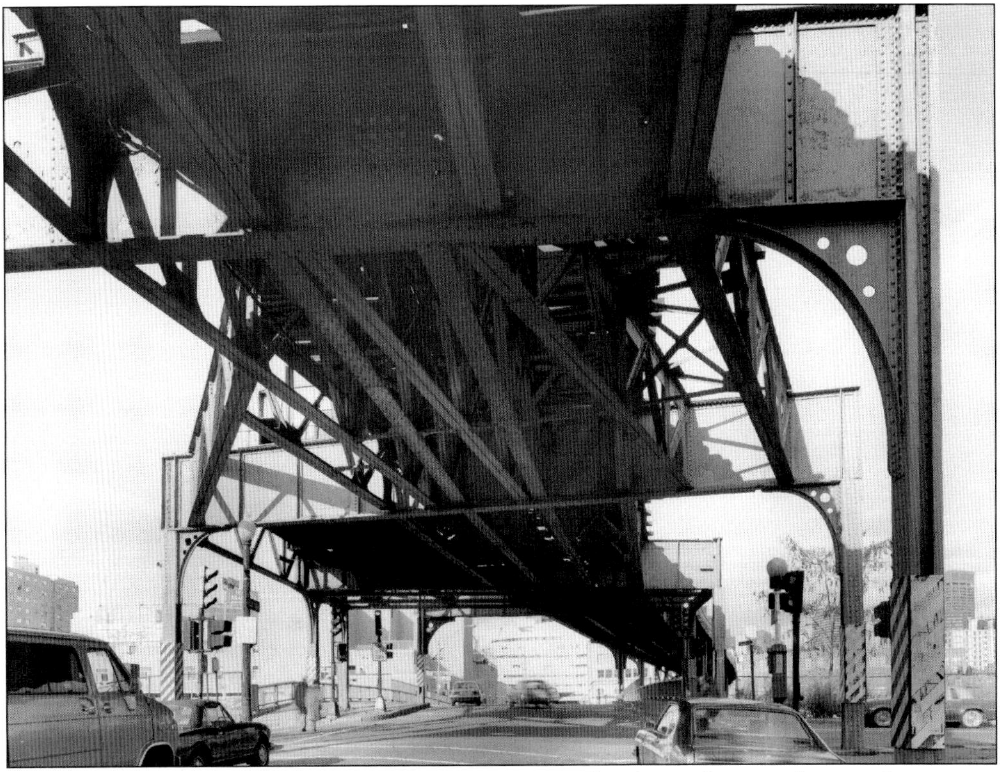

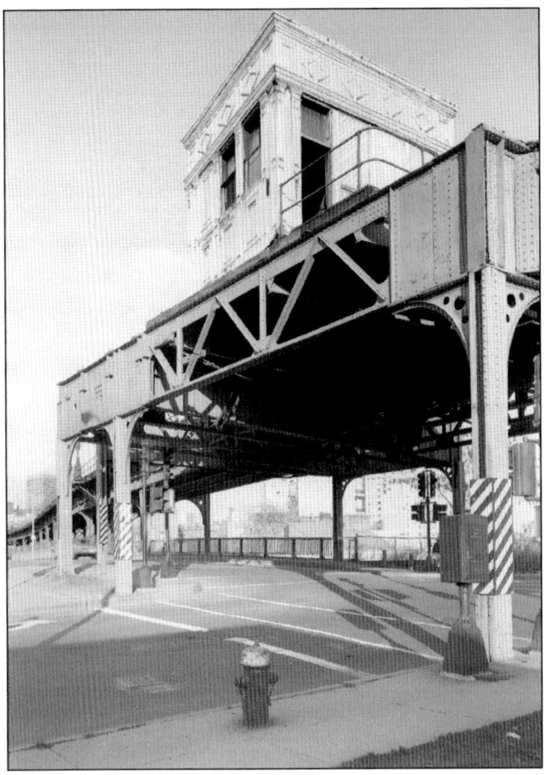

The above photograph was taken at Herald Street (formerly called Castle Street) looking north along Washington Street, past the Massachusetts Turnpike toward the present site of Tufts Medical Center in Chinatown. Just beyond the railway at lower left is the current location of the Josiah Quincy School, which relocated there in 1976. (Courtesy of the Historic American Engineering Record; photograph by Richard Cheek.)

The photograph at left looks northeast at the intersection of Herald (formerly Castle Street) and Washington Streets and shows the remnants of Tower "D." This intersection was also the site of the Castle Street Wye, which connected the Washington Street and Atlantic Avenue Elevated lines until the Atlantic Avenue line discontinued operation in 1938. (Courtesy of the Historic American Engineering Record; photograph by Richard Cheek.)

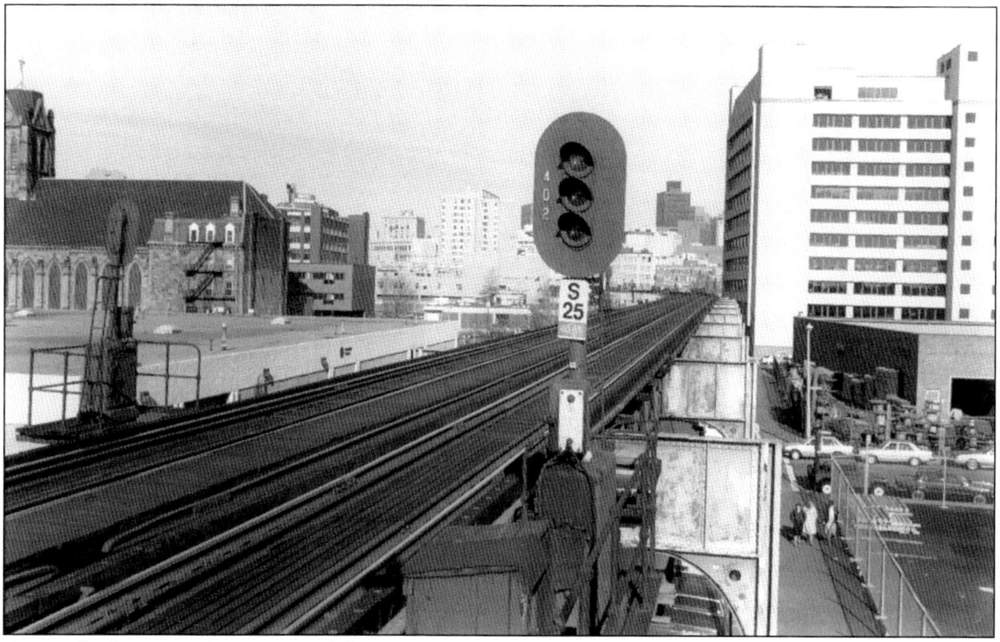

A view looking northeast toward downtown Boston from the Dover Street Station platform shows, at left, the rear of the Holy Trinity German Catholic Church on Shawmut Avenue and, at right, a low-rise brick building containing the Graybar Electric Company. Beyond that is the 11-story 1000 Washington Street building. (Photograph by and courtesy of David Akiba.)

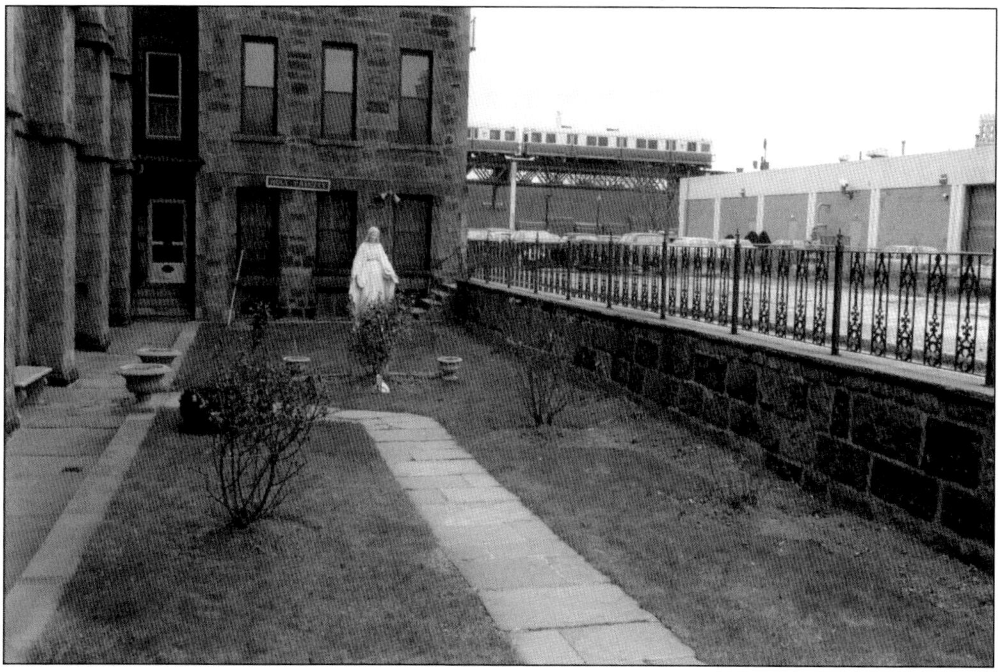

The elevated Orange Line is visible in the background of this view of a small courtyard beside the Holy Trinity German Catholic Church on Shawmut Avenue in the South End. Visible in the distance, just beyond the El and Washington Street, is the Graybar Electric Company building. (Photograph by and courtesy of David Akiba.)

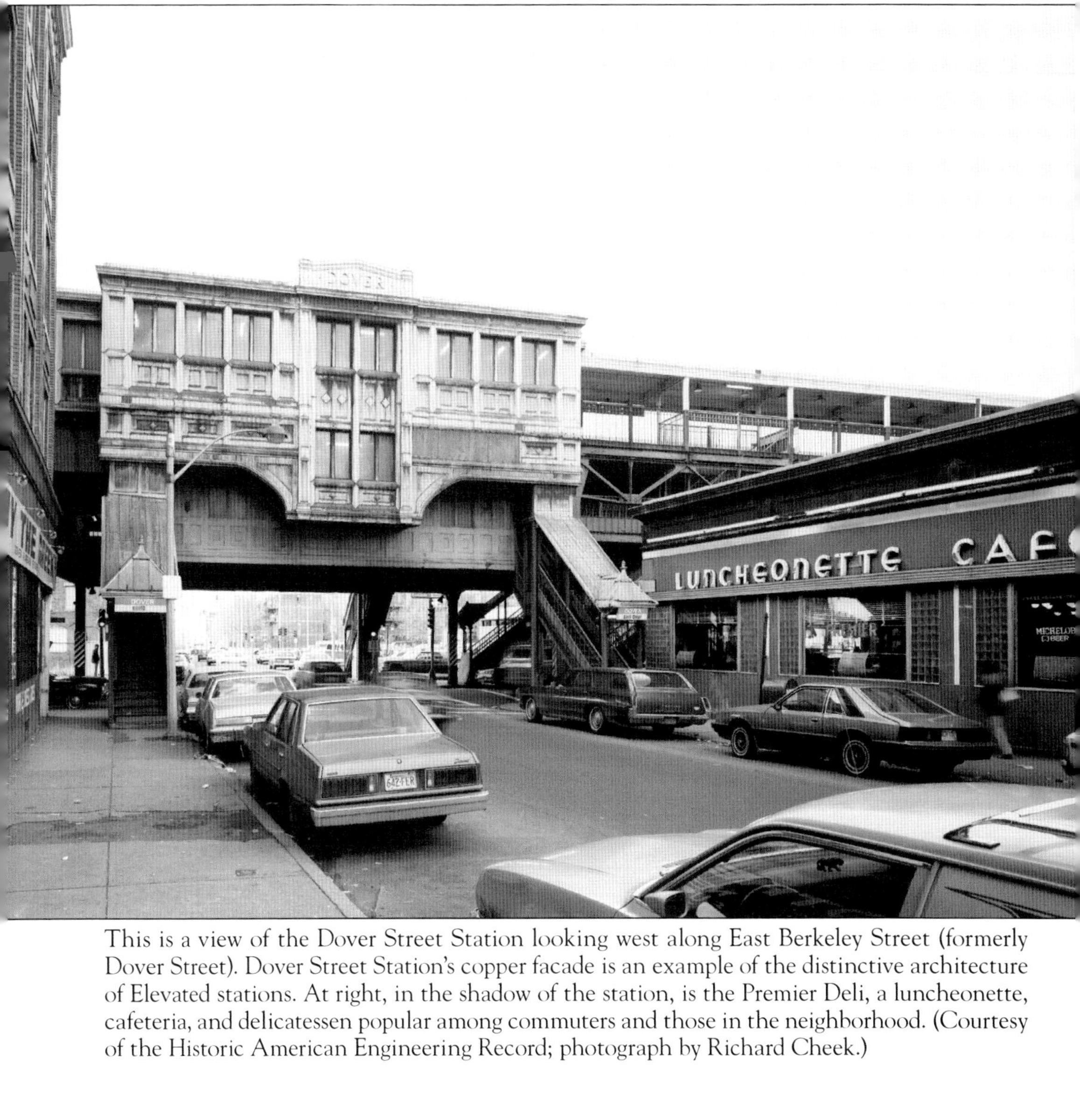

This is a view of the Dover Street Station looking west along East Berkeley Street (formerly Dover Street). Dover Street Station's copper facade is an example of the distinctive architecture of Elevated stations. At right, in the shadow of the station, is the Premier Deli, a luncheonette, cafeteria, and delicatessen popular among commuters and those in the neighborhood. (Courtesy of the Historic American Engineering Record; photograph by Richard Cheek.)

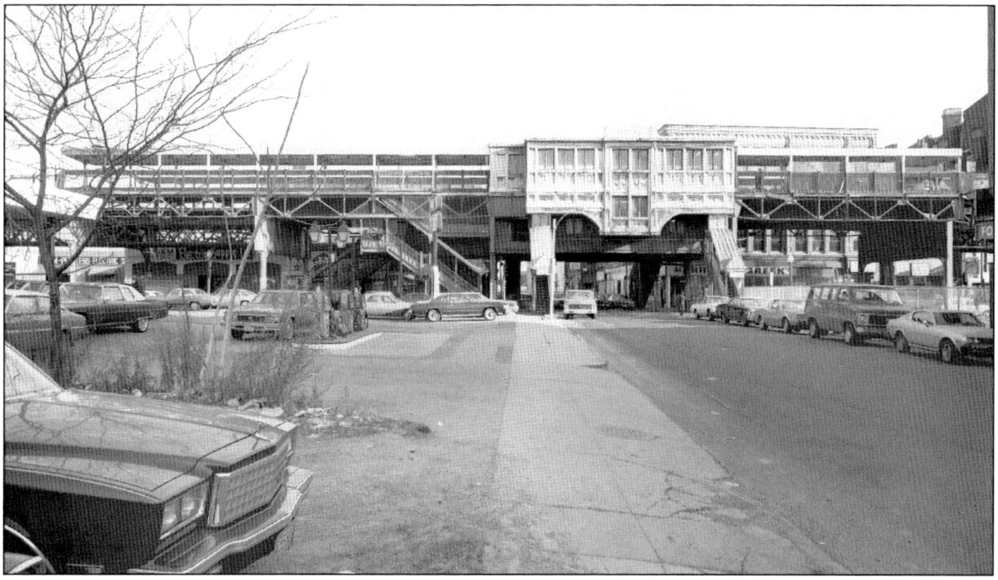

Dover Street Station looms over Dover Street, which was renamed East Berkeley Street in the 1960s in an effort to remove the stigma associating the area with crime and violence. At the time, Boston newspapers often referred to Dover Street as the city's "Skid Row." In recent years, however, community members have been making efforts to change the name back to Dover Street. (Courtesy of the Historic American Engineering Record; photograph by Richard Cheek.)

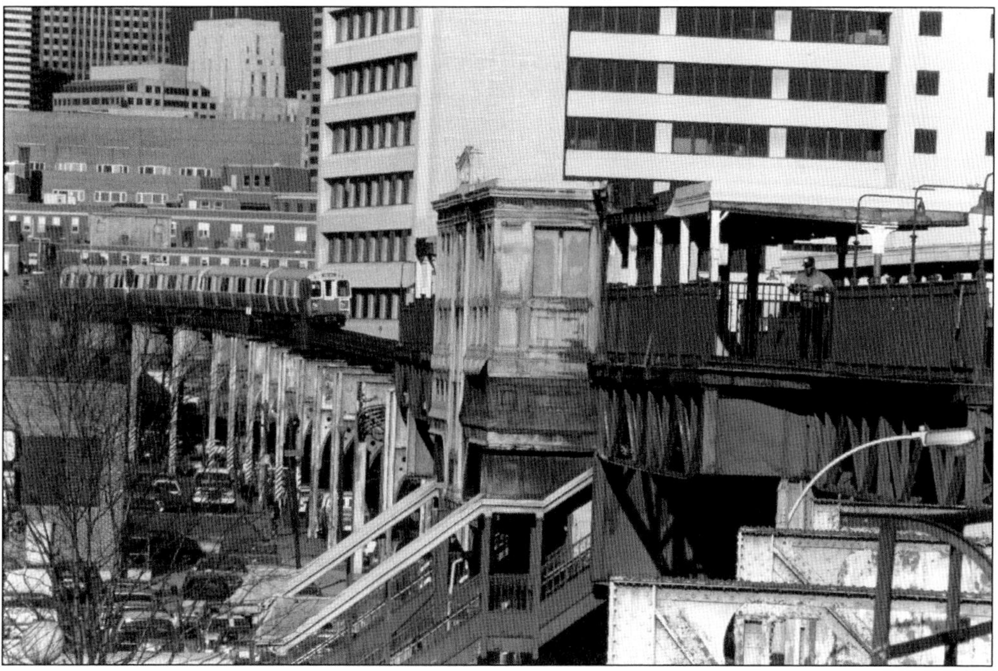

In this 1986 photograph, a southbound train passes the 1000 Washington Street building, at upper right, as it approaches Dover Street Station. At the time, the 11-story building was the headquarters of Teradyne, Inc., a manufacturer of semiconductors and other electronics. In the 2000s, Nordblom, Inc., acquired and redeveloped the building, leasing office space to private tenants and state agencies. (Photograph by and courtesy of David Akiba.)

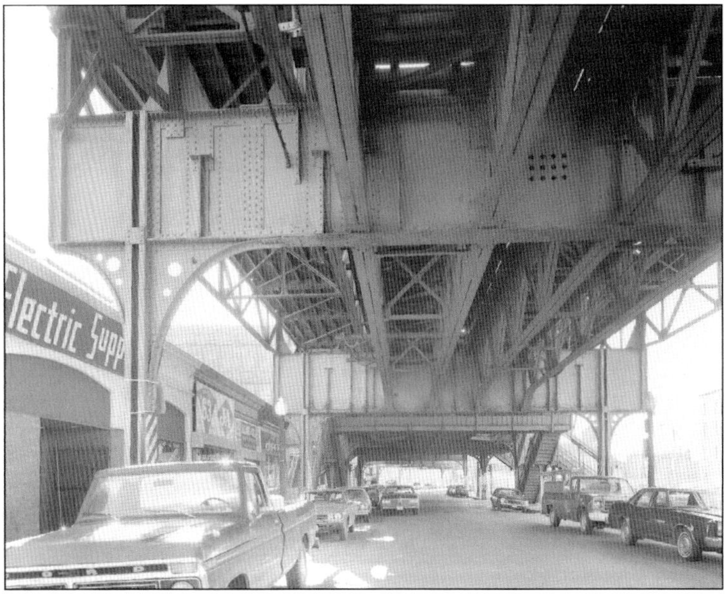

This view looking south down Washington Street beneath Dover Street Station offers a glimpse of how the Elevated structure narrowed the roadway and cast the businesses and vehicles below into shadow on even the sunniest day. In the distance at left are the Premier Deli and the stairs up to the station. (Courtesy of the Historic American Engineering Record; photograph by Richard Cheek.)

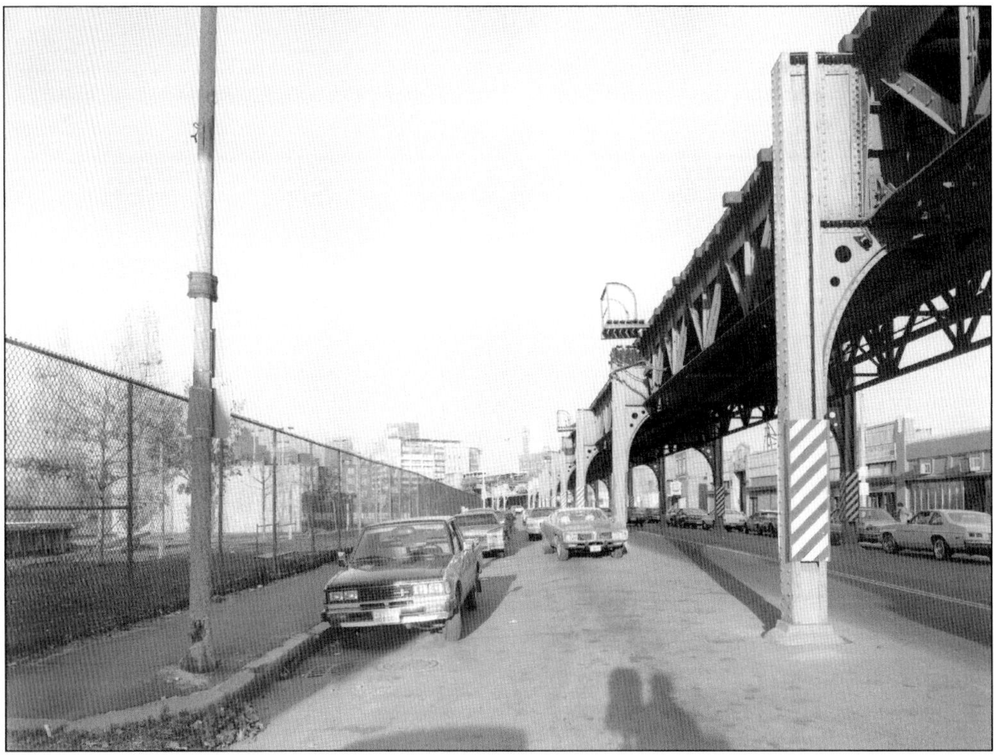

This photograph from the corner of Washington and the former Wilkes Street shows Dover Street Station in the distance. Wilkes Street was located on what is now Peters Park, a community park with gardens, a playground, a dog park, and sports fields. The tall white building visible in the distance is the Federal Reserve Bank Building of Boston. (Courtesy of the Historic American Engineering Record; photograph by Richard Cheek.)

The Red Fez, visible at left, was a restaurant serving Middle Eastern cuisine that opened in 1940 at Perry and Washington Streets and closed in the mid-1980s. In a review of a restaurant called the Red Fez that opened in 2002, *Boston Globe* food critics wrote: "People still talk about [the original Red Fez's] mint salad dressing." (Courtesy of the Historic American Engineering Record; photograph by Richard Cheek.)

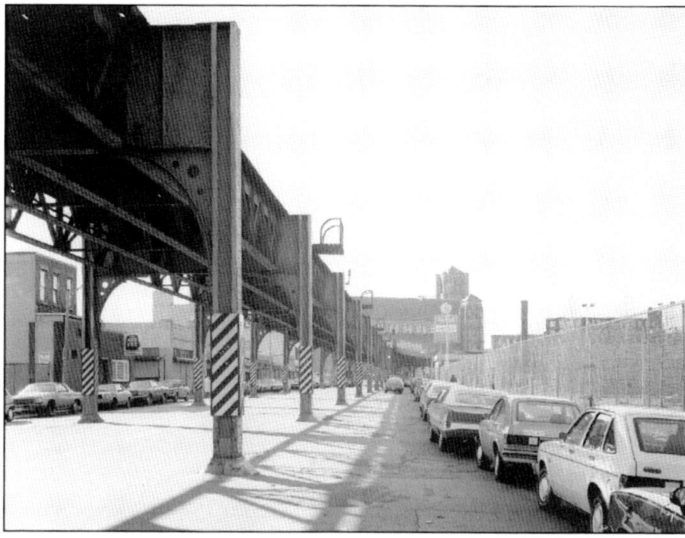

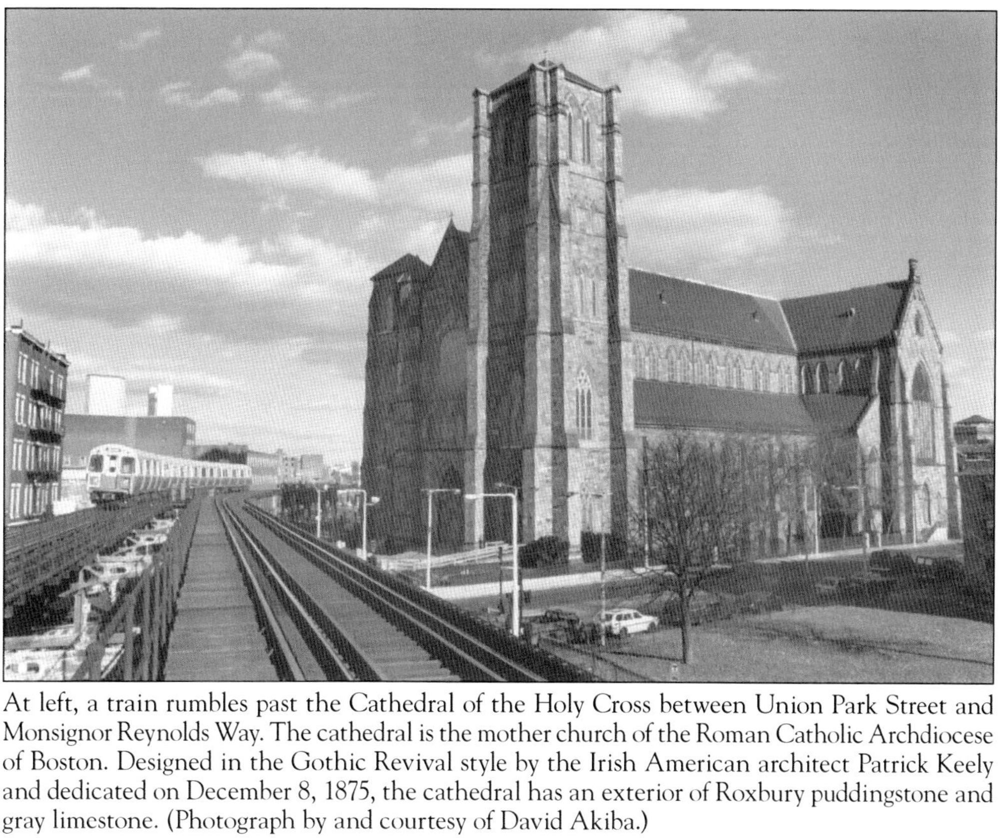

At left, a train rumbles past the Cathedral of the Holy Cross between Union Park Street and Monsignor Reynolds Way. The cathedral is the mother church of the Roman Catholic Archdiocese of Boston. Designed in the Gothic Revival style by the Irish American architect Patrick Keely and dedicated on December 8, 1875, the cathedral has an exterior of Roxbury puddingstone and gray limestone. (Photograph by and courtesy of David Akiba.)

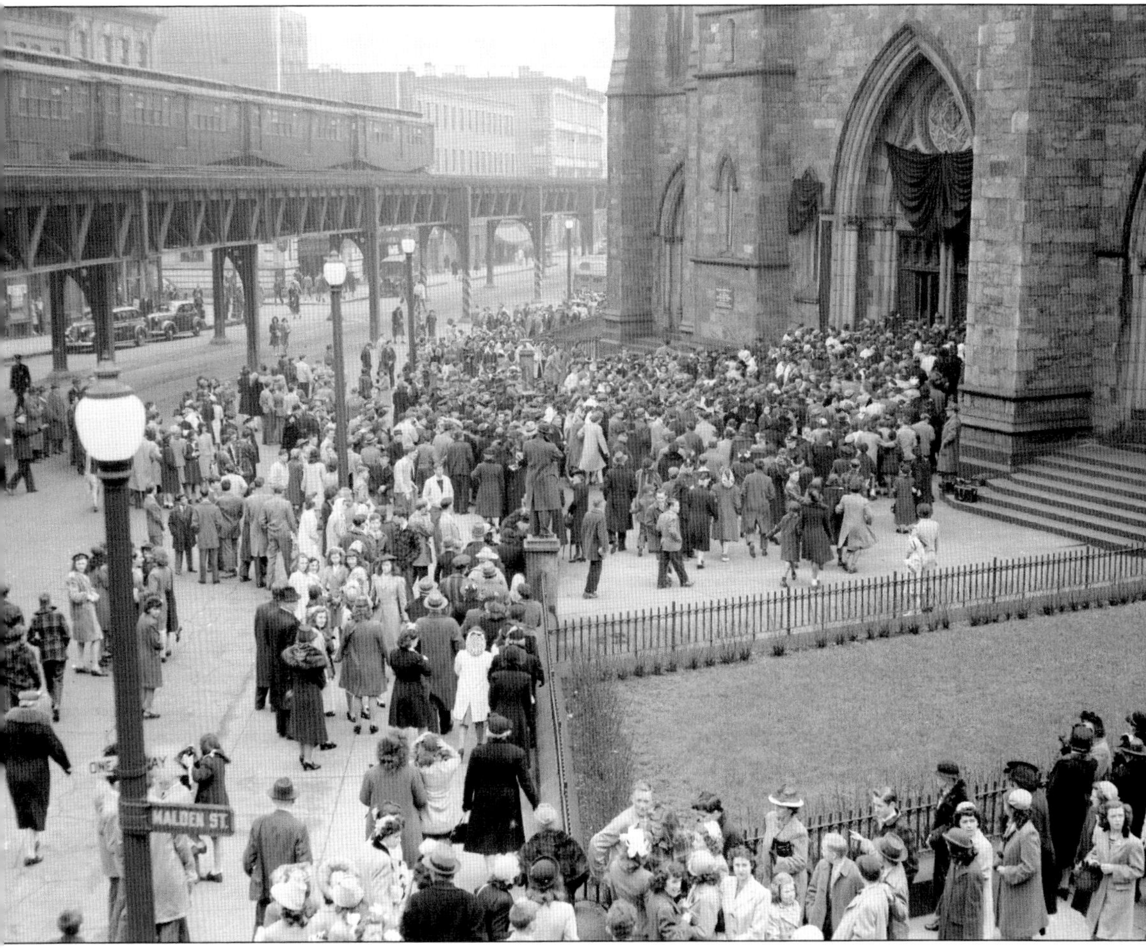

An Elevated train passed as thousands gathered outside the Cathedral of the Holy Cross on April 28, 1944, for the funeral of Cardinal William Henry O'Connell, archbishop of Boston. A sign for Malden Street is visible at lower left; the block alongside the cathedral was later renamed for Monsignor Thomas Reynolds, a pastor of the cathedral who died in 1946. (Courtesy of the Boston Public Library; photograph by Leslie Jones.)

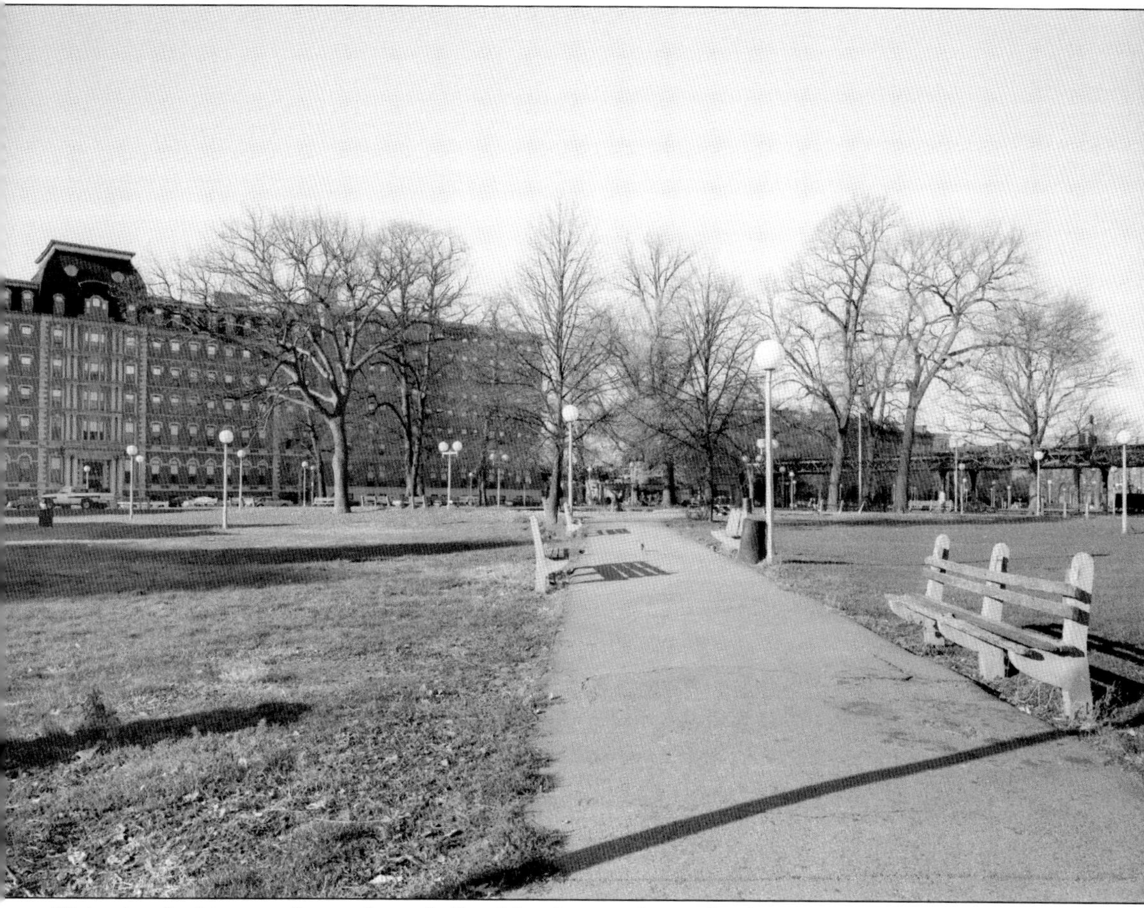

This view looking southeast through Franklin Square shows the former St. James Hotel, built in 1868 at Newton and Washington Streets. It housed the New England Conservatory of Music from 1882 to 1902 and later became a home for working single women. Its exterior appeared in the 1980s television series *St. Elsewhere*, with the Elevated featured in the opening titles. (Courtesy of the Historic American Engineering Record; photograph by Richard Cheek.)

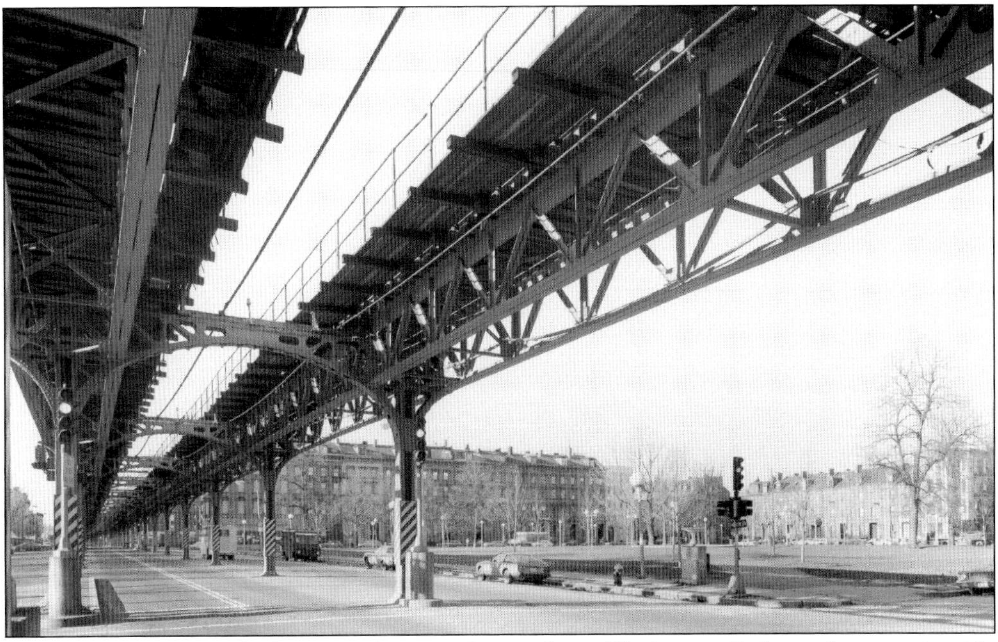

This view looking south down Washington Street shows Blackstone Park on the opposite side of the street from Franklin Square. These parks were originally designed in the mid-1800s by prominent architect Charles Bulfinch to be one larger park called Columbia Square. (Courtesy of the Historic American Engineering Record; photograph by Richard Cheek.)

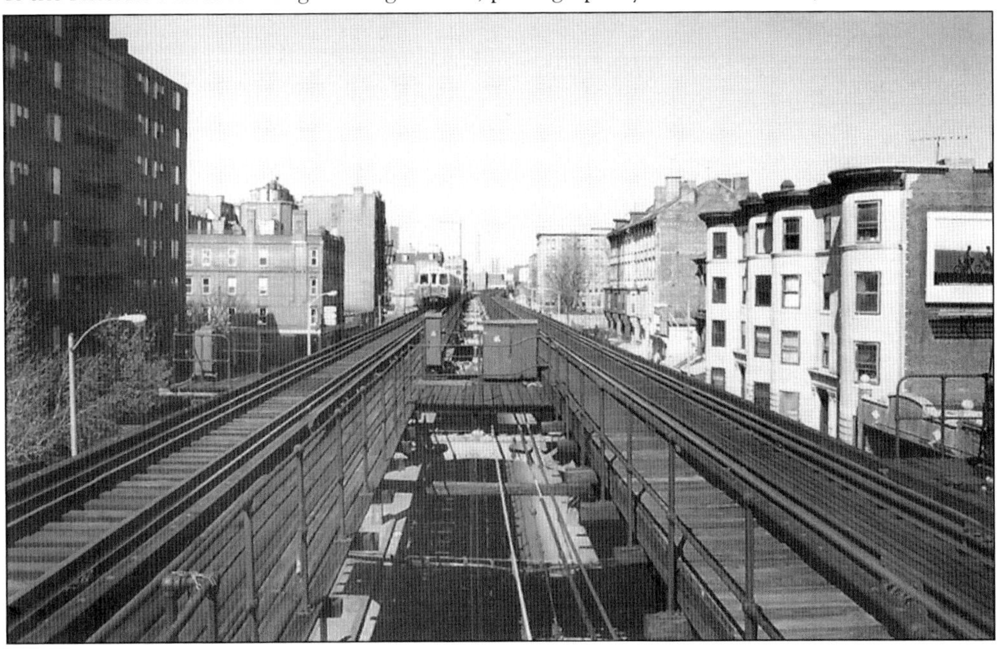

This photograph looks through the South End toward downtown from Northampton Station, with the block between Springfield and Worcester Streets in the foreground. Visible just beyond the platform at lower right is a one-story building that was home to Smith and Sheehan's, a bar known in the neighborhood as the "bucket of blood" due to the tendency of its patrons to get into brawls. (Photograph by and courtesy of Joe Boncek.)

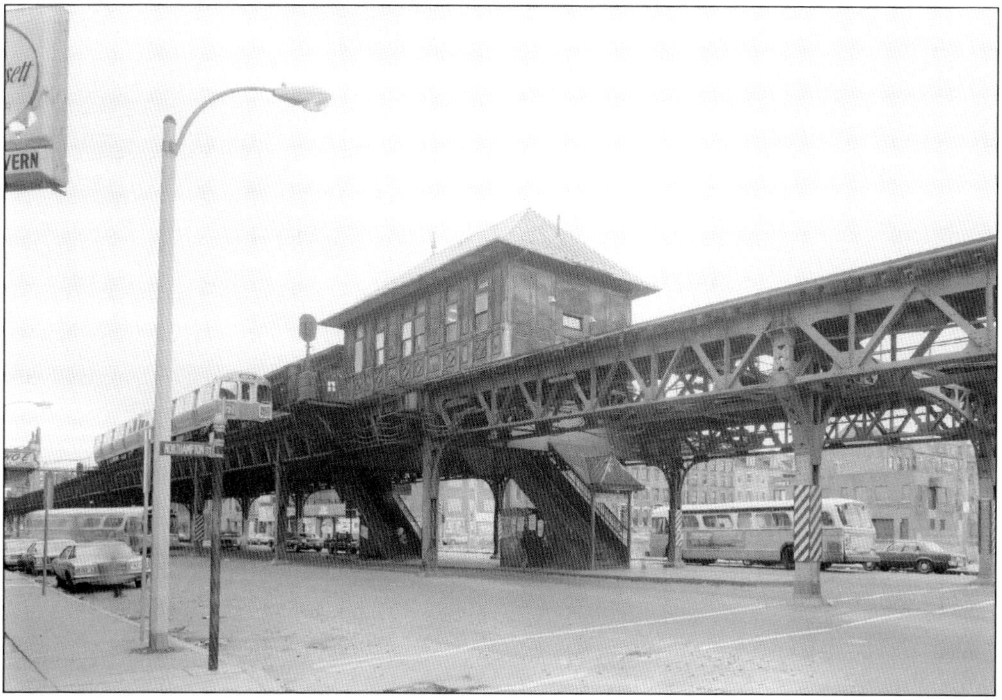

In 1988, soon after the Washington Street Elevated had closed and the Orange Line route shifted, the structure at Northampton Station, pictured in these images from 1982, was in surprisingly high demand. Although the tracks connecting the stations along Washington Street had been dismantled, there were a number of ideas put forth about what to do with the different historical structures along the Elevated. Unlike most stations along the route, Northampton Station had remained largely intact and free from architectural modifications and thus generated much interest from preservationists, government agencies, and the community. The tower from Northampton Station was ultimately acquired by the Seashore Trolley Museum in Kennebunkport, Maine, and is currently on display on the museum's grounds. (Both, courtesy of the Historic American Engineering Record; photograph by Richard Cheek.)

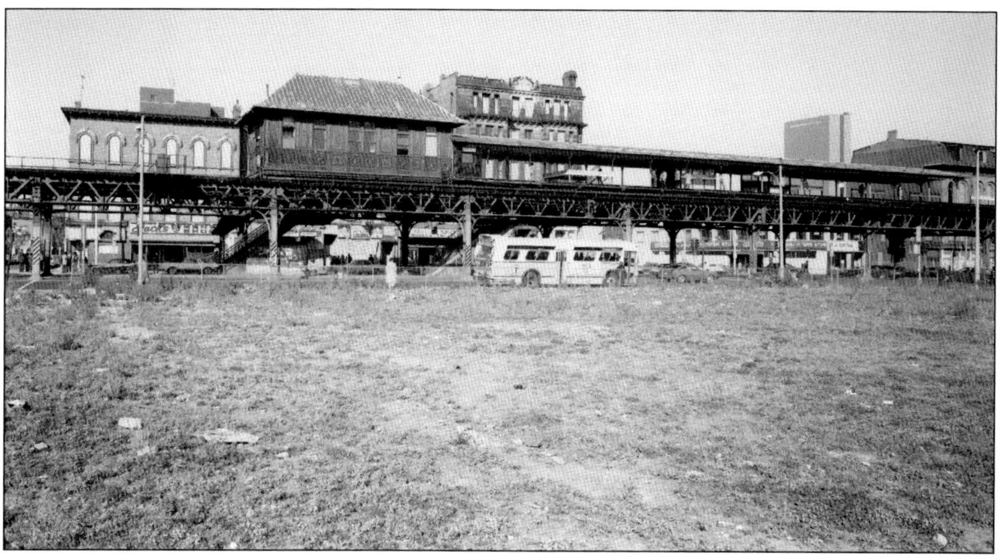

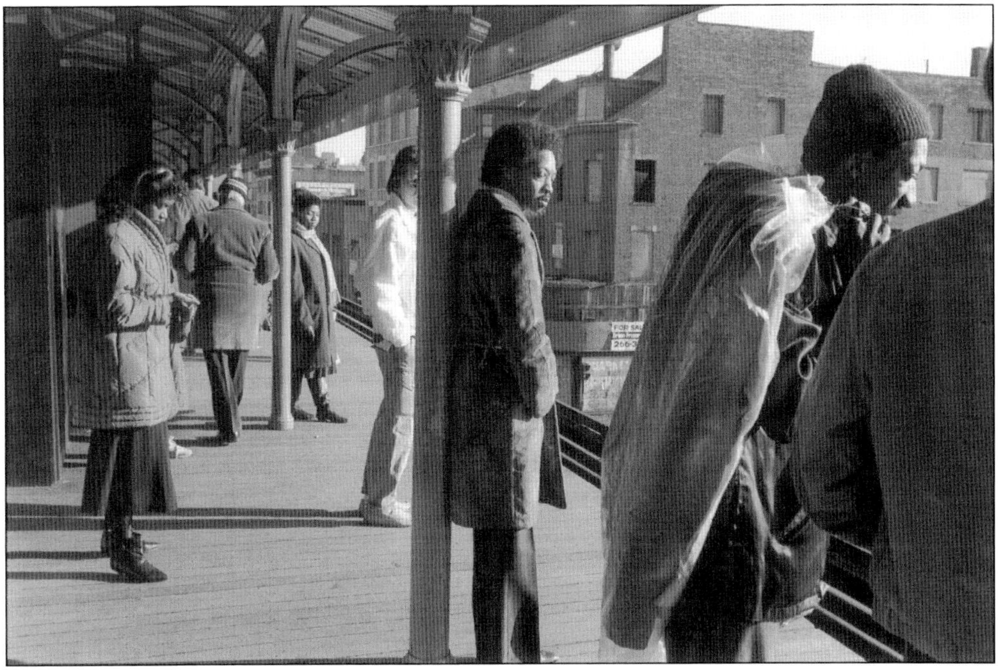

In this 1986 photograph, commuters await an inbound train at Northampton Station. In the center of the image, just beyond the platform, a derelict, dilapidated building with a "For Sale" sign and a closed pharmacy on the first floor stands at the eastern corner of Massachusetts Avenue and Washington Street. (Photograph by and courtesy of David Akiba.)

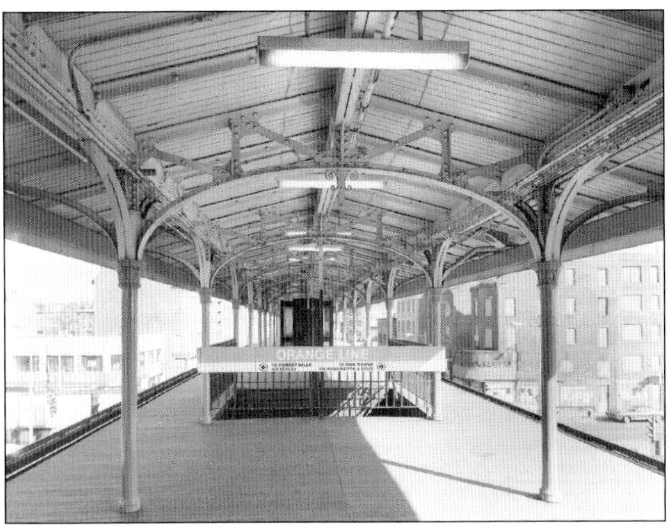

This 1982 photograph looks north from the platform of the Northampton Station at the intersection of Northampton and Washington Streets. The station platform extended toward the intersection of Massachusetts Avenue and Washington Street. The design of Orange Line signs has not changed in the ensuing years. (Courtesy of the Historic American Engineering Record; photograph by Richard Cheek.)

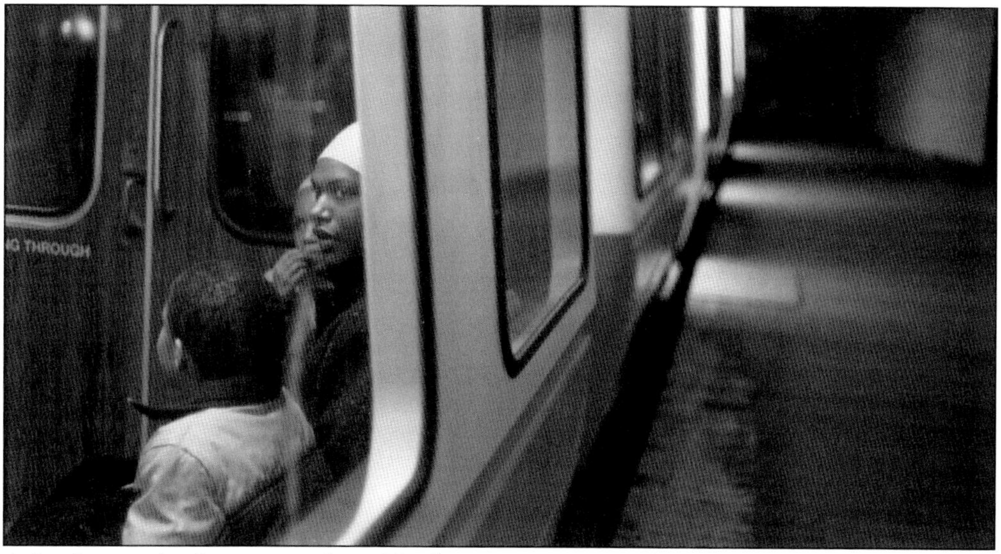

A family waits for their train to leave Northampton Station in this photograph from 1986, shortly before the Washington Street Elevated was closed. For many years, the Orange Line served the predominantly African American neighborhood of Roxbury and the ethnically mixed South End and Jamaica Plain, providing convenient and affordable access to downtown Boston and from there to points north and south. (Photograph by and courtesy of David Akiba.)

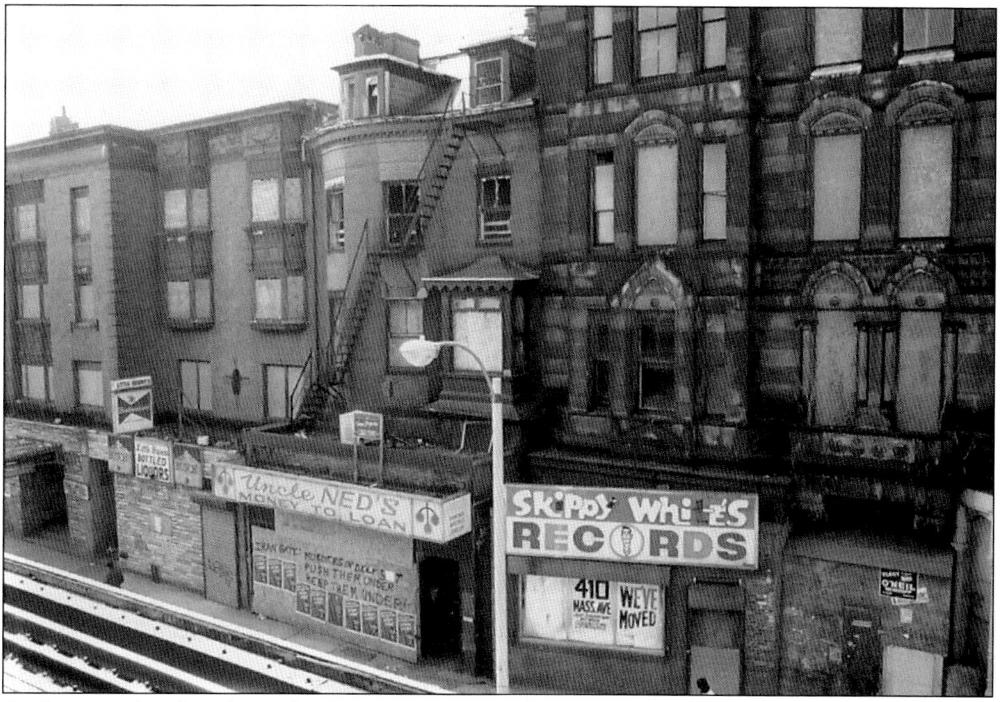

A photograph taken from Northampton Station shows empty storefronts that formerly housed Uncle Ned's Money to Loan and, in the former Hotel Alexandra at the northwest corner of Washington Street and Massachusetts Avenue, Skippy White's Records. The record store, first located on the other side of Washington Street between Lenox and Northampton Streets, was a neighborhood institution for many years. (Photograph by and courtesy of Joe Boncek.)

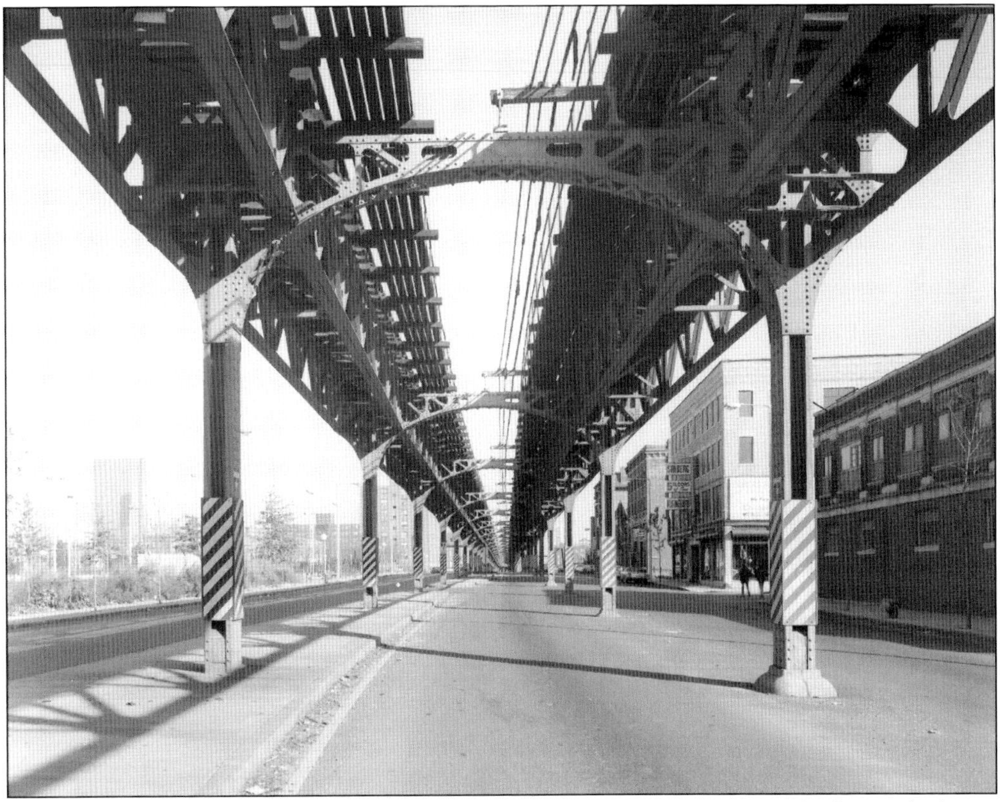

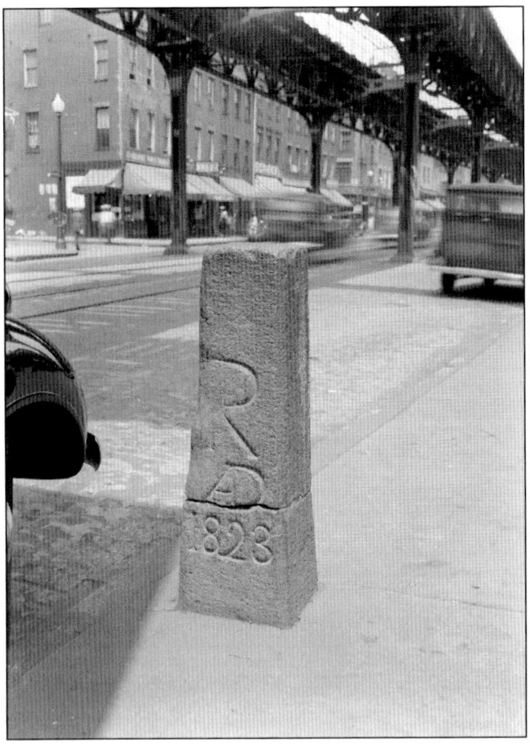

The above 1982 image looks north along Washington Street, with Hancock Center visible at left. To the right, at the corner of Washington and Thorndike Streets, is the Sriberg Furniture Company, which opened in the early 1900s, erected this four-story building in 1946, and closed sometime after 1985. In the 1990s, the building became home to Restoration Resources, a store selling antique architectural elements. (Courtesy of the Historic American Engineering Record; photograph by Richard Cheek.)

This 1823 stone at 2000 Washington Street marking the boundary of Roxbury and Boston (prior to Roxbury's annexation) was already 117 years old when it was photographed in July 1940. In the background, slightly out of focus, is what appears to be an early Stop & Shop supermarket. The chain was founded in Somerville, Massachusetts, in 1914. (Courtesy of the Library of Congress; photograph by Frank O. Branzetti.)

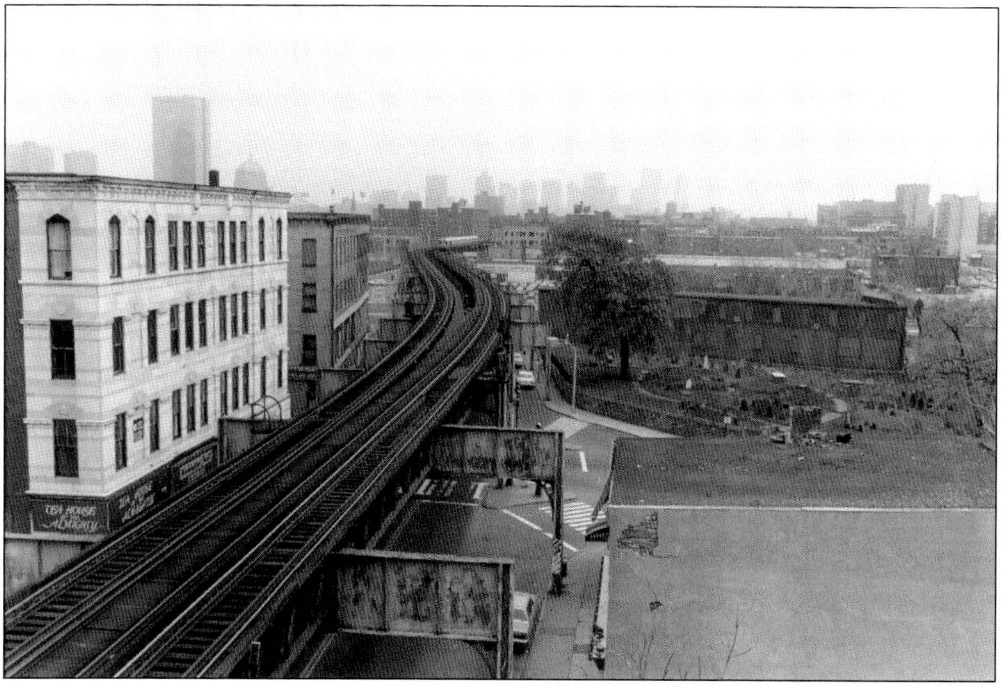

The Elevated tracks snake down Washington Street alongside the Eliot Burying Ground, visible at right in the middle distance. Dating back to 1630, the year of Boston's founding, the cemetery is one of the three oldest burying grounds in the city. Inside is the Dudley family tomb, which includes colonial governors Thomas and Joseph Dudley, chief justice Paul Dudley, and Col. William Dudley. (Photograph by and courtesy of David Akiba.)

This view looks north along Washington Street at the northerly junction of tracks at Dudley Station with Robell's Department Store at lower left. As merchants prepared for the loss of the Elevated in 1987, Robell's manager Eden Gordon told the *Boston Globe* that she was concerned about the potential loss of many customers. By the early 1990s, Robell's had closed. (Courtesy of the Historic American Engineering Record; photograph by Richard Cheek.)

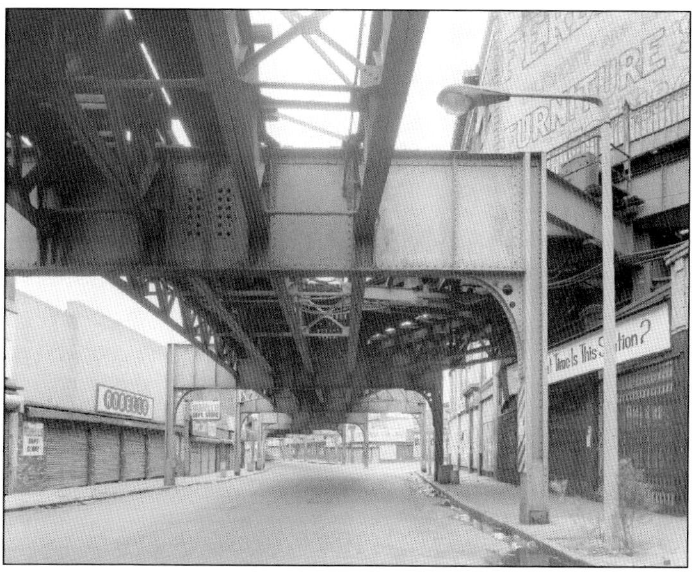

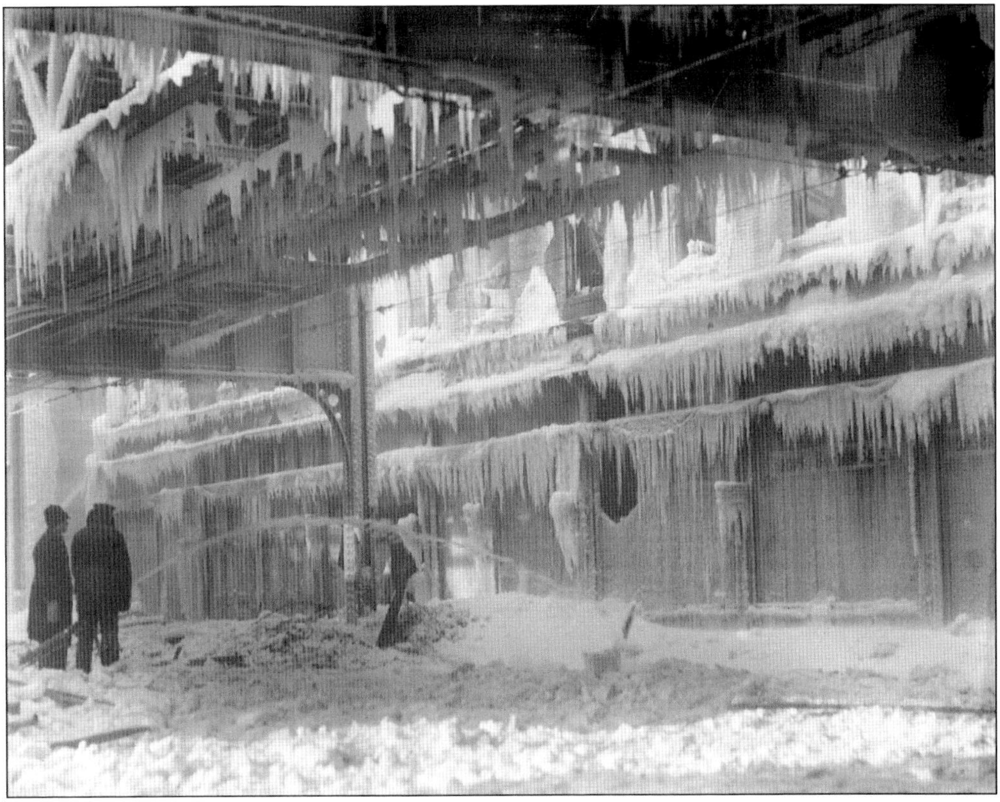

Early on the morning of January 14, 1914, a fire broke out at the W. & A. Bacon department store, located at 2175–2193 Washington Street, just northwest of Dudley Square. The temperature that morning was eight degrees below zero, causing water from the firefighters' hoses to freeze quickly. One firefighter was killed when a portion of a wall fell on him. (Courtesy of the Boston Public Library; photograph by Leslie Jones.)

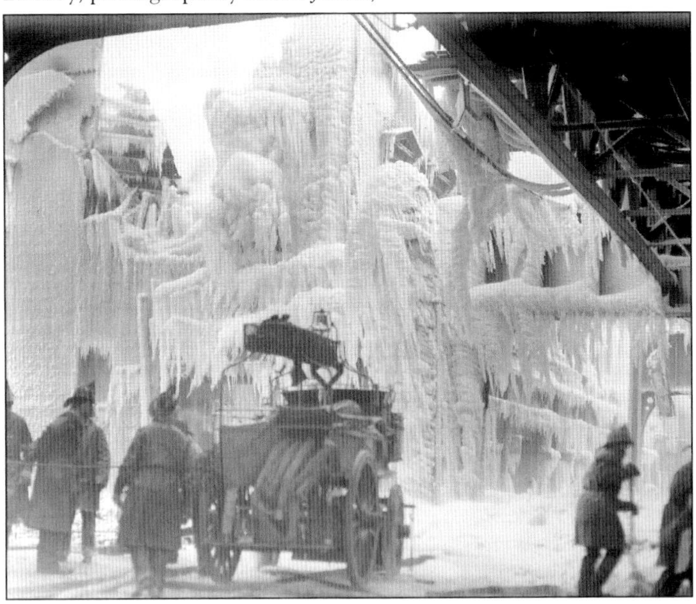

The store's headquarters, Bacon Hall, was a three-story building constructed in 1858 that stood very near the Elevated structure, impeding firefighters' efforts. Trains were halted in both directions, and passengers were directed to walk a narrow path to the nearest stations. Horace Bacon, co-owner of the store, told the *Boston Globe* the total monetary loss was about $150,000. (Courtesy of the Boston Public Library; photograph by Leslie Jones.)

This 1901 photograph shows Dudley Station in its original state, with only the central rapid-transit section enclosed and both the east loop for streetcars (right) and the west loop (left) open. Dudley was the terminus of the Elevated's Main Line until the Forest Hills extension opened in 1909. (Courtesy of University Archives & Special Collections, Joseph P. Healey Library, University of Massachusetts Boston: Anthony Mitchell Sammarco Collection.)

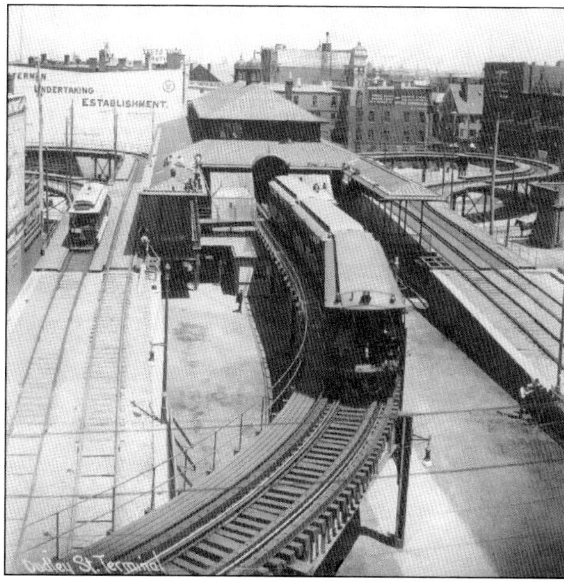

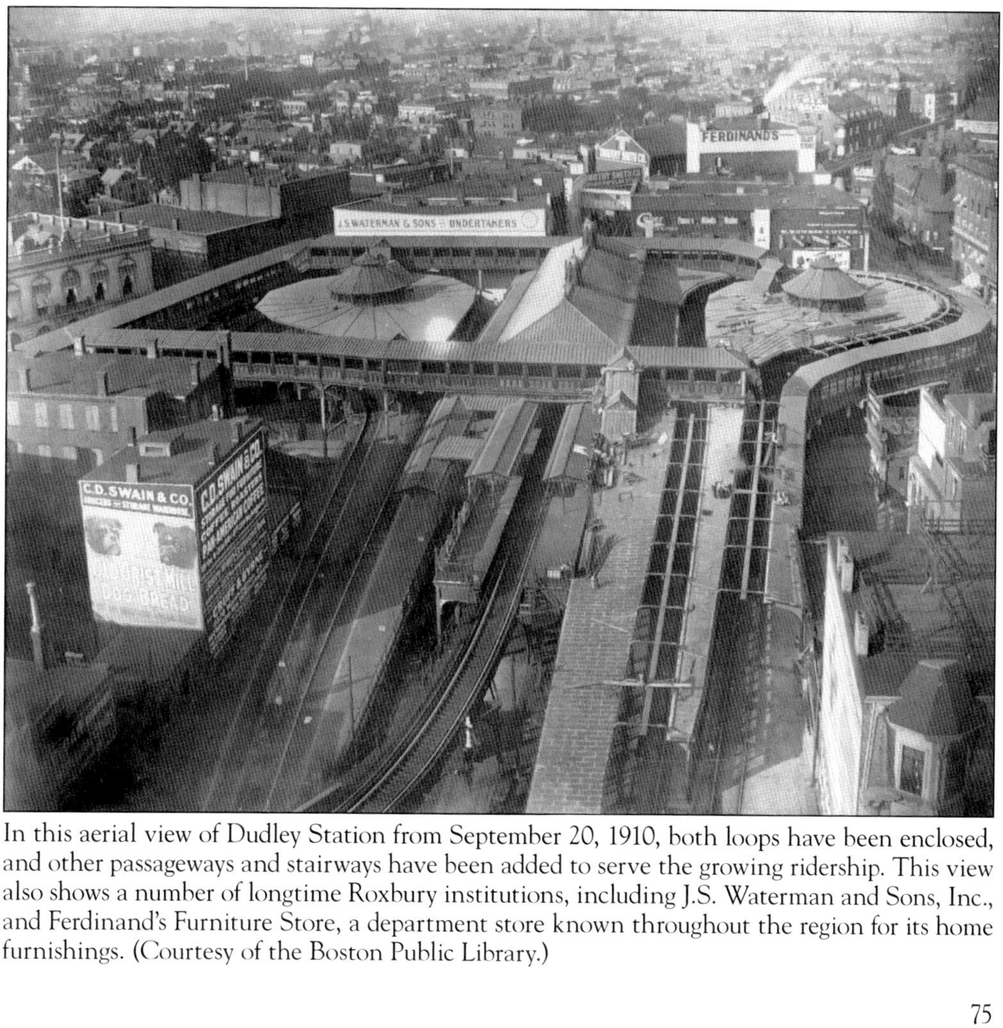

In this aerial view of Dudley Station from September 20, 1910, both loops have been enclosed, and other passageways and stairways have been added to serve the growing ridership. This view also shows a number of longtime Roxbury institutions, including J.S. Waterman and Sons, Inc., and Ferdinand's Furniture Store, a department store known throughout the region for its home furnishings. (Courtesy of the Boston Public Library.)

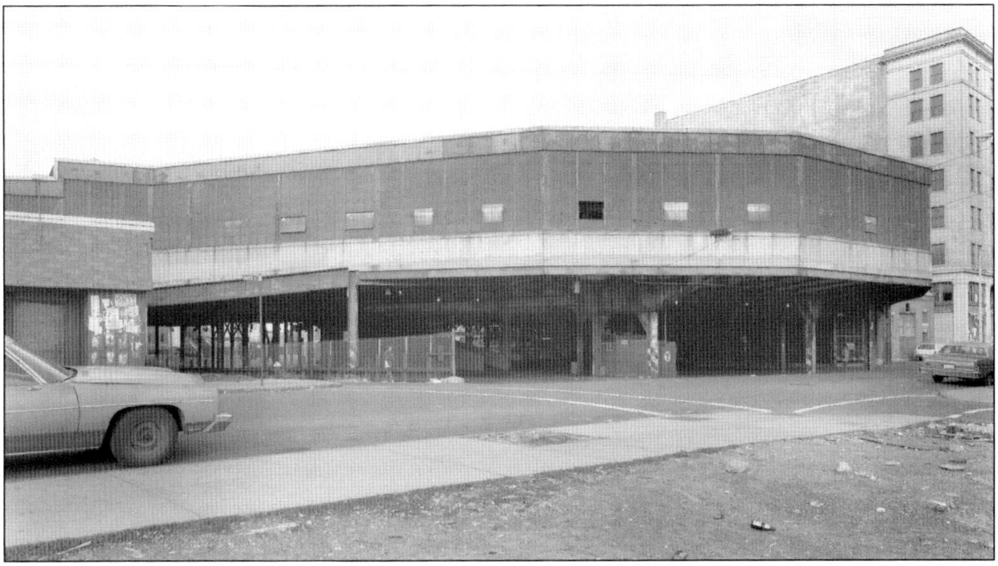

This 1980s photograph offers a street-level view of the Dudley Station as seen from Warren Street looking northeast with the Ferdinand's Furniture Store Annex at far right. By this time, the streetcar tracks had been removed to accommodate buses. (Courtesy of the Historic American Engineering Record; photograph by Richard Cheek.)

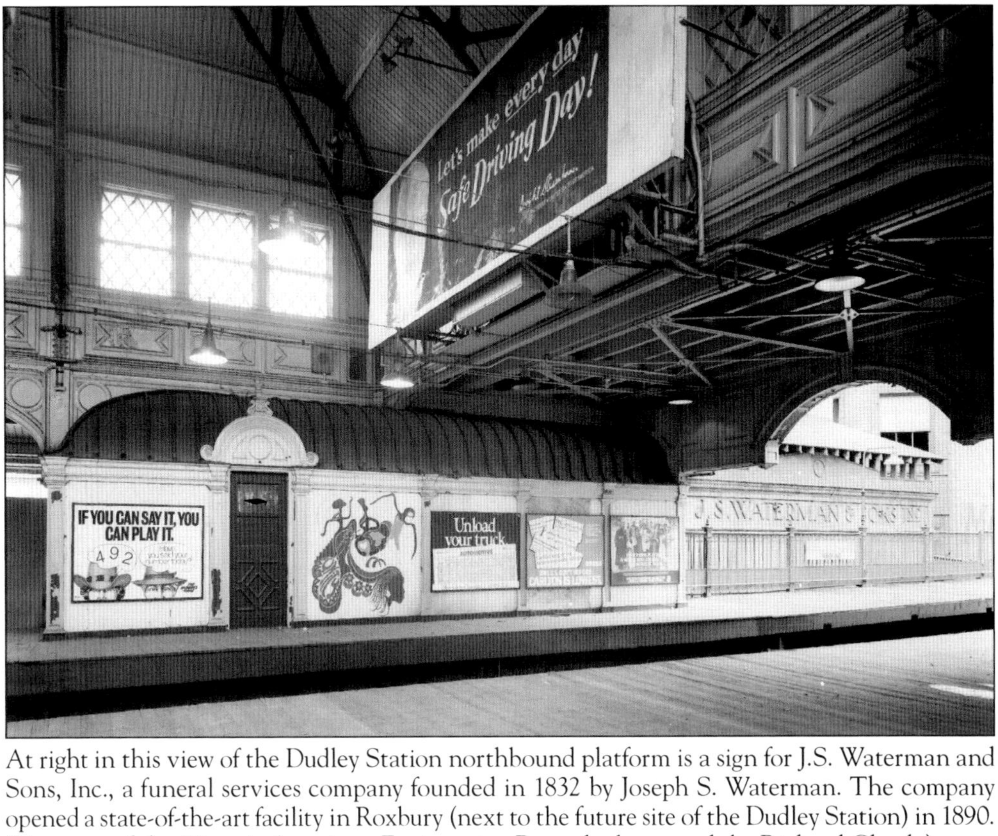

At right in this view of the Dudley Station northbound platform is a sign for J.S. Waterman and Sons, Inc., a funeral services company founded in 1832 by Joseph S. Waterman. The company opened a state-of-the-art facility in Roxbury (next to the future site of the Dudley Station) in 1890. (Courtesy of the Historic American Engineering Record; photograph by Richard Cheek.)

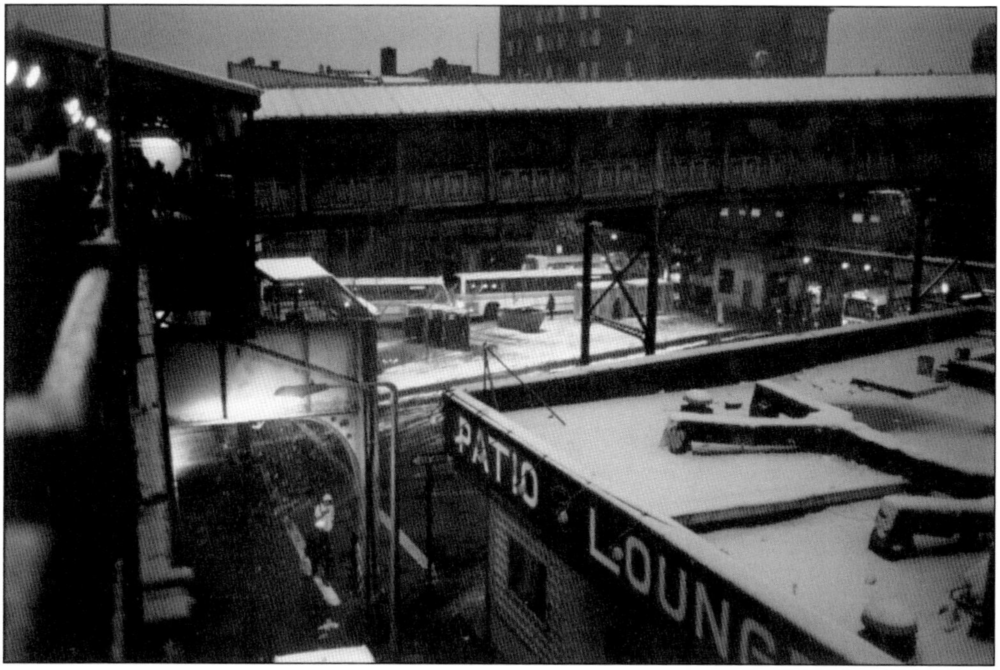

Looking down from Dudley Station in these 1986 photographs, the Patio Lounge, located at 2360 Washington Street, sits under a light blanket of snow. By the 2000s, the building had been replaced with a strip mall containing a Dunkin' Donuts, a fried-chicken restaurant, and a barbecue restaurant. The busway beneath the station is in the same location today, with the elevated railway removed but portions of the original station repurposed as bus shelters. Former *Boston Globe* columnist Mike Barnicle wrote in 1975 about Ronnie, a 19-year-old heroin addict who supported his habit by selling the drug in the shadow of the El next to the Patio Lounge. (Both, photograph by and courtesy of David Akiba.)

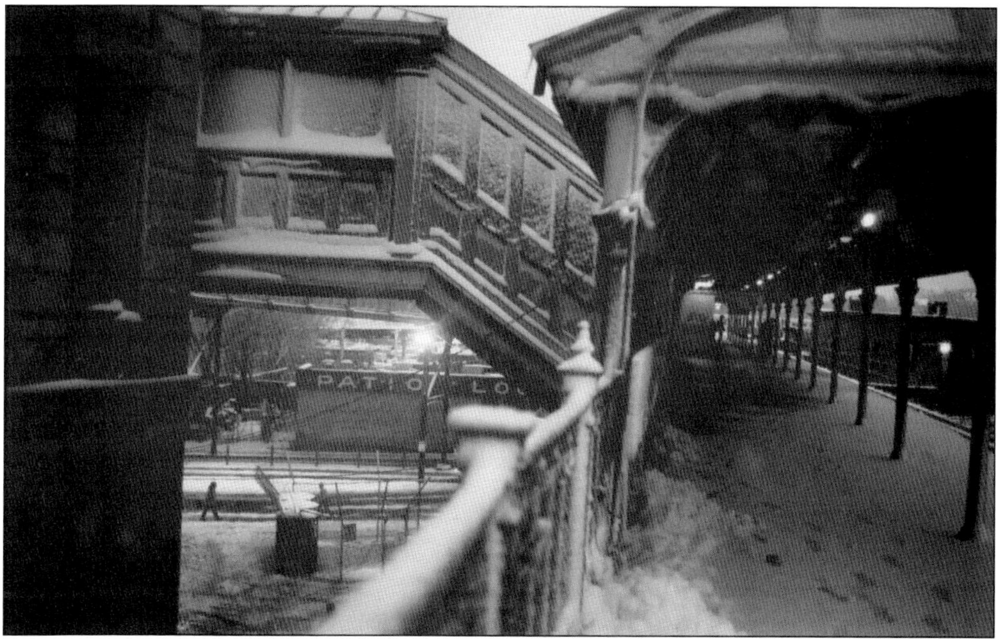

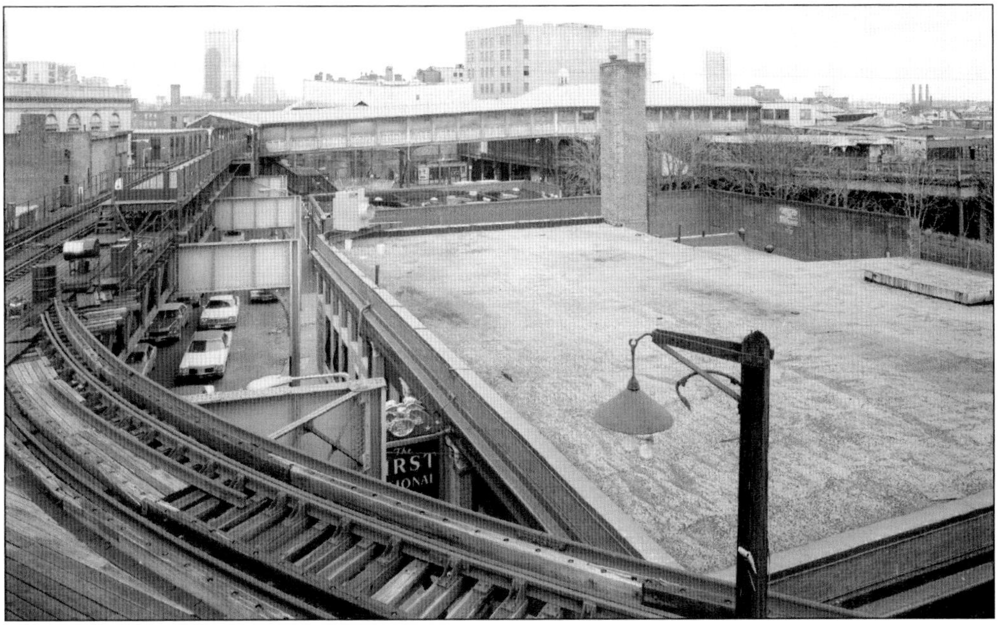

Looking north over 2343 Washington Street, the Hancock Tower is visible nearly two miles away. The roofline of the J.S. Waterman and Sons, Inc., building is visible over the central passage, and the Ferdinand's Annex is at the upper right. At lower right is the former First National Bank building, which became a Bank of America branch in the 2000s. (Courtesy of the Historic American Engineering Record; photograph by Richard Cheek.)

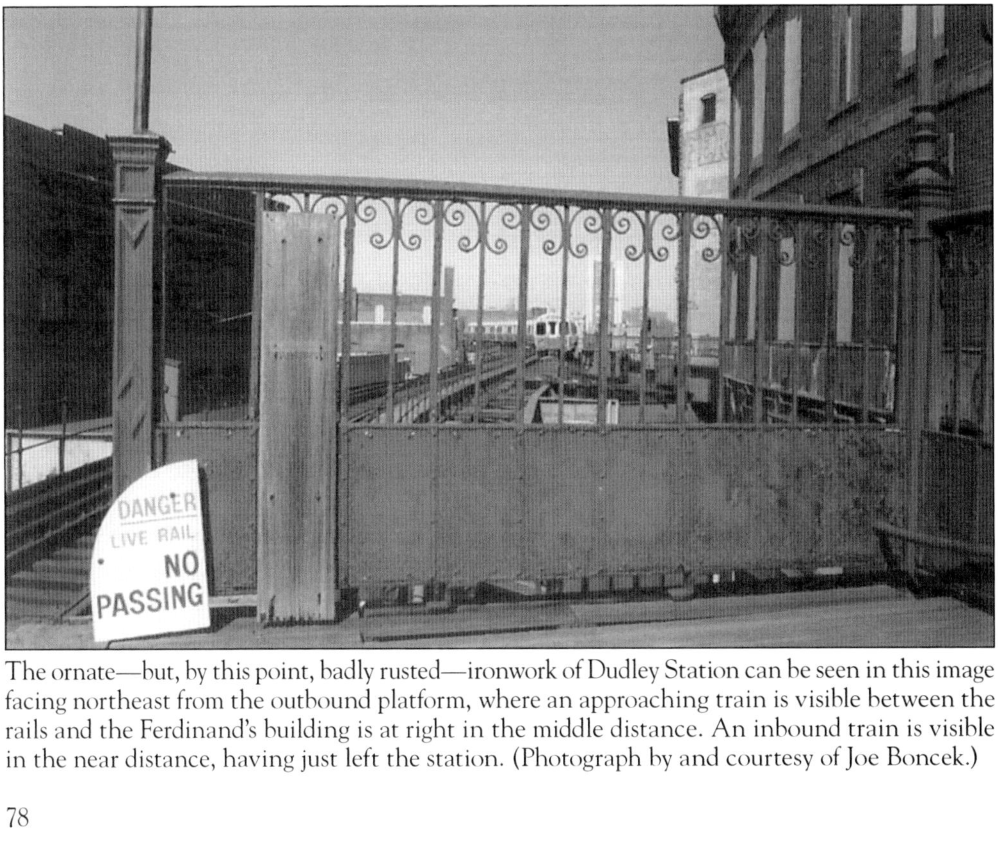

The ornate—but, by this point, badly rusted—ironwork of Dudley Station can be seen in this image facing northeast from the outbound platform, where an approaching train is visible between the rails and the Ferdinand's building is at right in the middle distance. An inbound train is visible in the near distance, having just left the station. (Photograph by and courtesy of Joe Boncek.)

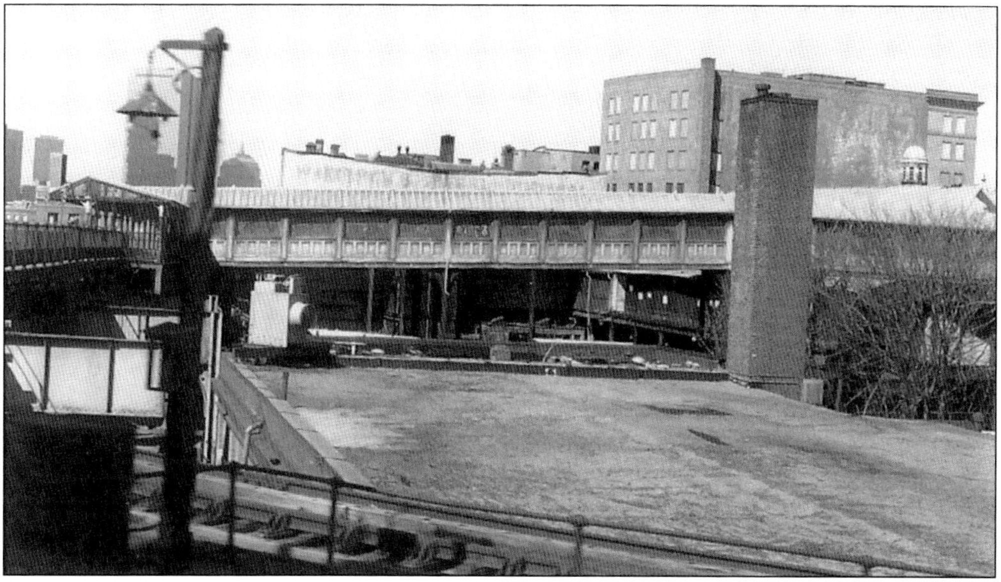

This view looks northwest from one area of Dudley Station over the roof of 2343 Washington Street with the roofline of the former J.S. Waterman and Sons building visible just over the central passage and Ferdinand's Annex at the upper right. The area beneath the central passageway became the Dudley Station busway after the removal of the Elevated. (Photograph by and courtesy of Joe Boncek.)

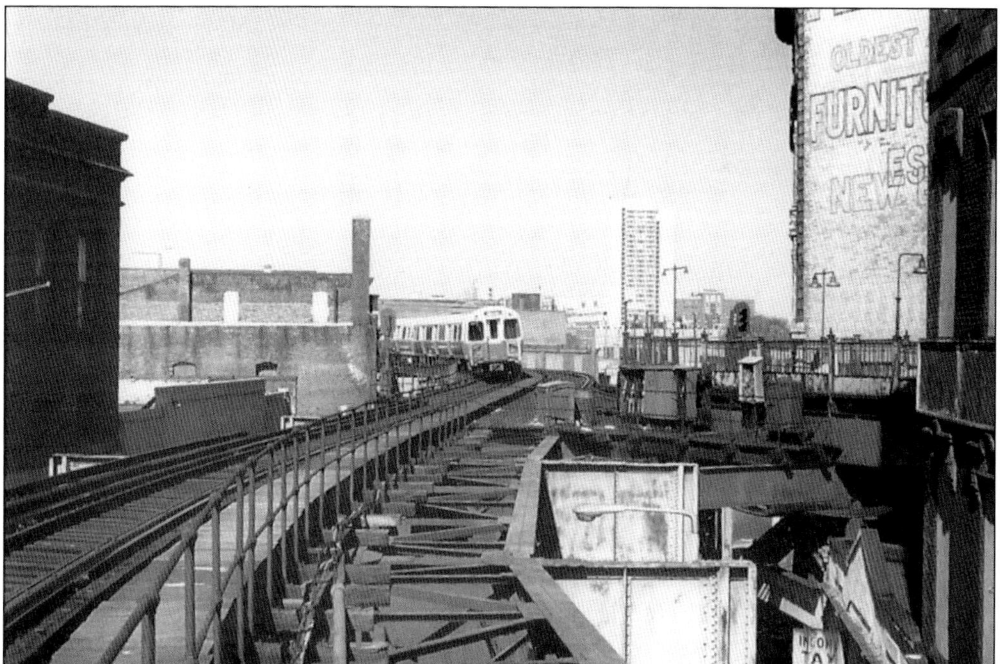

This April 1987 image taken from the outbound platform at Dudley Square facing east shows Ferdinand's at upper right and the M. Harriet McCormack Nursing Tower on Northampton Street near Boston City Hospital, now Boston Medical Center. A southbound train is approaching the station. (Photograph by and courtesy of Joe Boncek.)

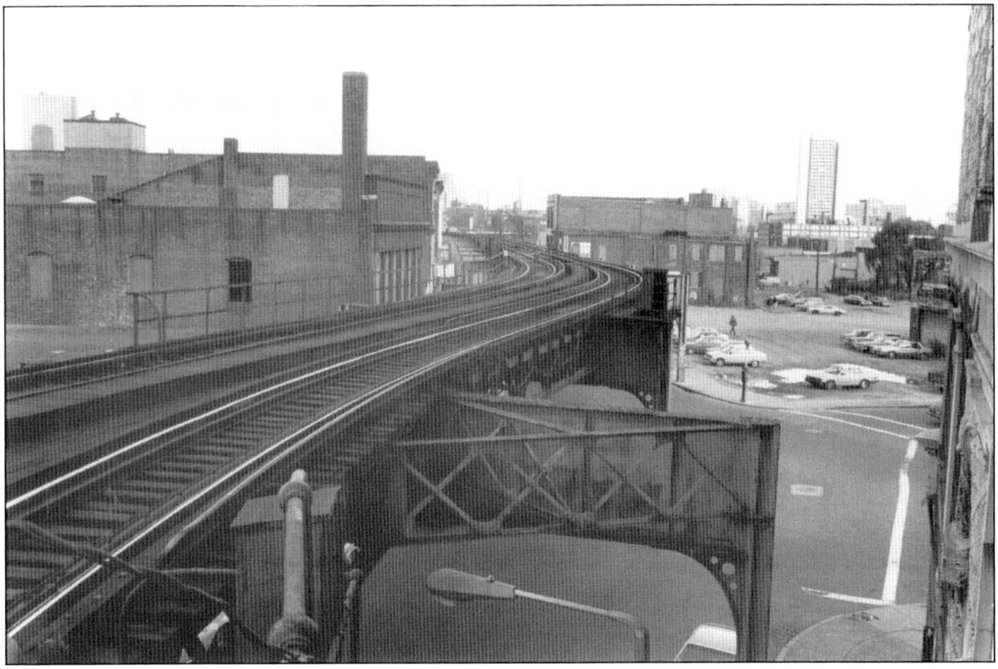

Another April 1987 photograph taken from the outbound platform at Dudley Square facing east shows the M. Harriet McCormack Nursing Tower on Northampton Street near Boston City Hospital, now Boston Medical Center. Just past the curve in the tracks is 2164 Washington Street, the future home of the Hamill Gallery of African Art. (Photograph by and courtesy of David Akiba.)

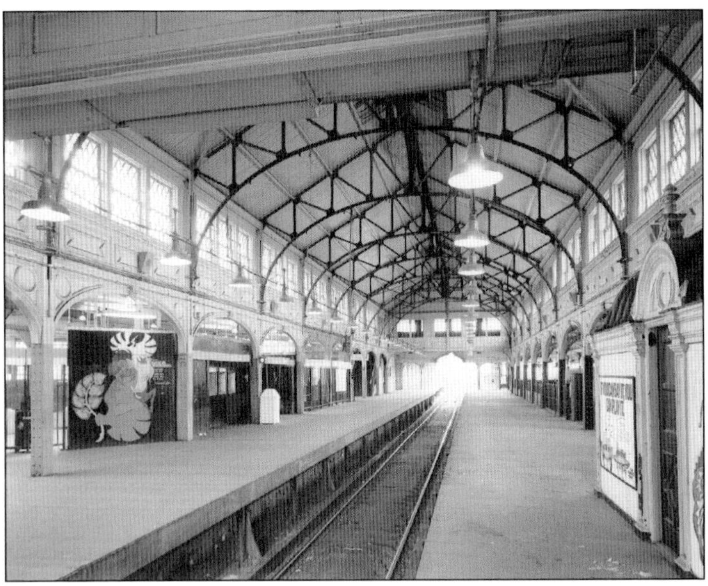

This interior view of the southbound platform at Dudley Station, looking north, gives a sense of the grandeur of the station, which was designed by architect Alexander Wadsworth Longfellow Jr. in a style described in a 1986 National Park Service report as "early French Renaissance." (Courtesy of the Historic American Engineering Record; photograph by Richard Cheek.)

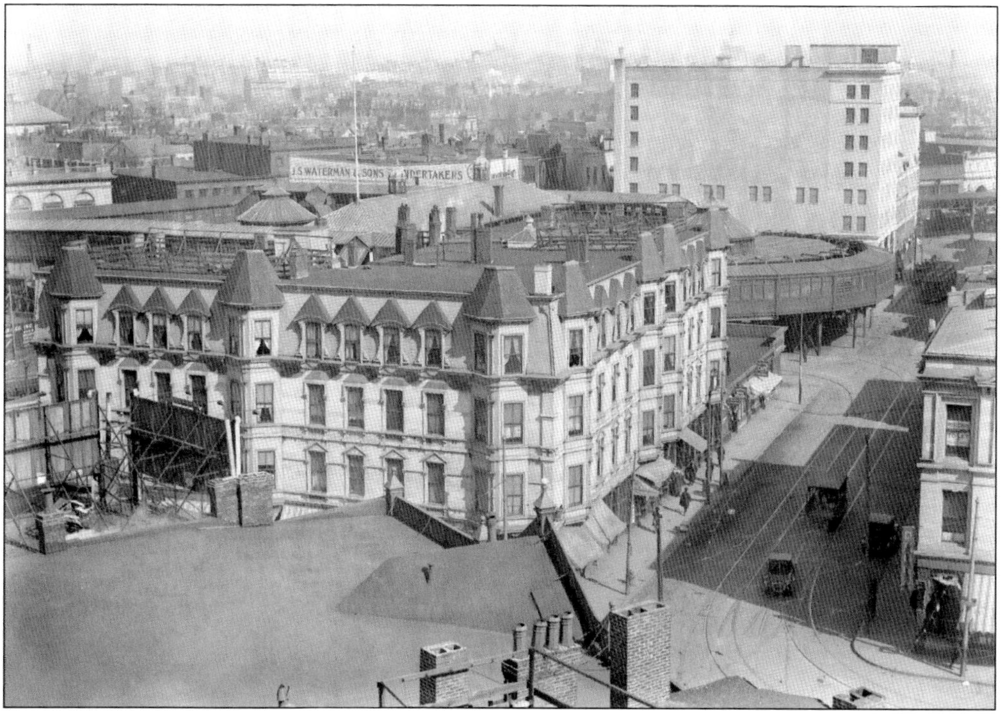

This view overlooks Warren Street in Dudley Square, with the eastbound loop of Dudley Station visible just beyond the Hotel Dartmouth (just left of center). Across Warren Street, at right, is the Italian Renaissance–style Palladio Hall, designed and built in the 1870s by architect Nathaniel J. Bradlee. (Courtesy of the Boston Public Library; photograph by Leslie Jones.)

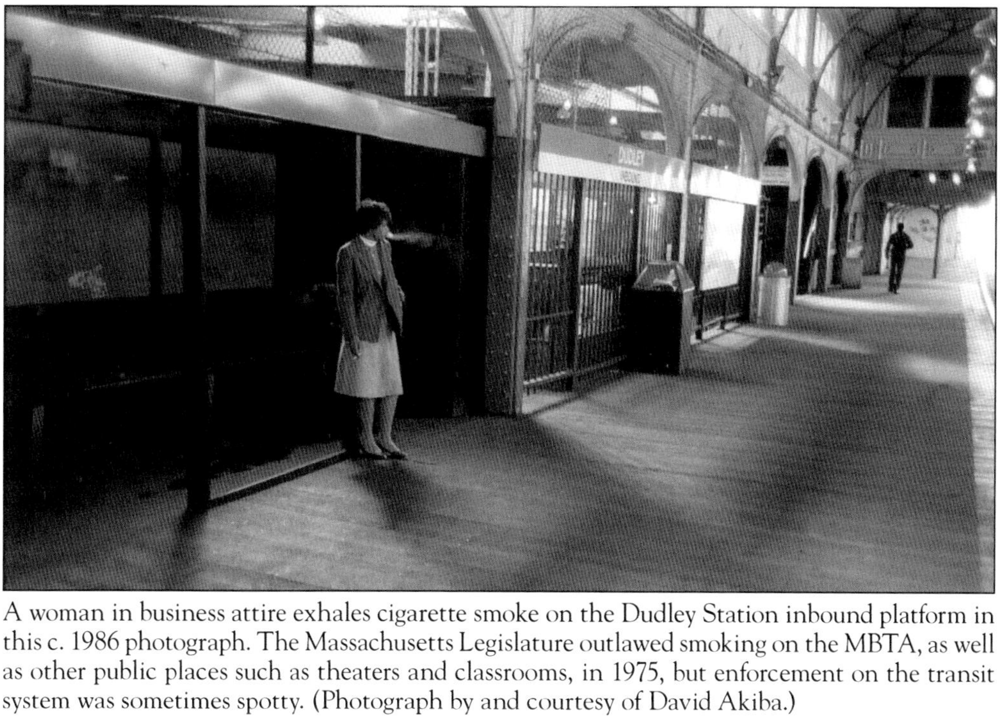

A woman in business attire exhales cigarette smoke on the Dudley Station inbound platform in this c. 1986 photograph. The Massachusetts Legislature outlawed smoking on the MBTA, as well as other public places such as theaters and classrooms, in 1975, but enforcement on the transit system was sometimes spotty. (Photograph by and courtesy of David Akiba.)

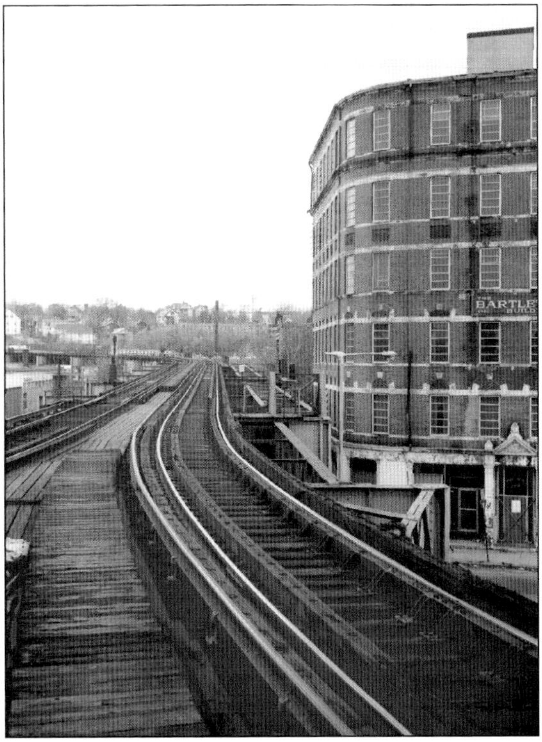

This photograph looks south from Tower "F" toward Bartlett Street Garage, site of the former Guild Street Elevated storage yard. Vacant at the time, the Bartlett building burned down on June 27, 1982. At one time, the Bartlett building was the Dunbar Hotel. (Courtesy of the Historic American Engineering Record; photograph by Richard Cheek.)

As seen below, the Egleston Square power substation stood on Washington Street just northeast of Columbus Avenue, built to support the extension from Dudley to Forest Hills. After the line was relocated, it sat vacant for years. In 2005, Urban Edge, a community development organization, partnered with the Boston Neighborhood Network to develop the building for BNN's production facilities and administrative offices. (Courtesy of the Historic American Engineering Record; photograph by Richard Cheek.)

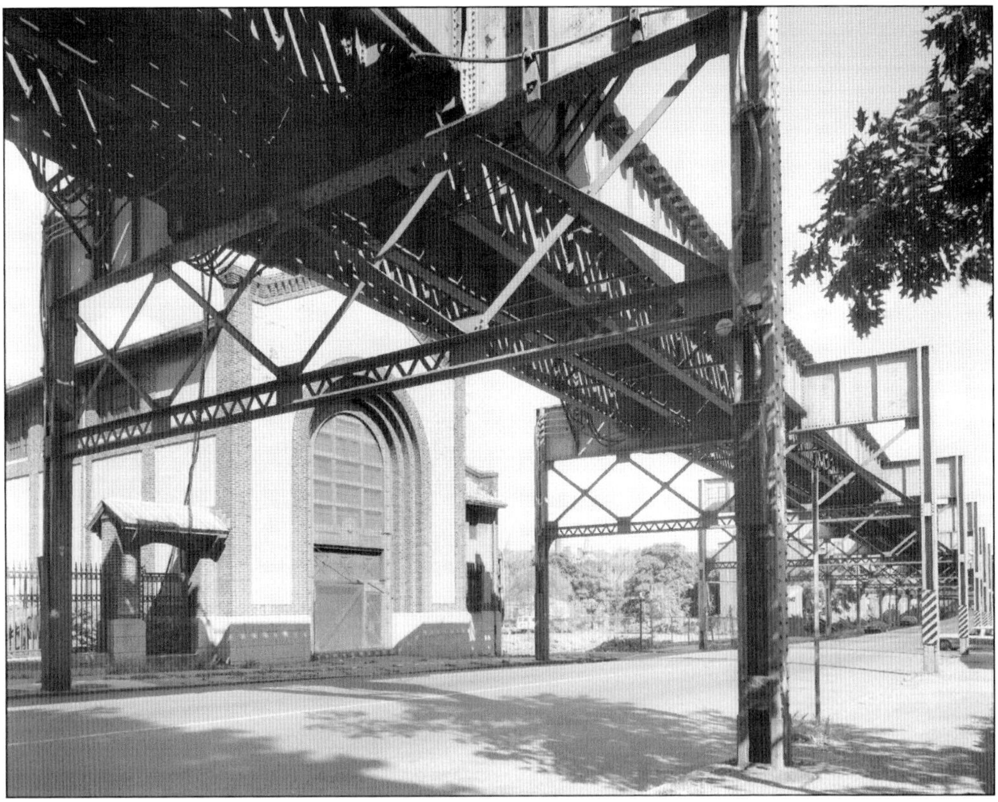

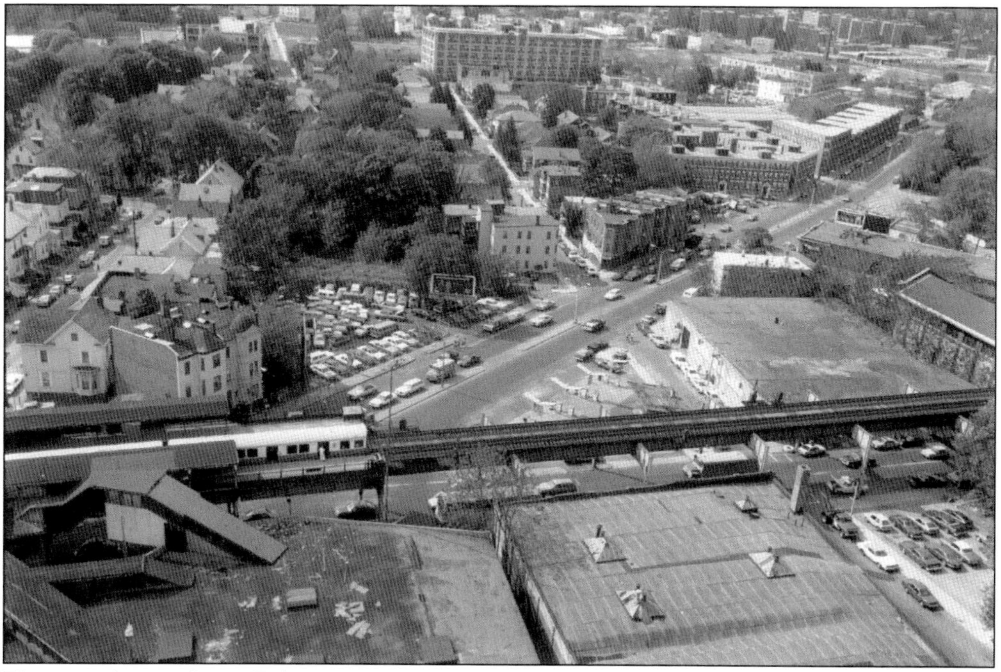

This aerial view shows Egleston Square Station from above, with a train heading downtown and Columbus Avenue stretching north toward the upper right. The homes beyond the station remained nearly 30 years later, and a gas station still stood at the intersection, though it had been modernized. Buildings at the lower left and to the right of the gas station had both been replaced. (Photograph by and courtesy of David Akiba.)

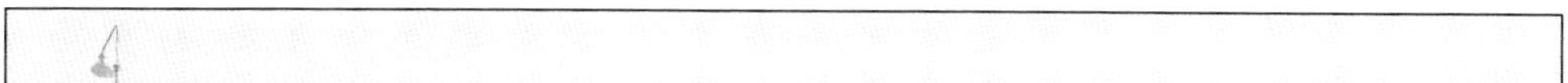

This view shows the Egleston Square Station from the northeast, looking across Washington Street from Columbus Avenue. Visible under the station on the southwest corner of the intersection are businesses, including Ugi's Restaurant and Egleston One-Hour Cleaners. The once rundown area is now a vibrant business district, thanks in part to the efforts of Egleston Square Main Street. (Courtesy of the Historic American Engineering Record; photograph by Richard Cheek.)

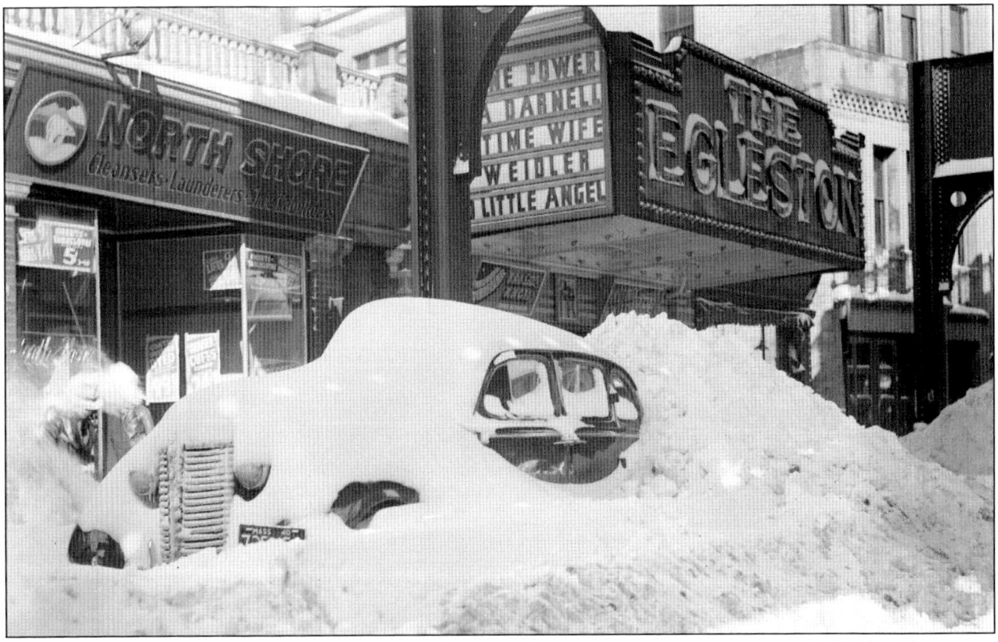

From the silent film era until 1961, the Egleston Theatre was in operation at 3093 Washington Street, just southwest of Egleston Square. At the time of this 1939 snowstorm, it was showing *Day-Time Wife*, starring Tyrone Power and Linda Darnell, and *Bad Little Angel*, starring Virginia Weidler. (Courtesy of the Boston Public Library; photograph by Leslie Jones.)

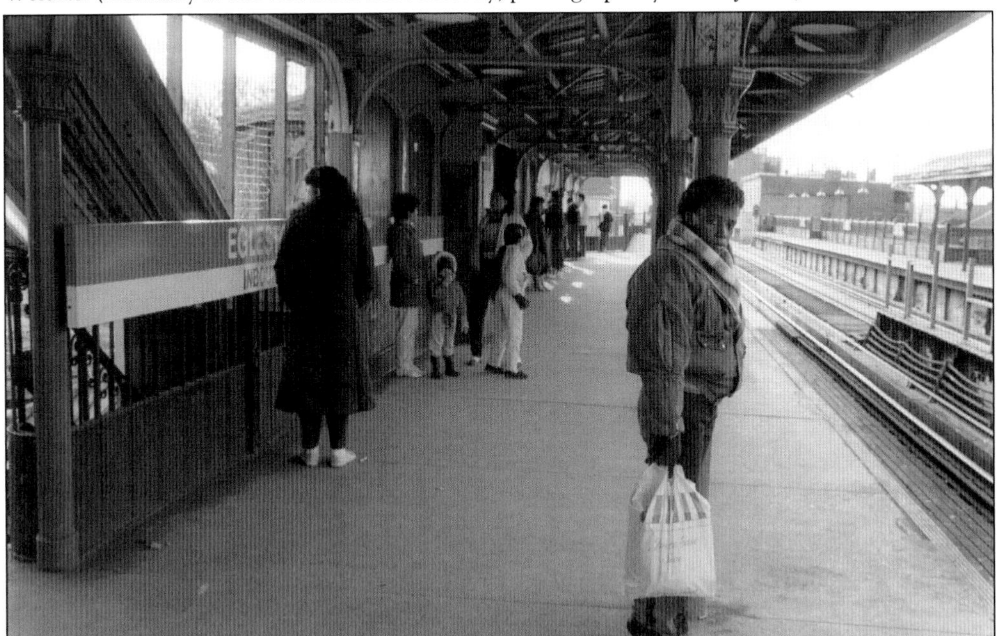

In this 1986 photograph, commuters await a train on the inbound platform at Egleston Square Station. The woman looking at the photographer appears to have been shopping at the punningly named Justin Case Shoes on downtown's Summer Street. Above her head, the station's decorative architectural elements have been graffitied. (Photograph by and courtesy of David Akiba.)

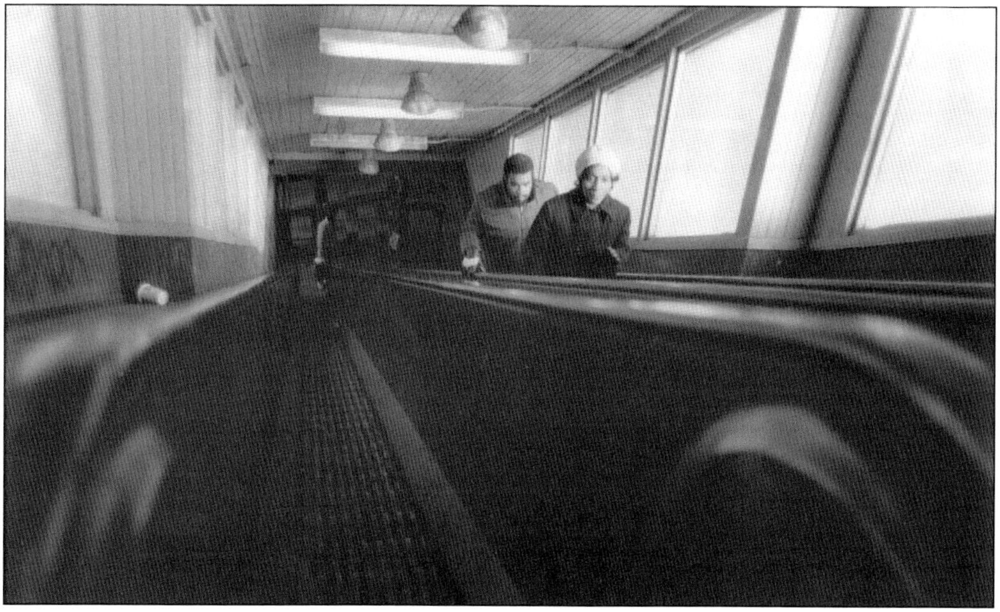

At Egleston Square Station, commuters ride up one of the system's famous narrow wooden escalators. In a 1982 *Boston Globe* op-ed, David B. Wilson wrote, "[A]s civic icons go, the clattering, clanking, precipitously sloping wooden-treaded escalators of the T contribute something to the soul of the city; without them, it would be a different and a poorer place." (Photograph by and courtesy of David Akiba.)

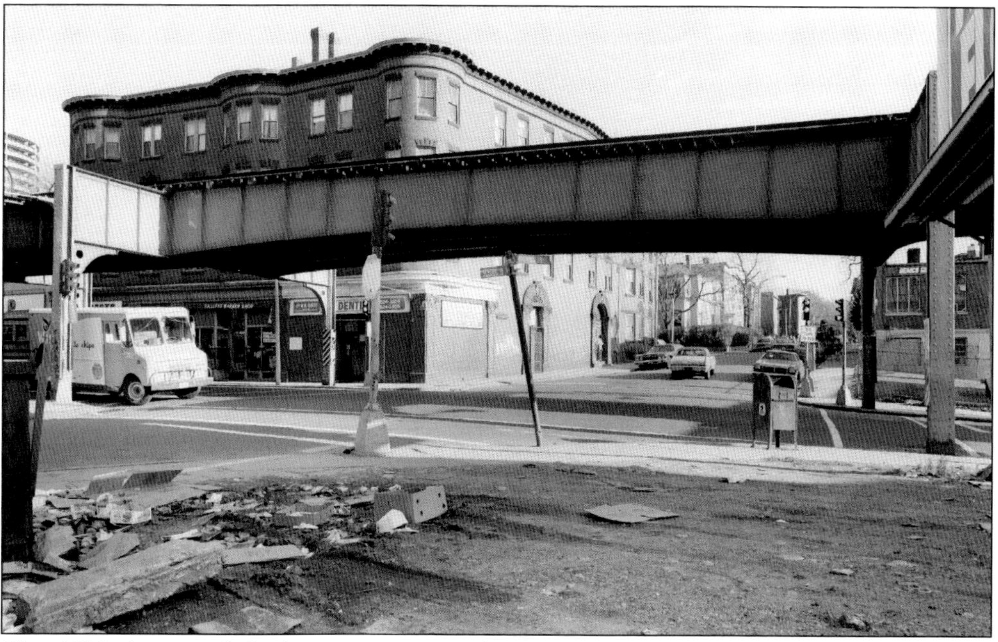

This 1982 photograph looks east across Washington Street and the Elevated structure from School Street in Egleston Square, just south of the Elevated station. Visible under the platform at left are Talley's Barber Shop, at 3120 Washington Street, and Dr. N.B. Dixit, family dentist, at 3122 Washington Street. (Courtesy of the Historic American Engineering Record; photograph by Richard Cheek.)

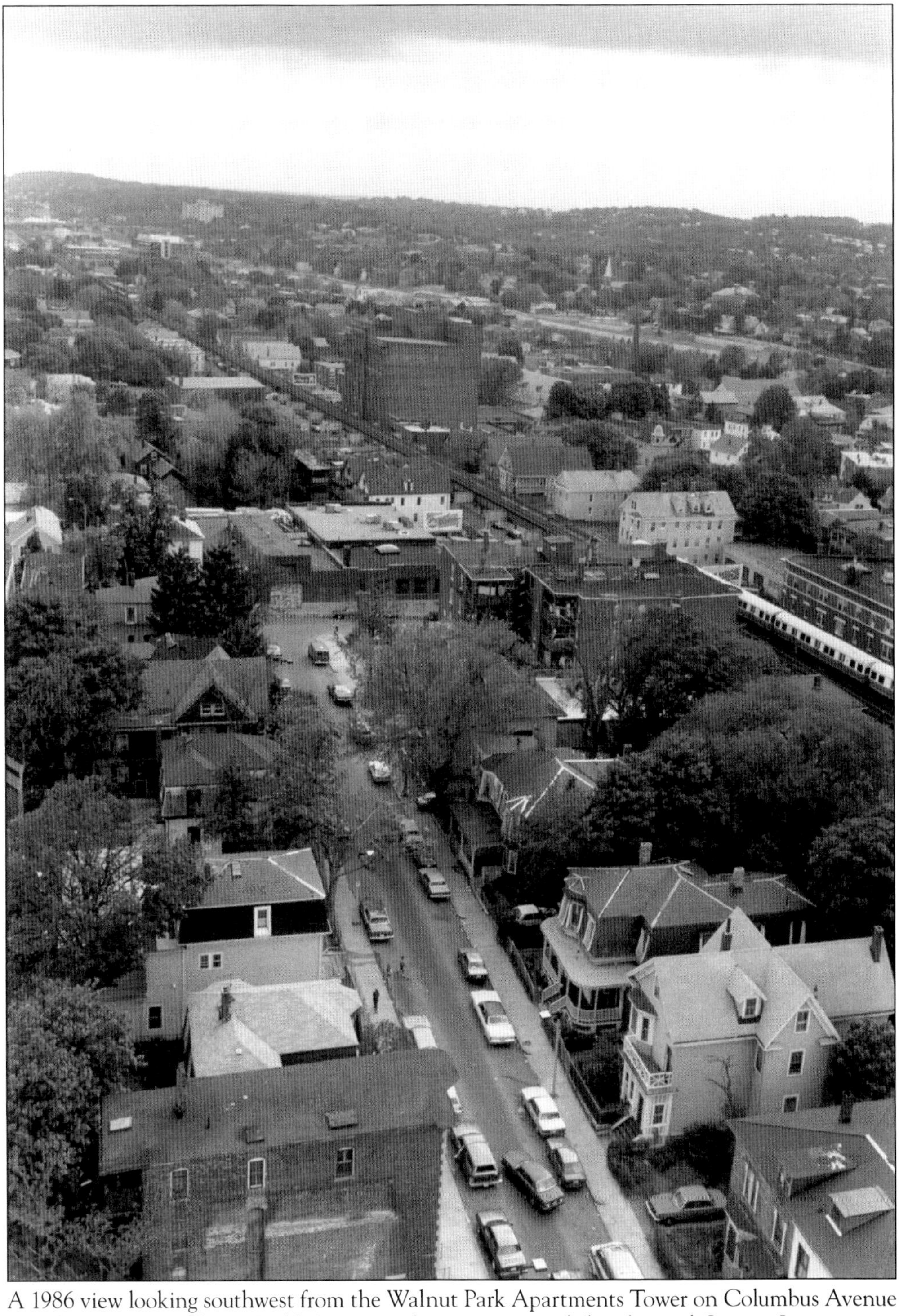

A 1986 view looking southwest from the Walnut Park Apartments Tower on Columbus Avenue in Egleston Square shows Weld Avenue at lower center and the elevated Orange Line cutting diagonally toward Green Street Station, a half-mile away, on its way to Forest Hills. (Photograph by and courtesy of David Akiba.)

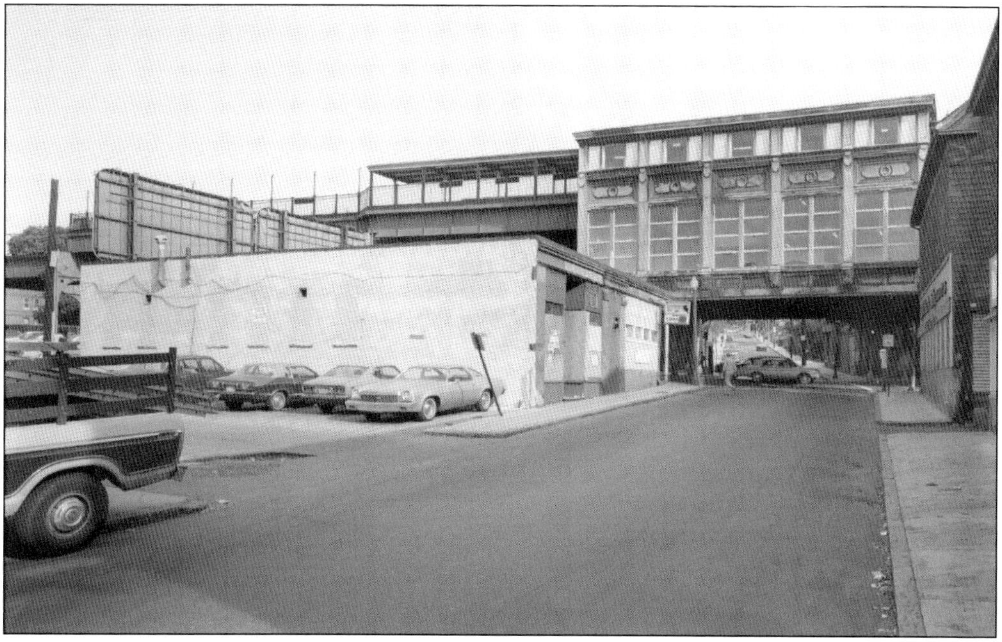

This 1982 photograph looks southeast along Green Street toward Washington and Green Street Station, with Glen Road beyond. A liquor store is at right at the intersection, while Smitty's Sub Shop is at left; the Smitty's site is now home to the Jamaica Plain police station. (Courtesy of the Historic American Engineering Record; photograph by Richard Cheek.)

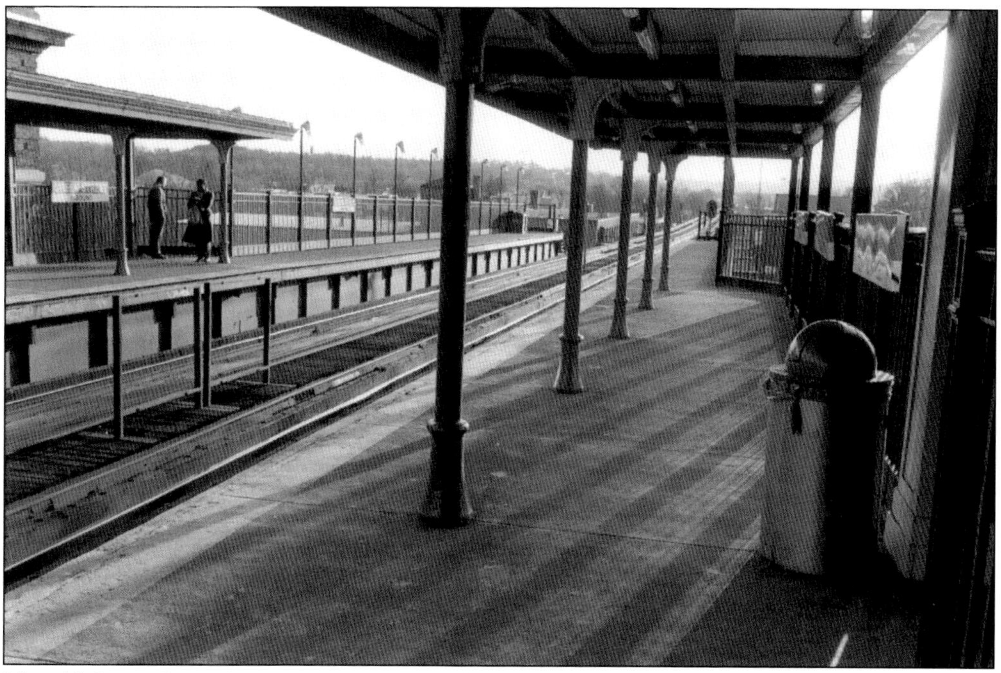

The old Green Street Station was not originally part of the Washington Street Elevated's extension to Forest Hills but opened for service in 1912. When the station was later relocated along the Southwest Corridor route of the new, submerged Orange Line, it moved only three blocks northwest, one of the smallest changes for commuters. (Photograph by and courtesy of David Akiba.)

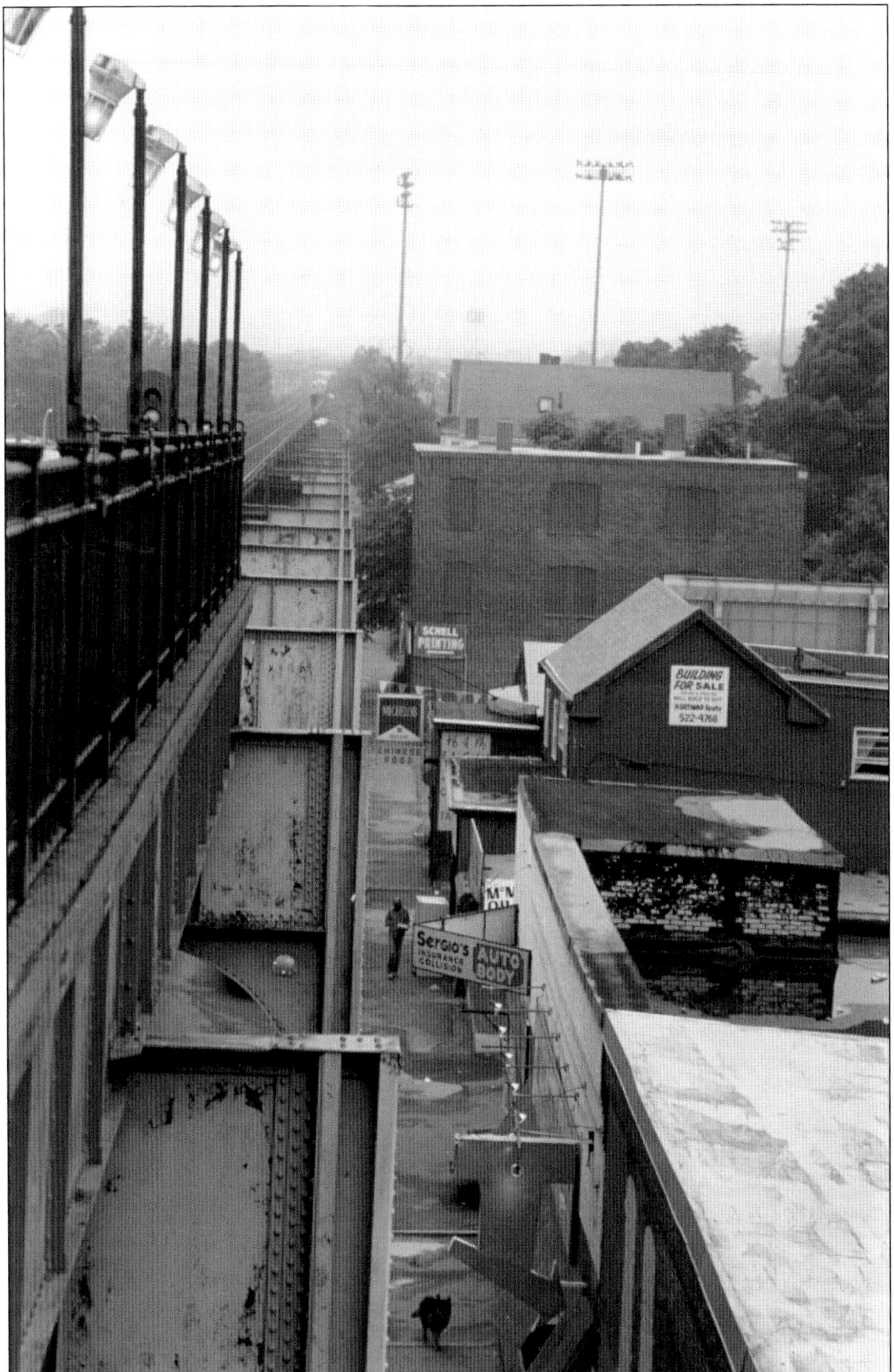

A 1986 image from the Green Street Station platform shows a train approaching in the distance, where the clock tower of the new Forest Hills Station, under construction, is dimly visible. On Washington Street, closer to the station, is Sergio's Auto Body, a Chinese restaurant, and Schell Printing. (Photograph by and courtesy of David Akiba.)

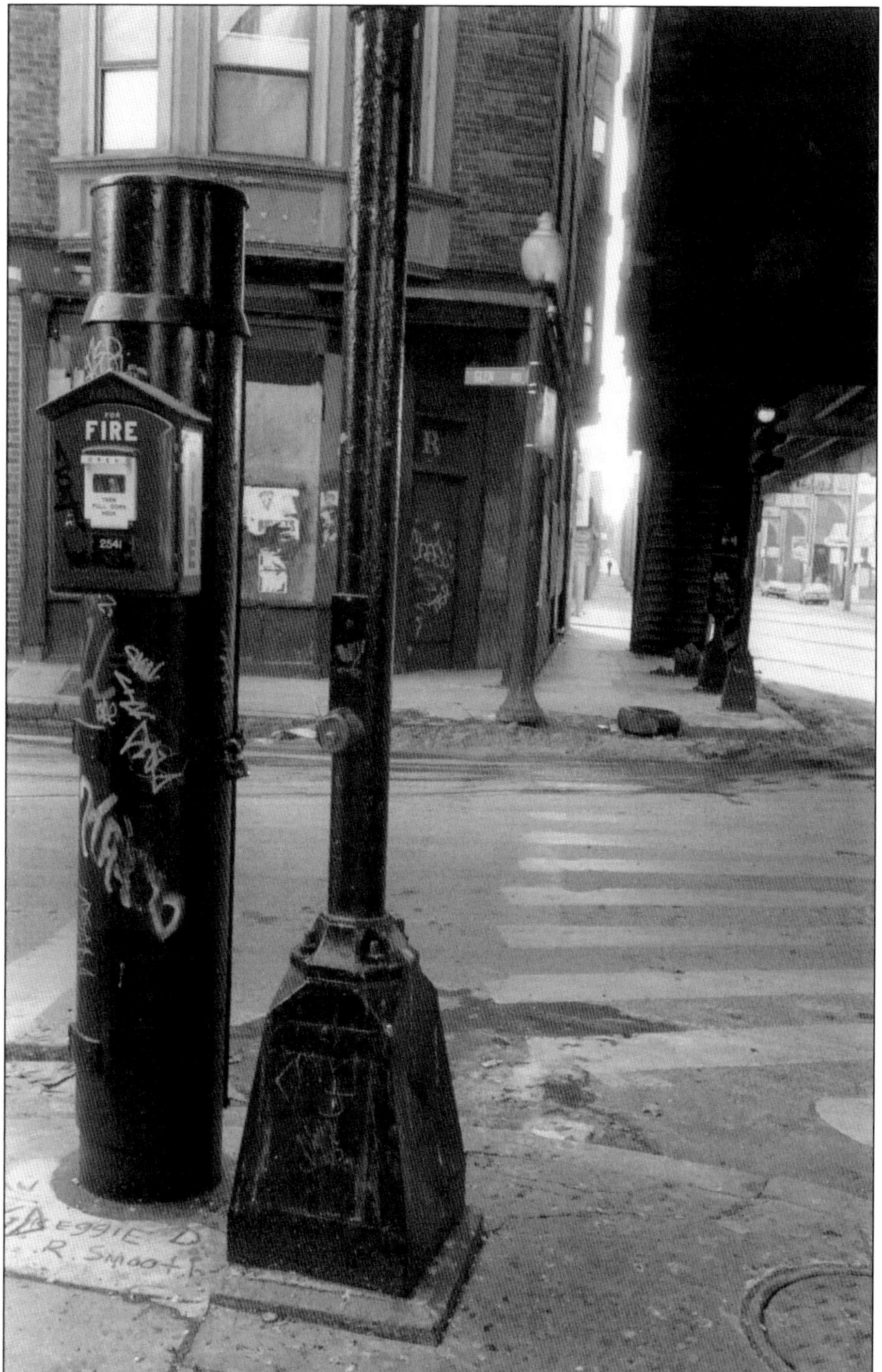

As it crosses Washington Street heading east, Green Street becomes Glen Road, which continues up a hill to Franklin Park. This view, looking south at the corner of Washington Street and Glen Road, offers a sense of how the Elevated tracks were constructed close to buildings. (Photograph by and courtesy of David Akiba.)

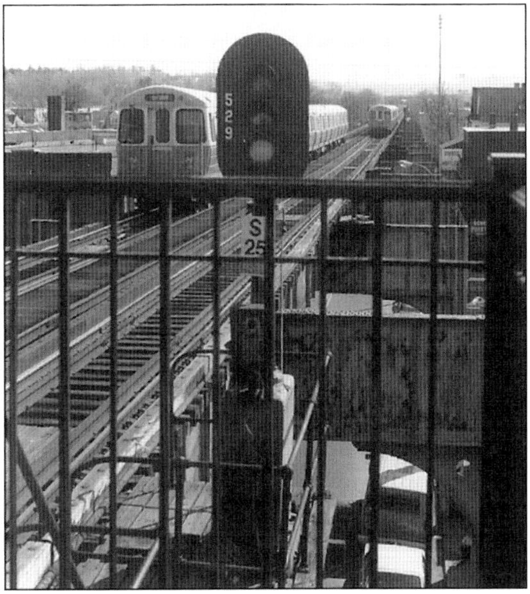

Looking southwest from the Green Street outbound platform toward Forest Hills in April 1987, Schell Printing, at 3399 Washington Street, where it moved in the 1960s and remains today, is partially visible at far right. While many Washington Street businesses have come and gone, Schell Printing stands with nearby Hatoff's Gas Station and Ruggiero's Market as establishments that have remained for decades. (Photograph by and courtesy of Joe Boncek.)

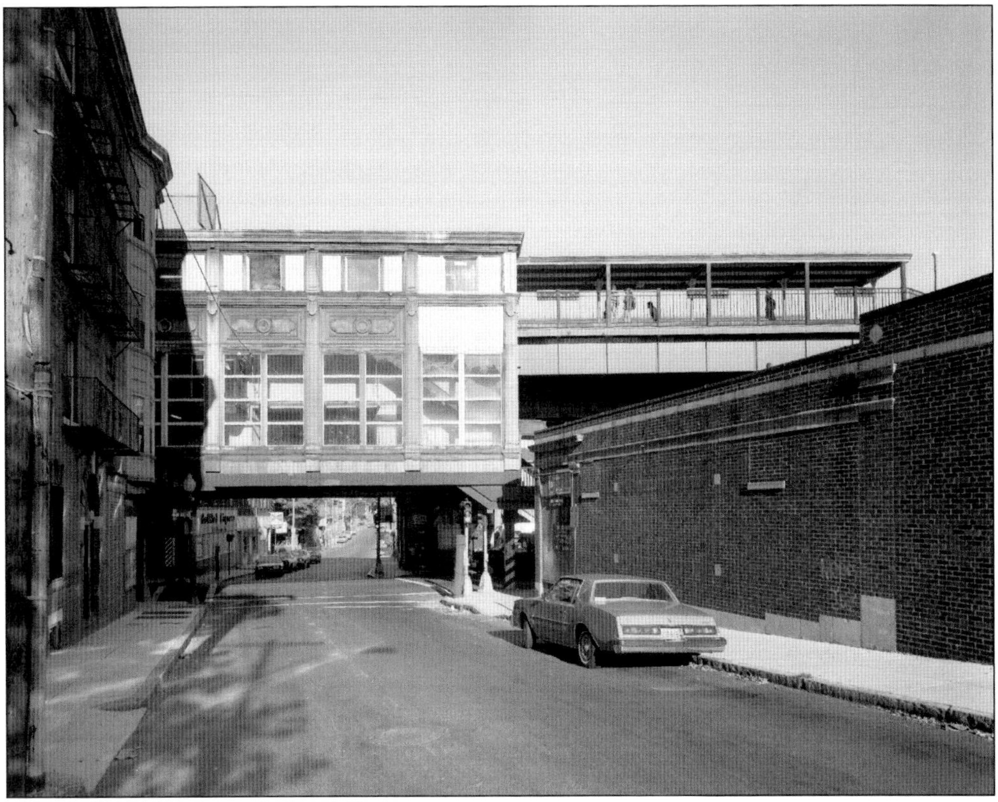

This view from 1982 looks west down Glen Road, across Washington Street toward Green Street. The Green Street Station dominates the intersection. Beneath it, across Washington Street at left, is the present-day site of the District E-13 Boston Police Station. In this picture, that corner is home to Ruggiero's Market, which has since moved just slightly north up the street. (Courtesy of the Historic American Engineering Record; photograph by Richard Cheek.)

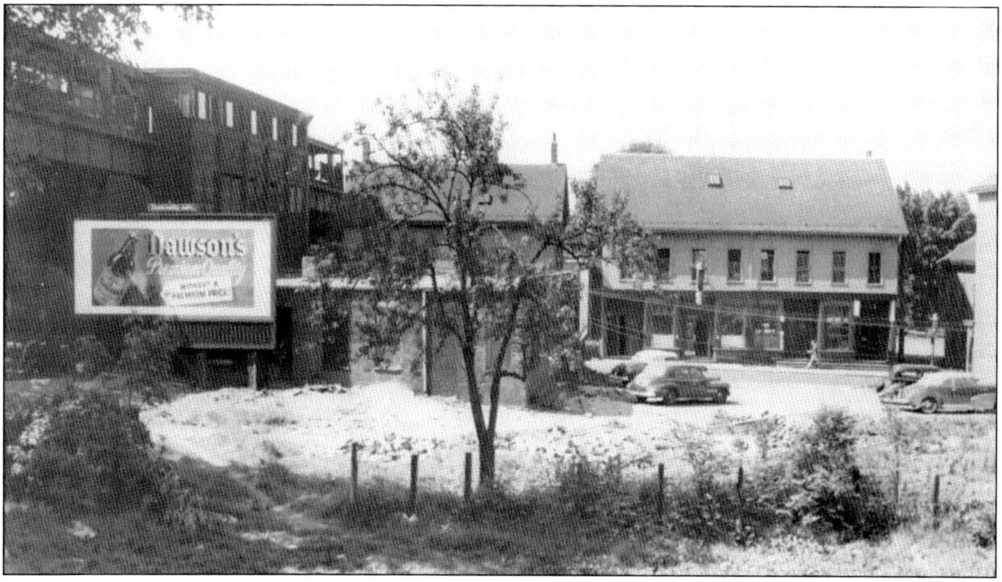

The Green Street Station looms over lower-set structures in this 1948 photograph looking south toward commercial and apartment buildings along Green Street. The wooden buildings in this image still stand, but the one-story structure behind the billboard at left has been replaced with a police station. (Collection No. 5110.002, City of Boston Archives, Boston.)

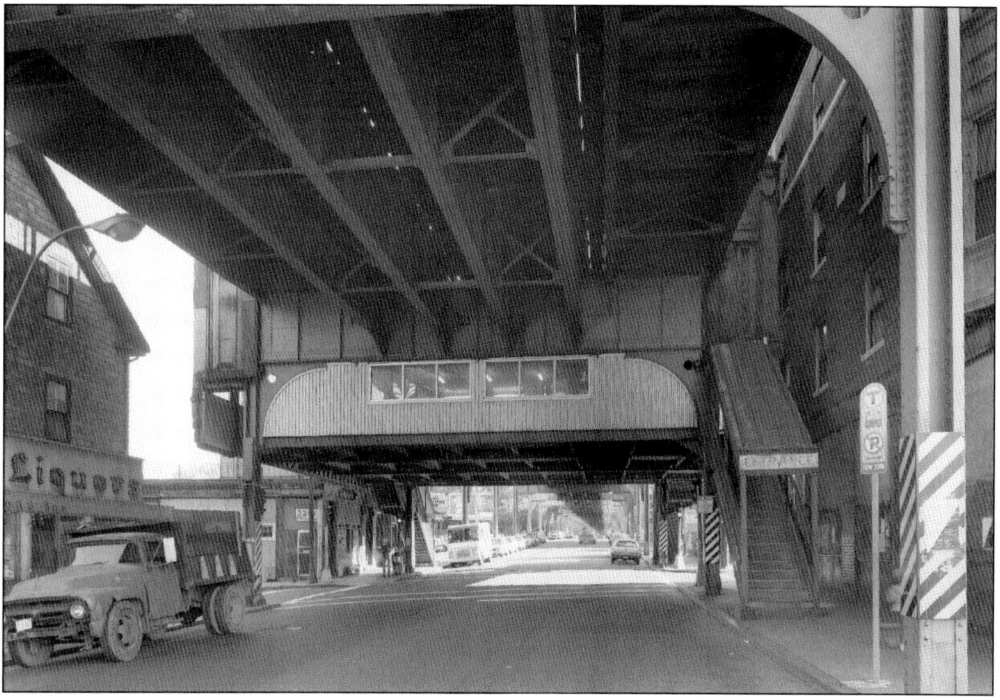

This 1982 photograph, looking north along Washington Street in the shade of the Elevated tracks, gives a sense of how Green Street Station dominated the intersection of Green and Washington Streets and how the Elevated cast entire neighborhoods in shadow. Once the station was removed in 1988, this intersection became practically unrecognizable. (Courtesy of the Historic American Engineering Record; photograph by Richard Cheek.)

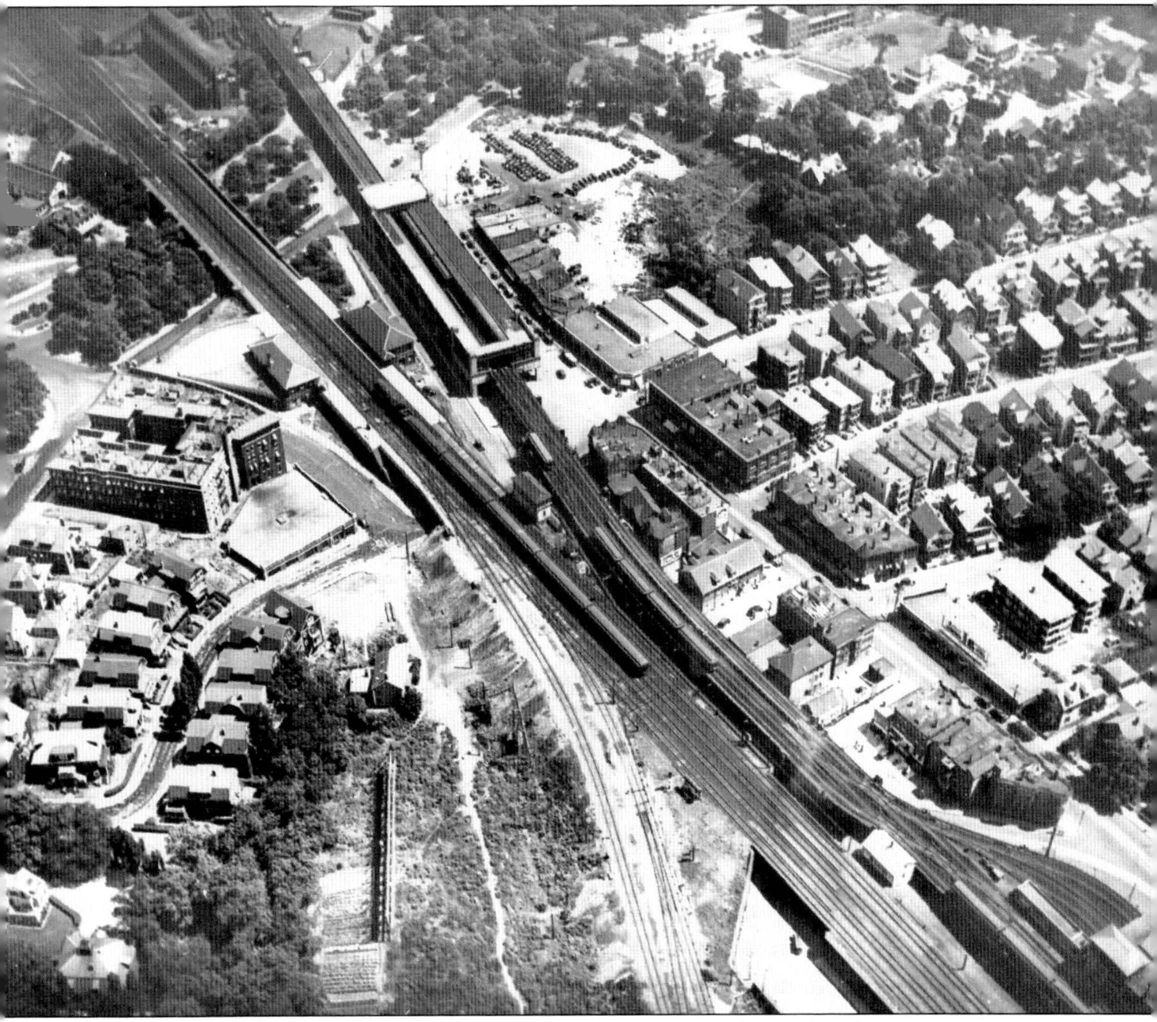

In 1903, just two years after the Elevated opened, the Boston Elevated Railway Company initiated plans to extend service from Dudley Square to Forest Hills. This c. 1930 view of Forest Hills Station shows two sets of tracks. Those on the right serve the Elevated, while those on the left serve the Boston & Providence Railroad. (Courtesy of the Boston Public Library; photograph by Aero Scenic Airviews Company.)

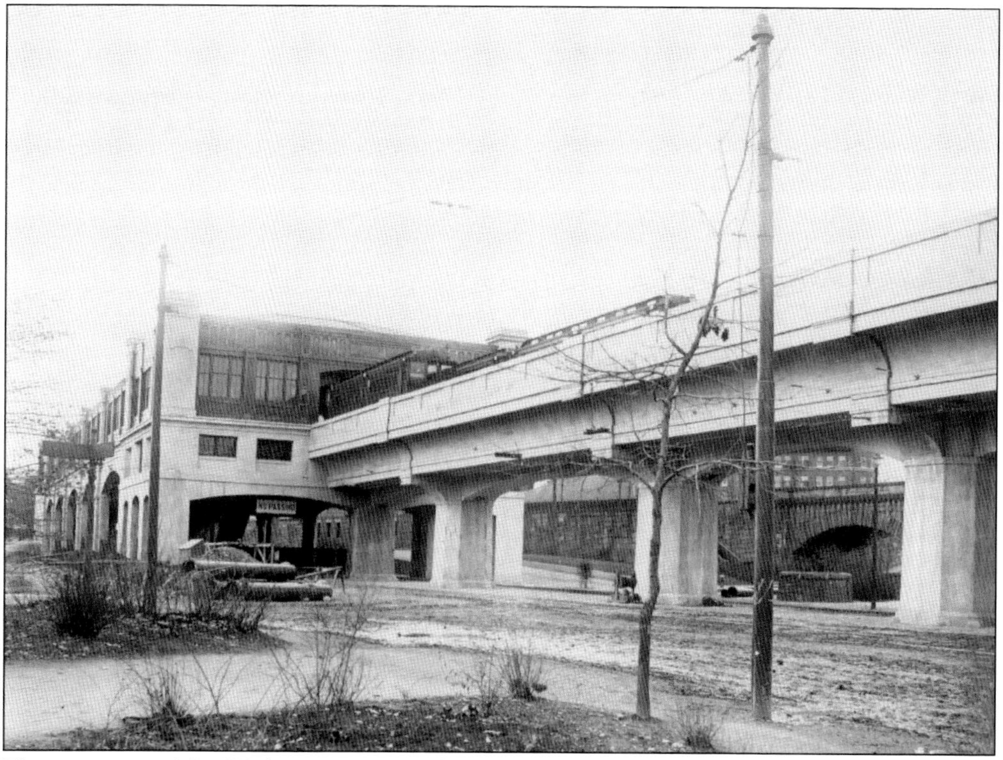

The extension of the Washington Street Elevated was not completed until late 1909, after a series of setbacks stalled the project for many years. This photograph looks south toward the exterior of Forest Hills Station in November 1909, just before the extension of Washington Street Elevated service from Dudley to Forest Hills. (Courtesy of the Boston Public Library.)

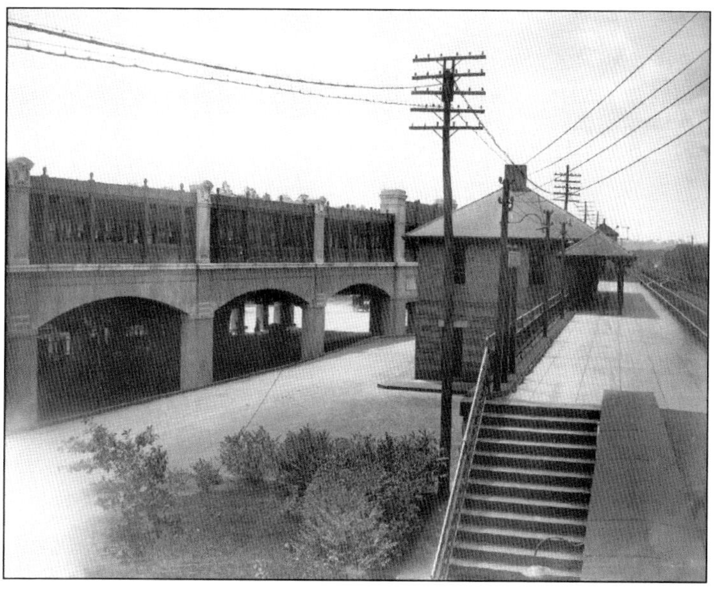

This August 1910 photograph, looking south toward Roslindale and Hyde Park, shows the western rise of the recently completed Forest Hills Station. The smaller structure at right is the Forest Hills Railroad Station, part of the Boston & Providence Railroad. In the 1980s, the new Forest Hills Station, serving both the Orange Line and the Commuter Rail, was erected in its place. (Courtesy of the Boston Public Library.)

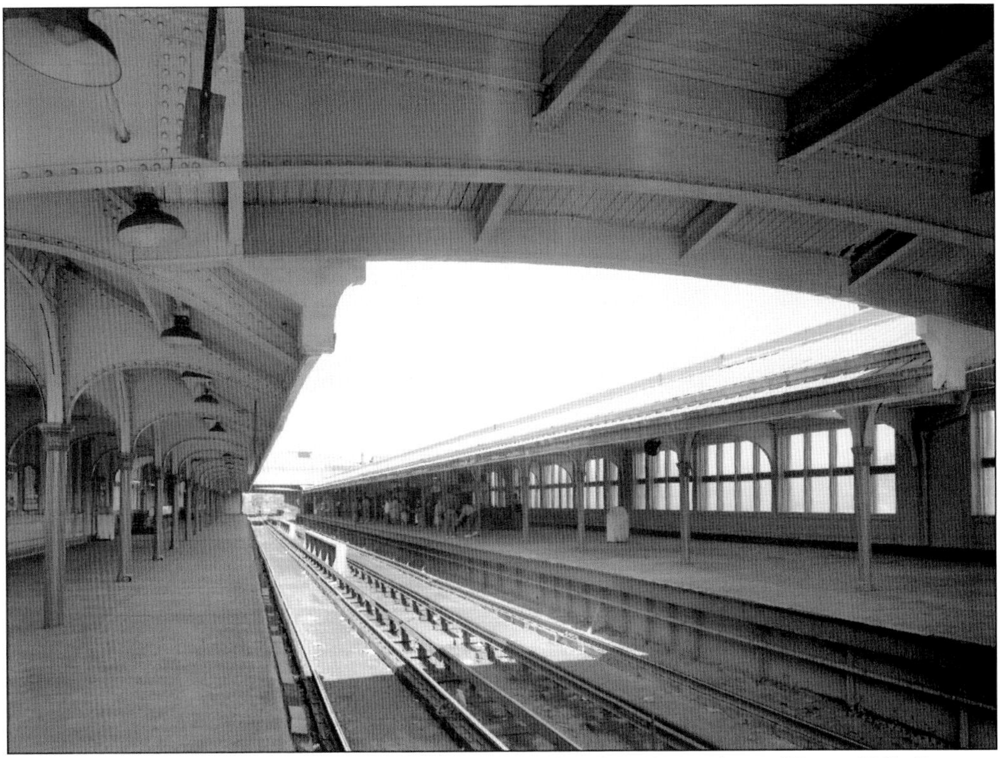

These two 1982 photographs show the architectural details and grandeur of Forest Hills Station, designed by Edmund M. Wheelwright, who also designed Park Street Station in downtown Boston. Over the years, Forest Hills Station was subject to a number of modifications, including a southward extension that allowed trains to reverse direction. The above image is a view looking north from the station's platform. The below image shows an interior view of the station, where a stairway to the upper levels is suspended from the main structure of the building. (Both, courtesy of the Historic American Engineering Record; photograph by Richard Cheek.)

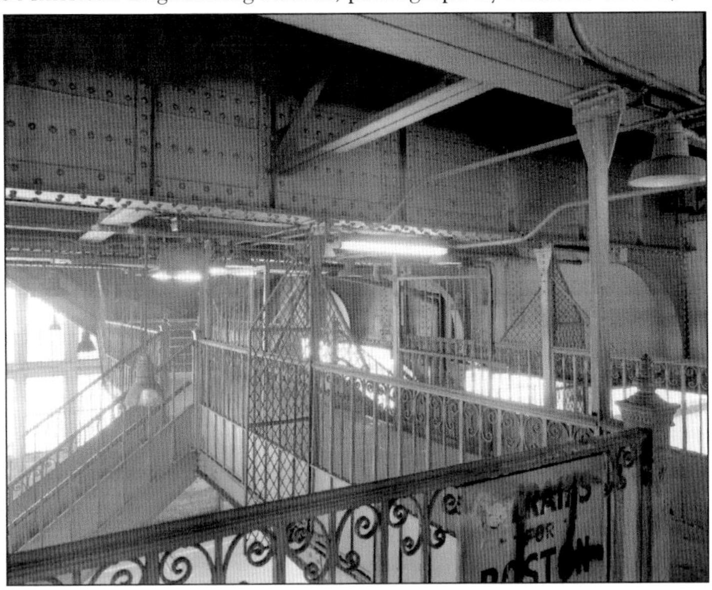

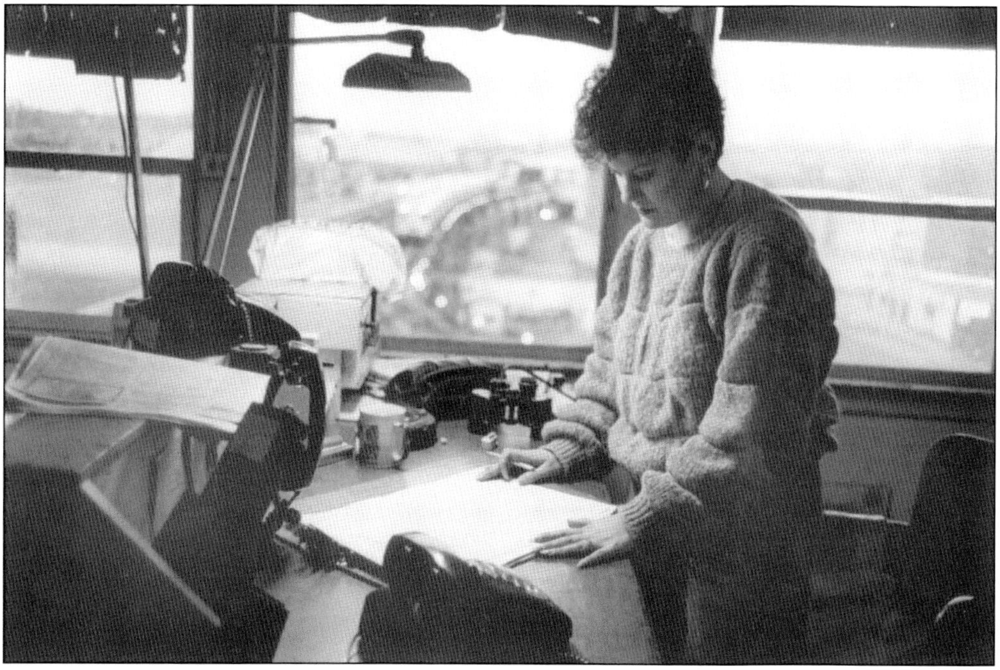

These images were taken inside the Tower "H" control tower at Forest Hills Station. The above image from 1986 shows an unidentified worker inside the control tower with a southbound train about to enter the station. The below image from 1982 offers a view of equipment just to the left of where the woman is standing in the above photograph. To enter the tower, a person had to climb a long, narrow, winding metal staircase that began in the lower Walk Hill storage yard, the sound of their footsteps echoing around them as they climbed to the top. (Above, photograph by and courtesy of David Akiba; below, courtesy of the Historic American Engineering Record, photograph by Richard Cheek.)

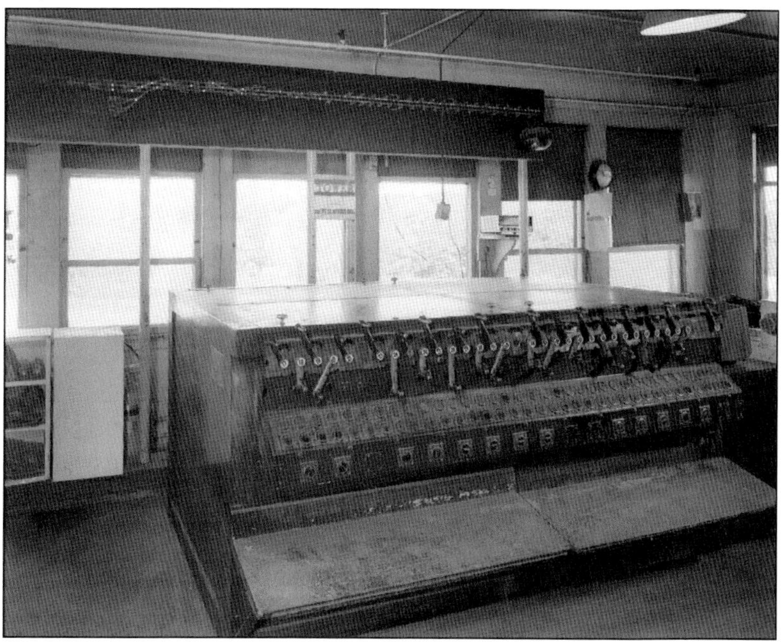

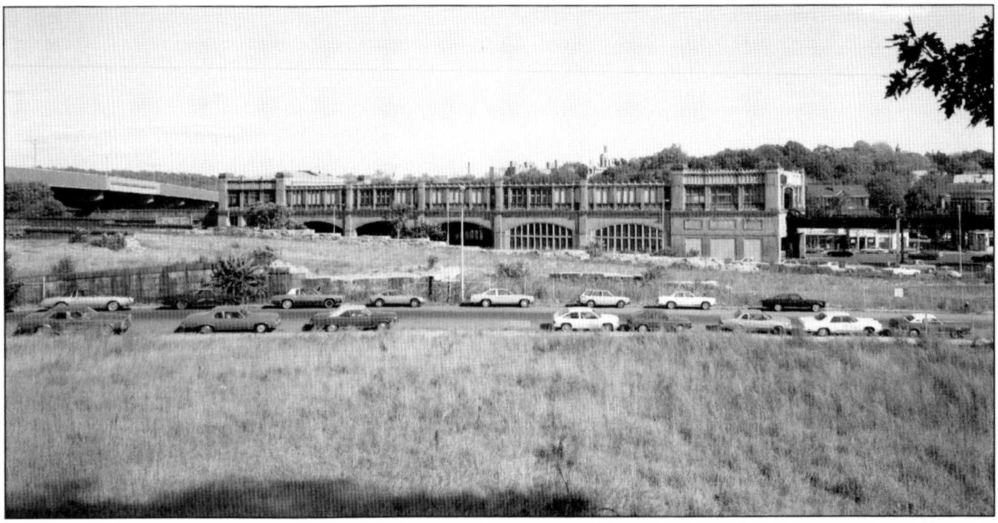

On the left side of this view looking east toward Forest Hills Station is the Monsignor William J. Casey Overpass, which carries the Arborway from the area of the Arnold Arboretum in Jamaica Plain toward Forest Hills Cemetery, Franklin Park, and the Dorchester section of Boston. (Courtesy of the Historic American Engineering Record; photograph by Richard Cheek.)

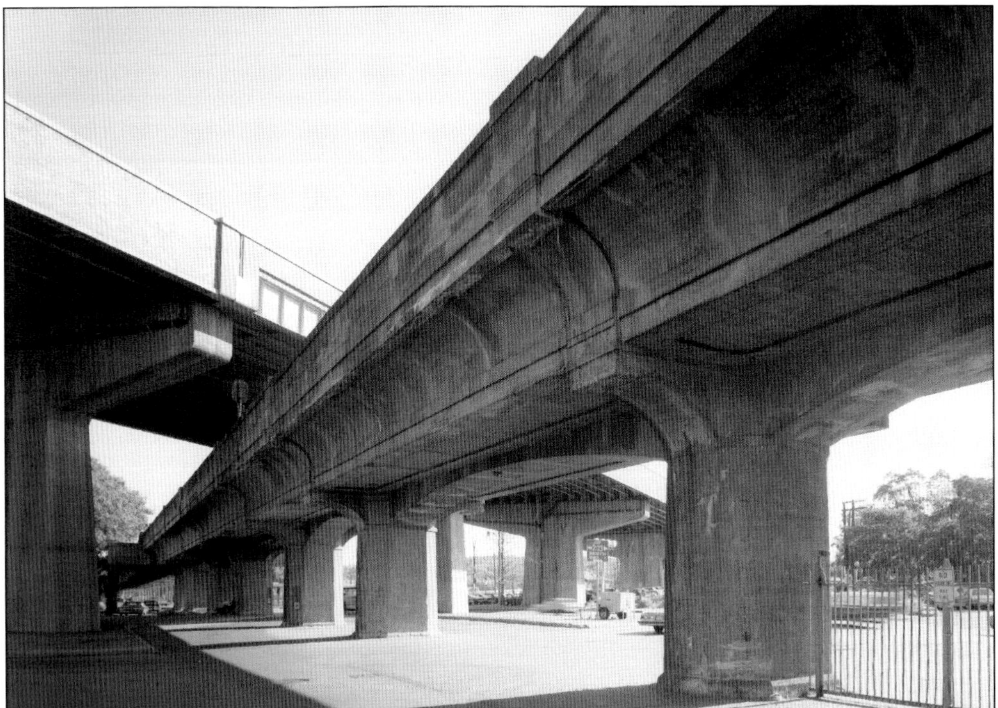

This 1982 photograph offers a closer view of the Casey Overpass above the elevated rail line, which was torn down after the line was rerouted in 1987. In 2011, the Massachusetts Department of Transportation began considering alternatives to replace the overpass, which was constructed in the 1950s and has fallen into considerable disrepair; a surface road is planned. (Courtesy of the Historic American Engineering Record; photograph by Richard Cheek.)

Five

Rerouting the Northern Line

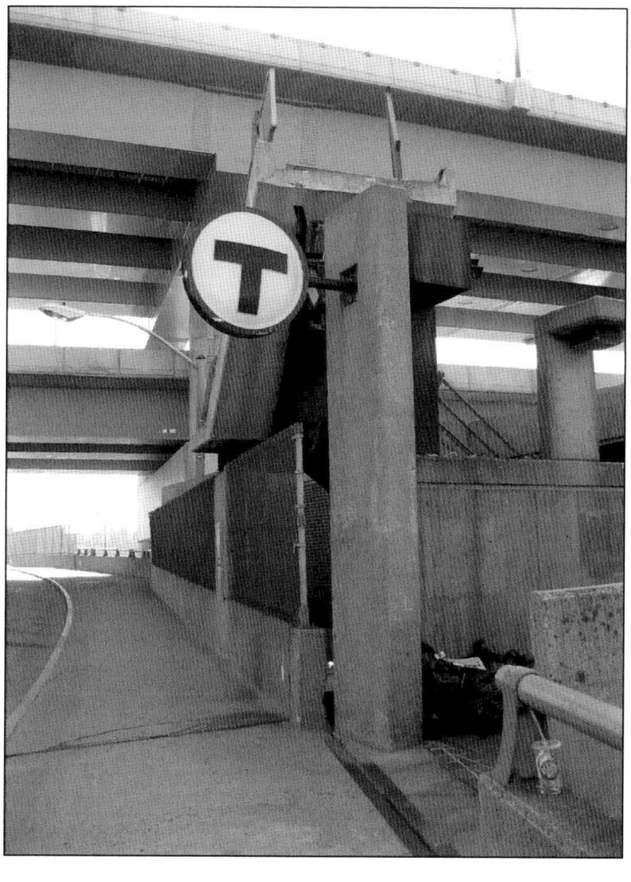

The "T" emblem is prominent outside Community College Station in Charlestown. The emblem was adopted in 1965 and sometimes described as the "Circle-T." When it was introduced, Massachusetts Bay Transportation Authority officials said the authority would avoid using the initials "MBTA" and asked news media to do the same. The MBTA hoped to distinguish itself from its predecessor, the Metropolitan Transit Authority, or MTA. (Photograph by and courtesy of Andrew Lynch.)

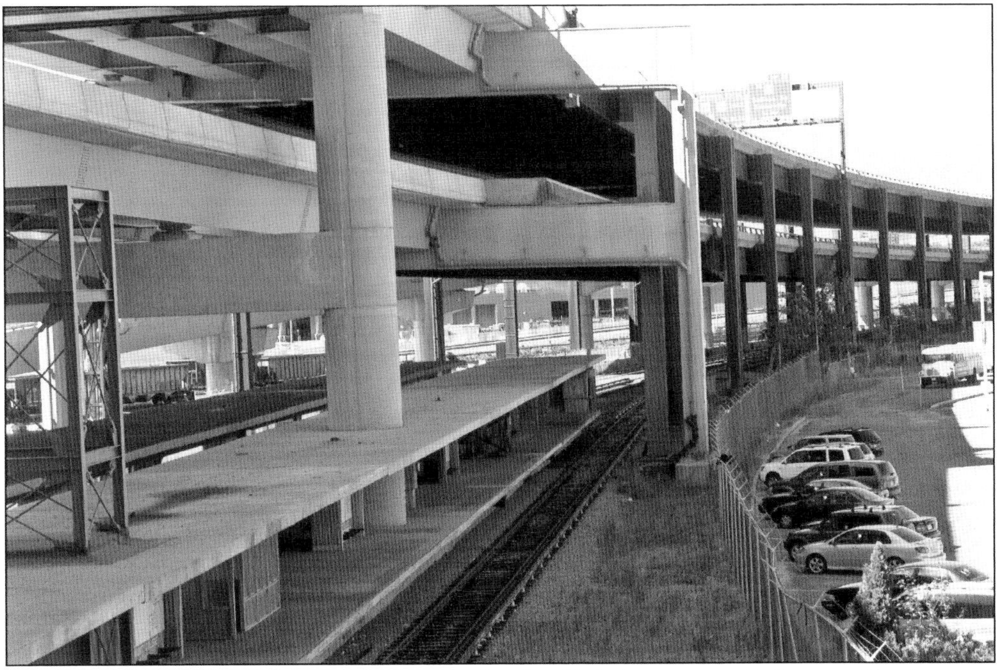

Community College Station (pictured) serves Bunker Hill Community College in Charlestown. It was one of two stations built beneath Interstate 93, along the Boston & Maine Railroad tracks, in the Haymarket North Extension. Construction on the extension was begun in 1966 and completed in 1977. The Charlestown Elevated closed on Friday, April 4, 1975, and shuttle buses carried passengers between Sullivan Square Station and Essex Station while the extension was connected. (Photograph by and courtesy of Nathaniel Marsh.)

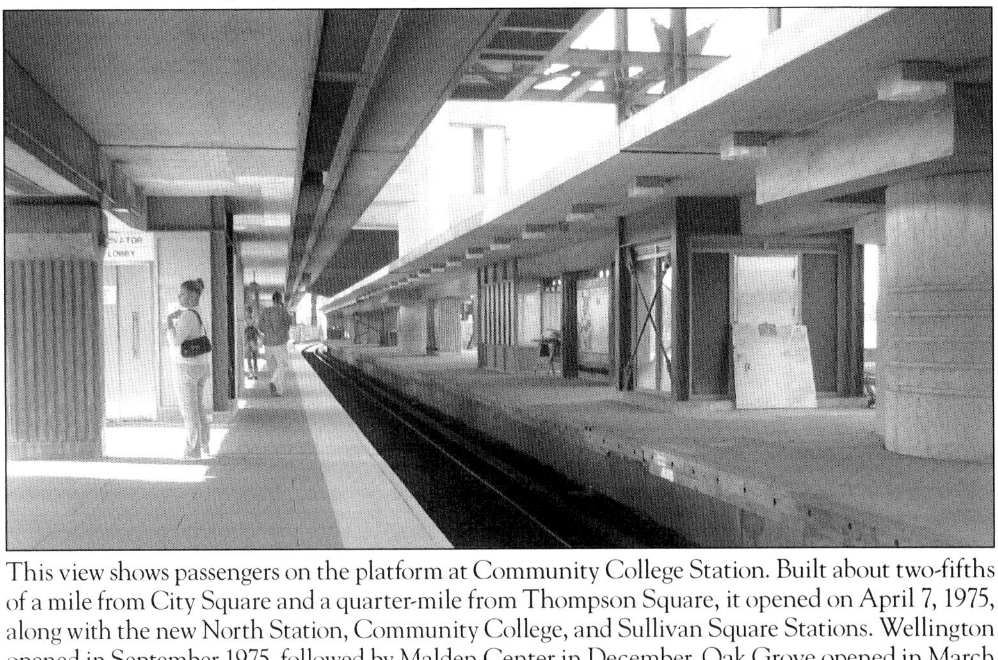

This view shows passengers on the platform at Community College Station. Built about two-fifths of a mile from City Square and a quarter-mile from Thompson Square, it opened on April 7, 1975, along with the new North Station, Community College, and Sullivan Square Stations. Wellington opened in September 1975, followed by Malden Center in December. Oak Grove opened in March 1977, completing the extension. (Photograph by and courtesy of Andrew Lynch.)

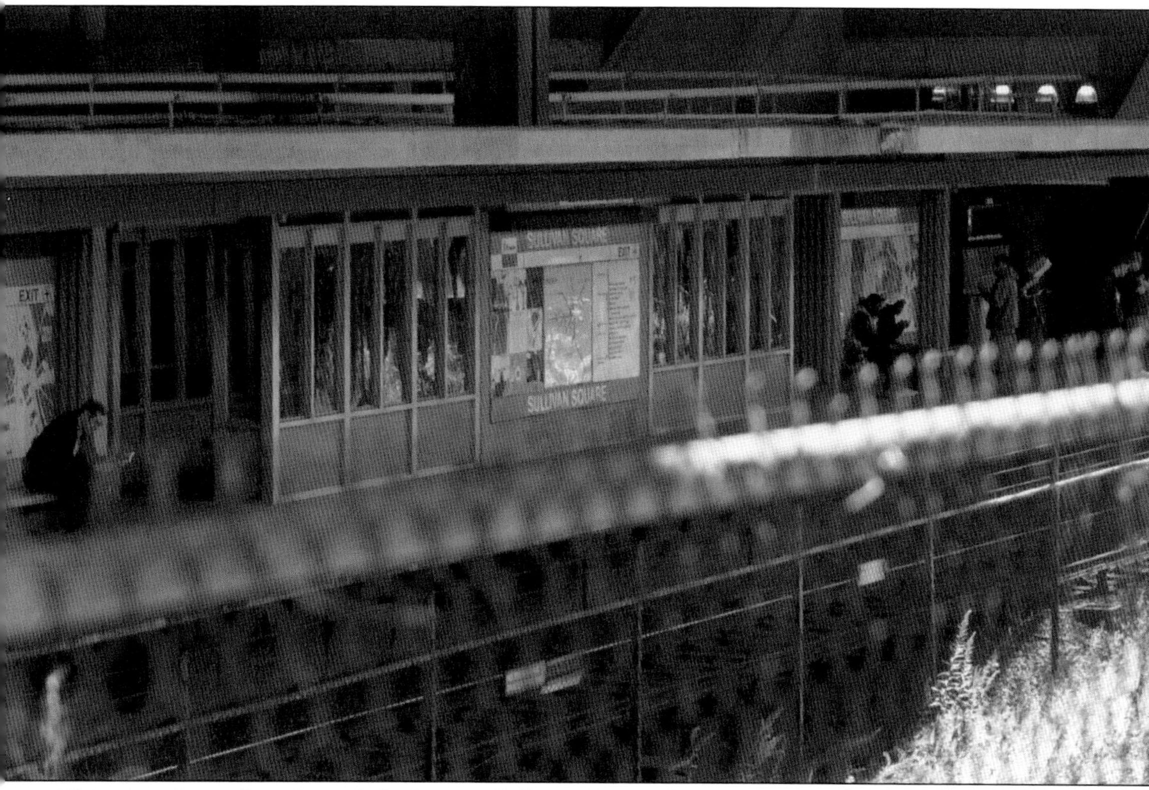

This view shows the inbound platform at Sullivan Square Station across a chain-link fence near the intersection of Brighton and Perkins Streets in Charlestown. A dedication ceremony for the Haymarket North Extension was held at Sullivan Square on April 4, 1975. (Photograph by and courtesy of Nathaniel Marsh.)

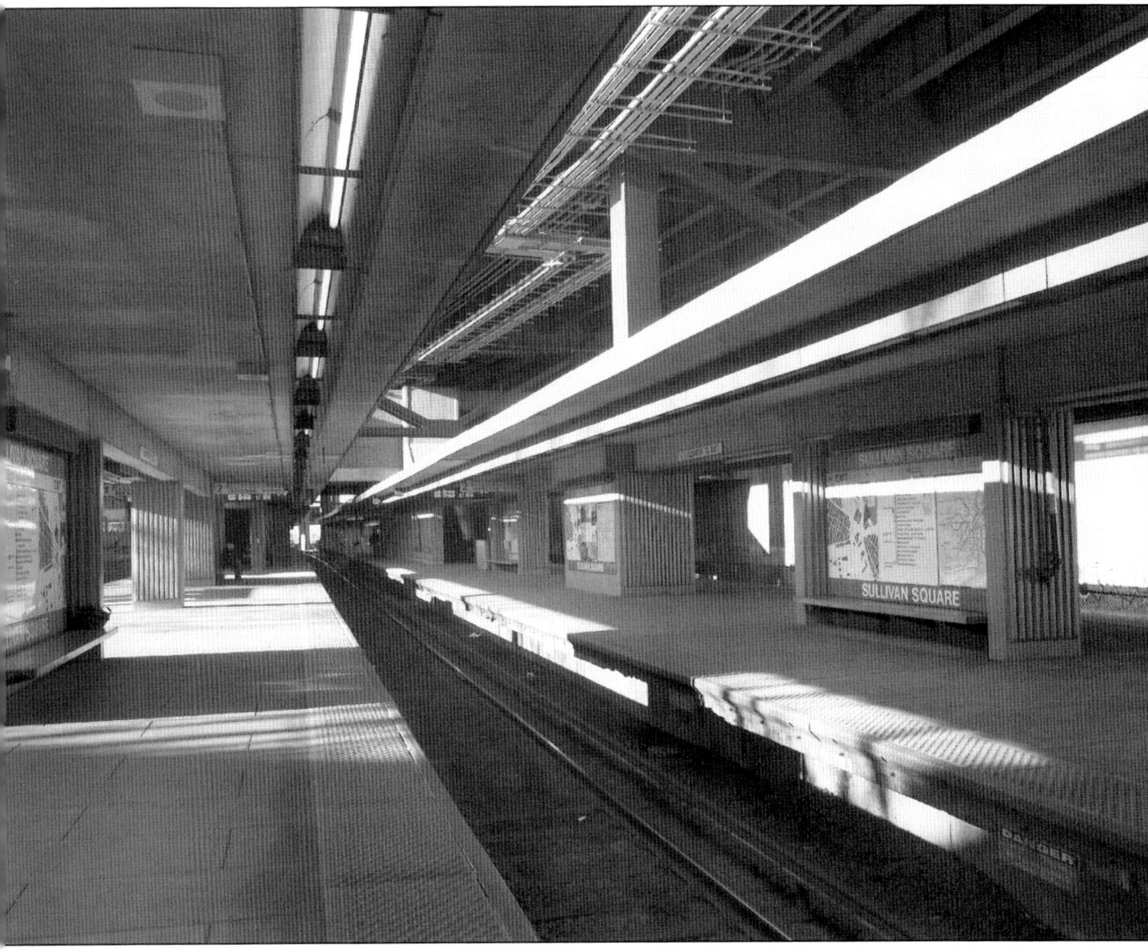

The new Sullivan Square Station is less than one-fifth of a mile from the site of the Elevated Sullivan Square Station, which was demolished in July 1975 and, like its predecessor, is a major bus transfer point. Its utilitarian interior (pictured) is far less grand than the soaring barrel-vaulted structure it replaced. Instead, it is an expanse of grey concrete slabs similar to those at the Community College Station. (Photograph by Jeremy C. Fox.)

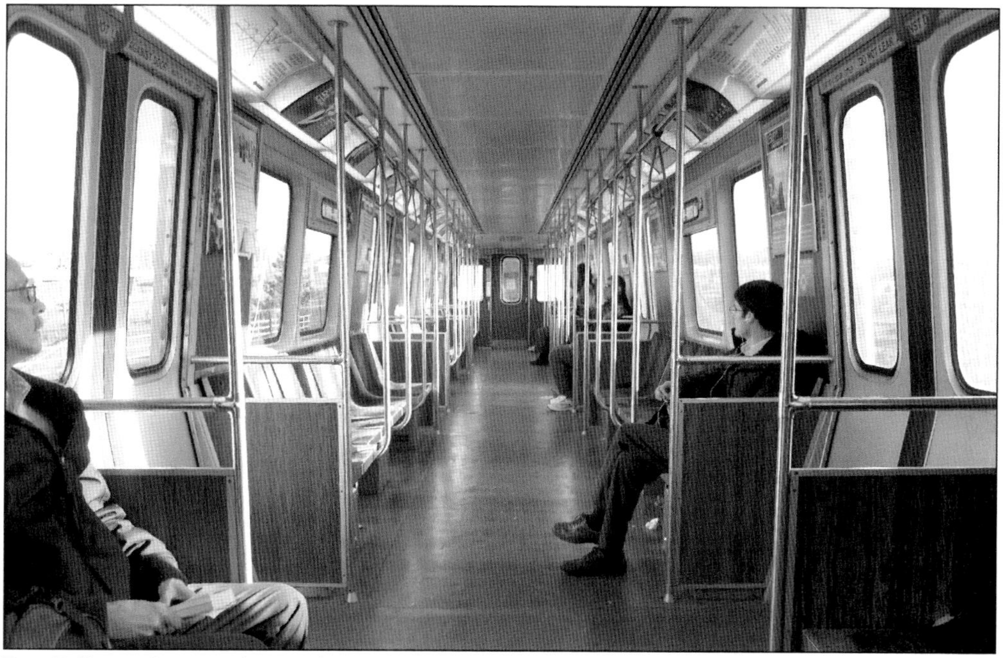

Past Sullivan Square, the northern route of the Orange Line departs from the path of Interstate 93 and travels almost north aboveground for more than a mile, crossing over the Mystic River to Wellington Station in Medford, Massachusetts. Here, a handful of passengers ride inbound from Wellington to Sullivan Square during afternoon rush hour, when most passengers are headed outbound from the city. (Photograph by Jeremy C. Fox.)

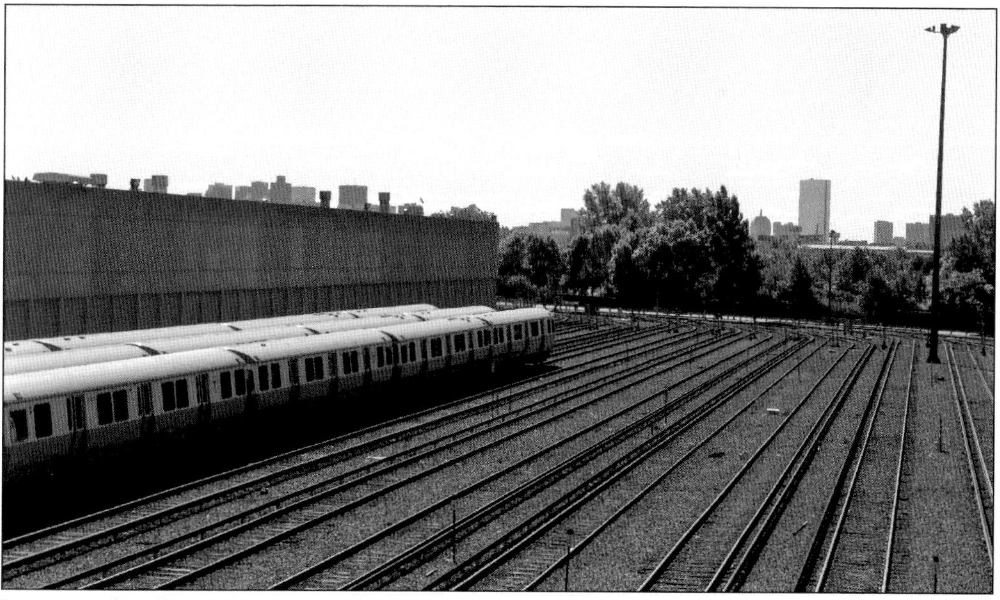

Just west of Wellington Station is the Wellington Carhouse, the Orange Line's primary repair and maintenance facility, pictured in this southward view with the Hancock Center visible on the skyline. A parking garage, from which this photograph was taken, is connected to the station by an overhead walkway and is west of this railyard and adjacent to Route 28. (Photograph by and courtesy of Nathaniel Marsh.)

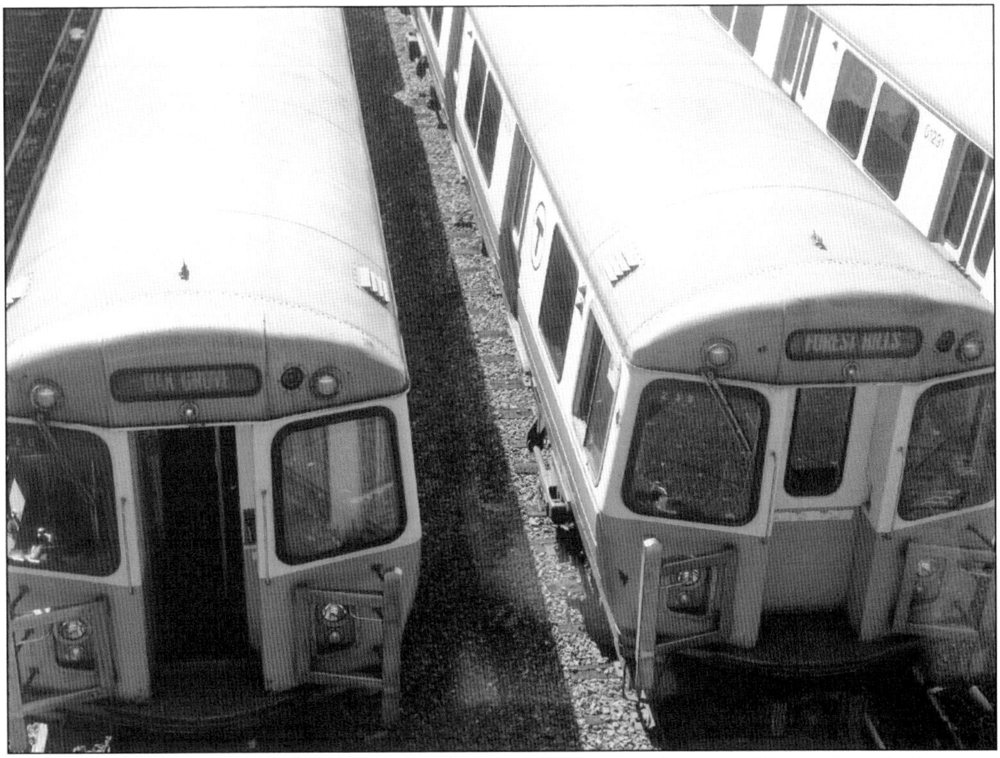

A second photograph from the elevated walkway at Wellington Station offers a closer look at two 01200 series cars displaying the names of the north and south termini of the modern Orange Line. Besides being a major center for maintenance of Orange Line trains, Wellington is an important bus transfer station serving Medford, Malden, Everett, and other surrounding cities. (Photograph by and courtesy of Nathaniel Marsh.)

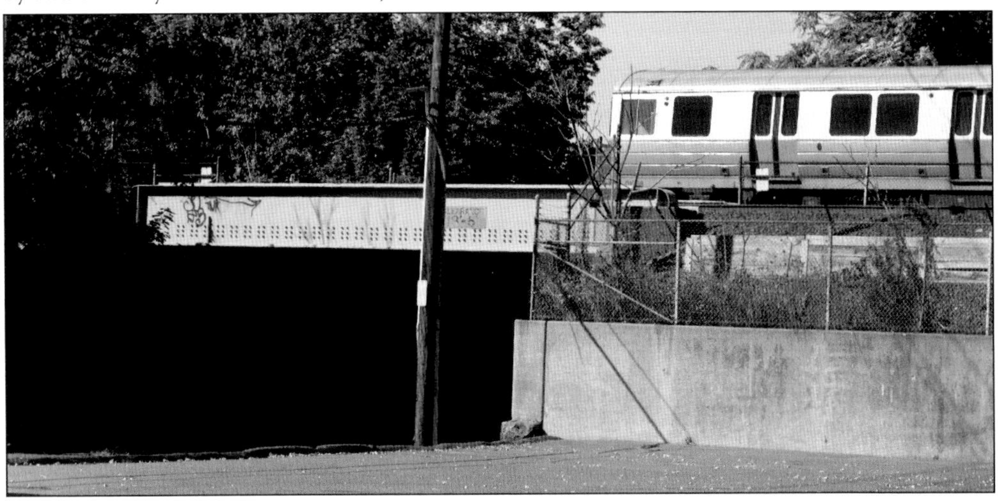

The Orange Line continues north of Wellington Station—sometimes at ground level, sometimes below grade, and sometimes aboveground. Here, a train headed from Malden Center Station to Wellington Station passes over Adams Street in Malden, adjacent to the Piantedosi Baking Company Specialty Division at 240 Commercial Street. (Photograph by and courtesy of Nathaniel Marsh.)

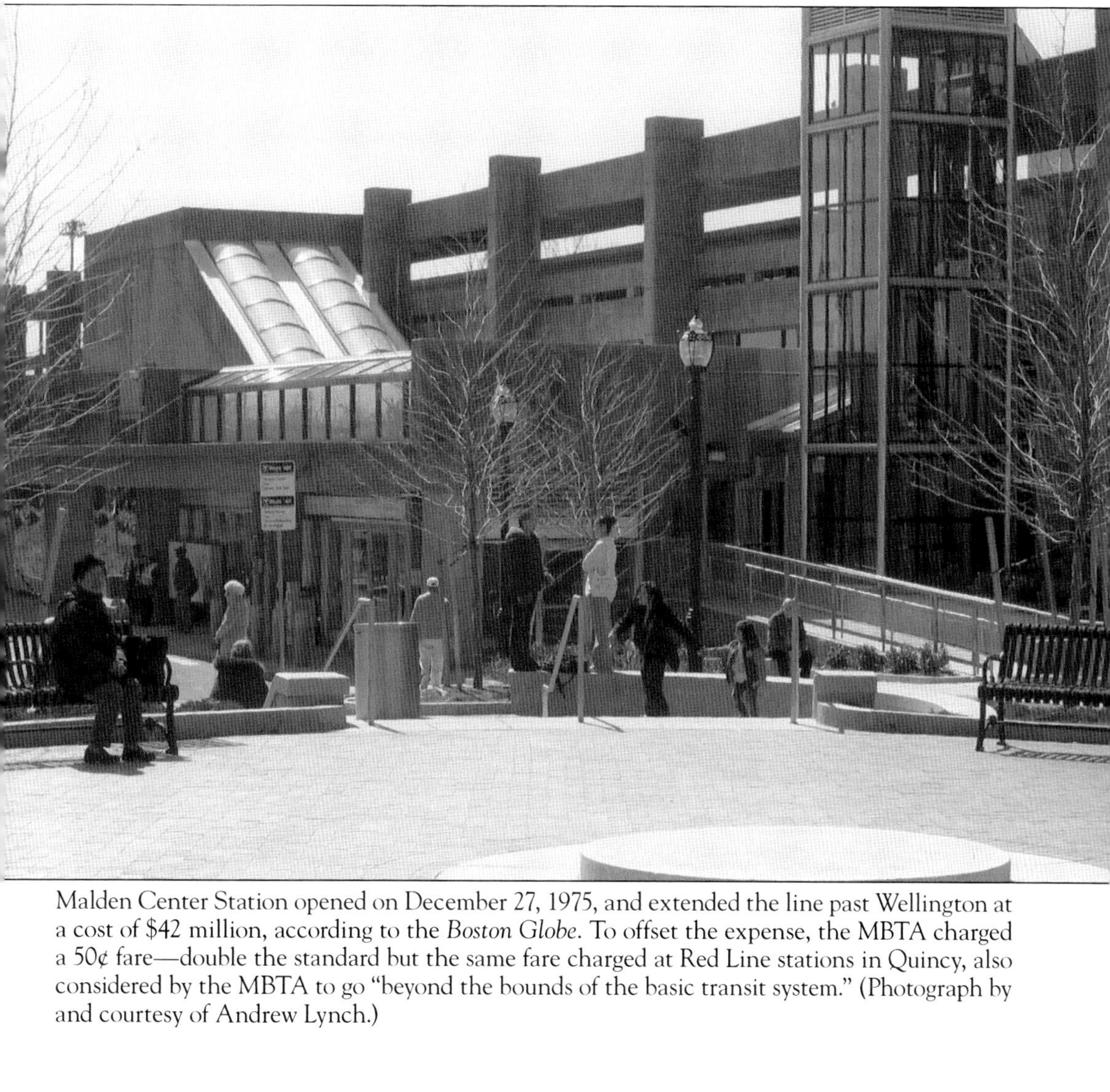

Malden Center Station opened on December 27, 1975, and extended the line past Wellington at a cost of $42 million, according to the *Boston Globe*. To offset the expense, the MBTA charged a 50¢ fare—double the standard but the same fare charged at Red Line stations in Quincy, also considered by the MBTA to go "beyond the bounds of the basic transit system." (Photograph by and courtesy of Andrew Lynch.)

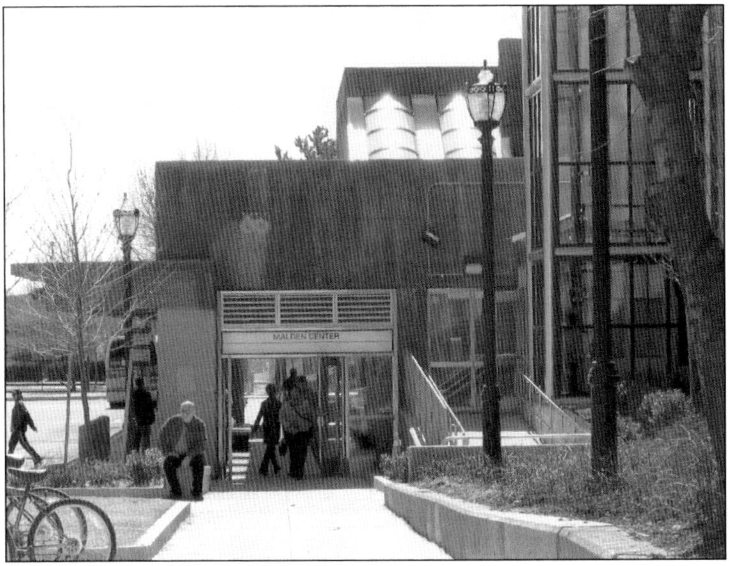

Malden Center Station serves both the Orange Line and the Haverhill Line of the Massachusetts Bay Commuter Railroad. As its name implies, it is centrally located, with Malden Government Center just across Commercial Street. Like the Sullivan Square and Wellington Stations, it is a major bus transfer station. (Photograph by and courtesy of Andrew Lynch.)

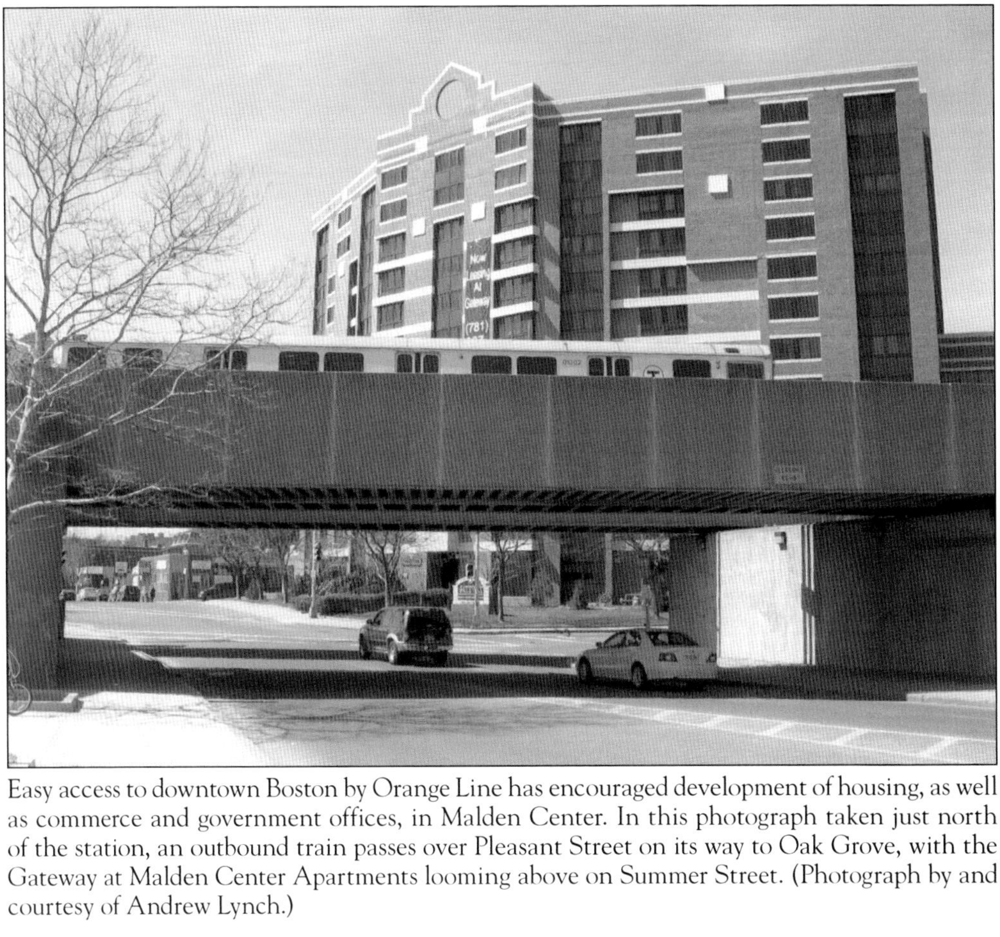

Easy access to downtown Boston by Orange Line has encouraged development of housing, as well as commerce and government offices, in Malden Center. In this photograph taken just north of the station, an outbound train passes over Pleasant Street on its way to Oak Grove, with the Gateway at Malden Center Apartments looming above on Summer Street. (Photograph by and courtesy of Andrew Lynch.)

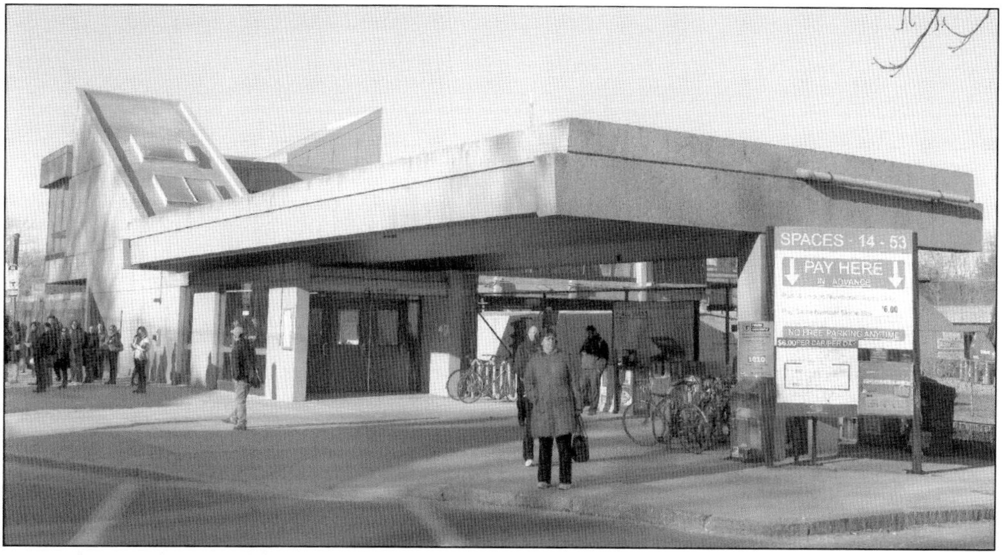

Located in northern Malden near Melrose, Oak Grove Station—the final station in the Haymarket North Extension—opened on March 20, 1977, after a series of delays. Oak Grove is primarily a park-and-ride station, with a parking lot of 788 spaces that serves several surrounding communities. (Photograph by Jeremy C. Fox.)

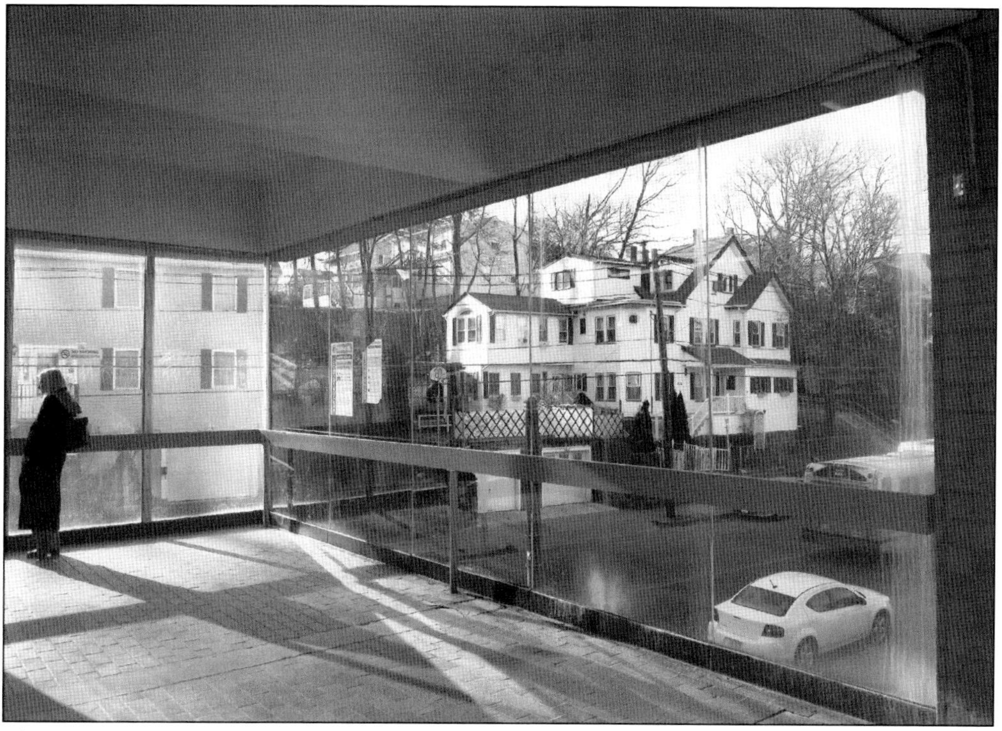

The concrete slabs and sharp angles of Oak Grove Station contrast with the traditional lines of surrounding homes, as shown in this image looking through windows on the west side of the station and across Washington Street. Though the neighborhood is mostly residential, an industrial park lies just south of the station, and Forest Dale Cemetery is to its east. (Photograph by Jeremy C. Fox.)

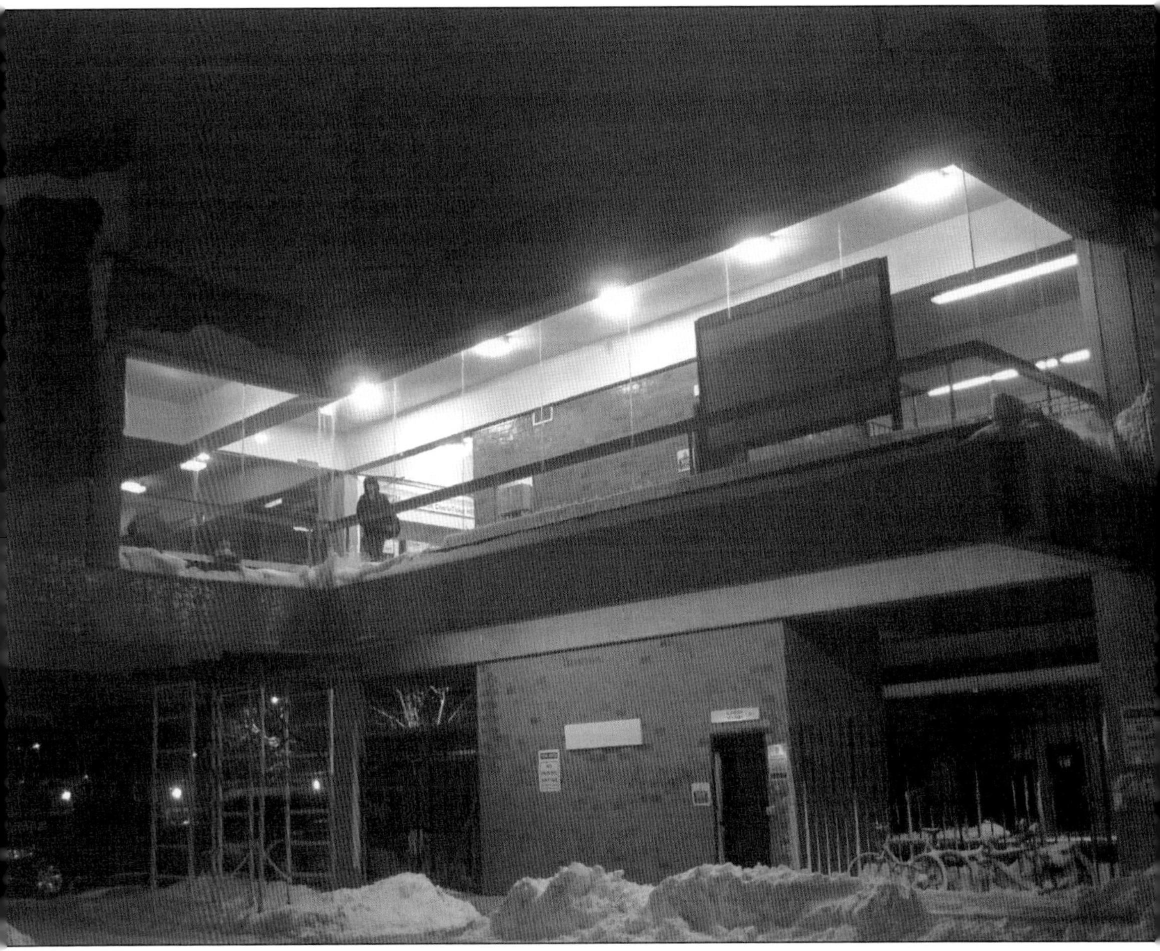

This photograph of Oak Grove Station on a snowy night captures its austerity and drama. Newspapers reported that community efforts to have the Charlestown Elevated removed were almost as old as the structure itself. As early as 1908, Charlestown residents petitioned the Massachusetts Legislature to take down the railway, but it would take nearly 70 years for their hopes to be fulfilled. (Photograph by and courtesy of Paul W. Locke.)

Six

The Southwest Corridor Realignment

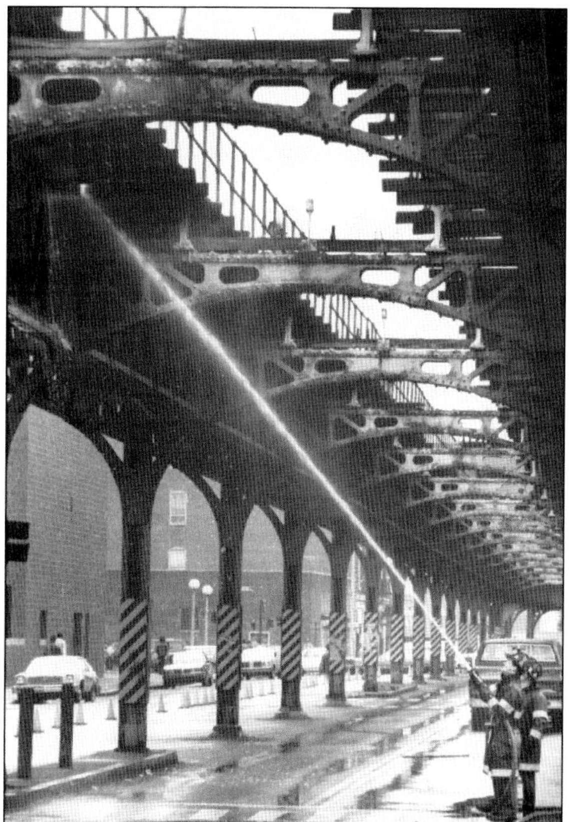

A *Boston Globe* photographer captured these firefighters in Boston's South End in April 1988 as they hosed down Elevated tracks being dismantled at the intersection of Washington and East Brookline Streets. The last train rode these Washington Street Elevated tracks one year earlier, on April 30, 1987, as the Orange Line was rerouted to the Southwest Corridor. (Courtesy of the *Boston Globe*; photograph by Thomas Landers.)

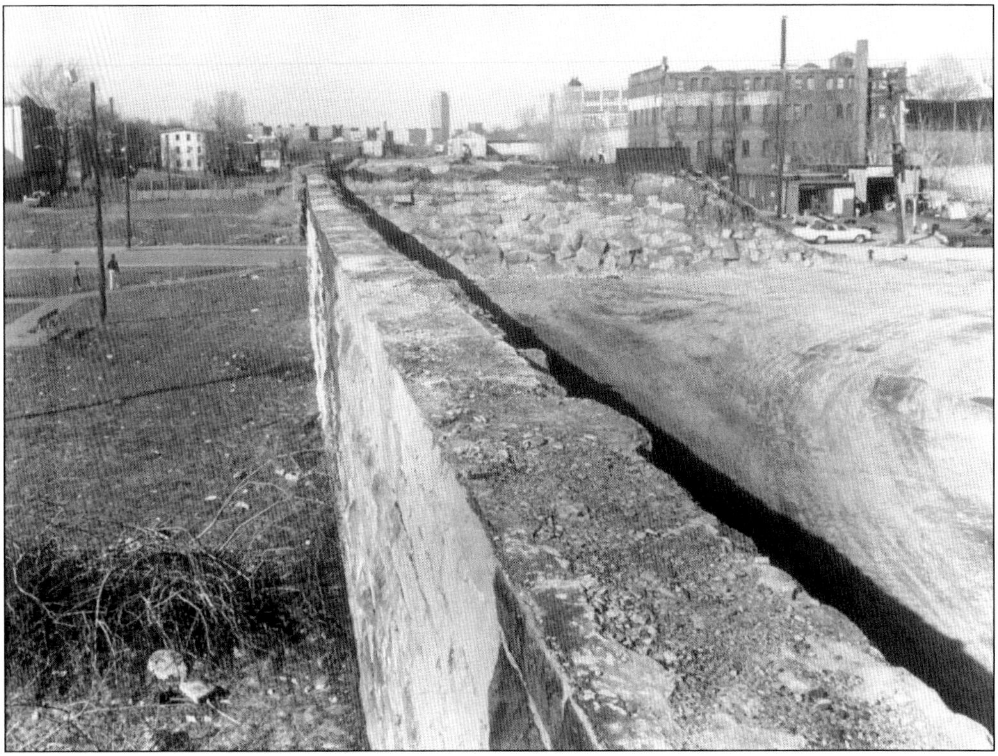

This 1980 photograph, looking north toward downtown Boston, shows a wall scheduled for demolition as part of the Southwest Corridor Project and rerouting of the Orange Line, which came about as a result of the failed Inner Belt highway project. The Inner Belt would have introduced several highways that would run through the city to the Central Artery on the waterfront. (Courtesy of the *Boston Globe*; photograph by Bill Curtis.)

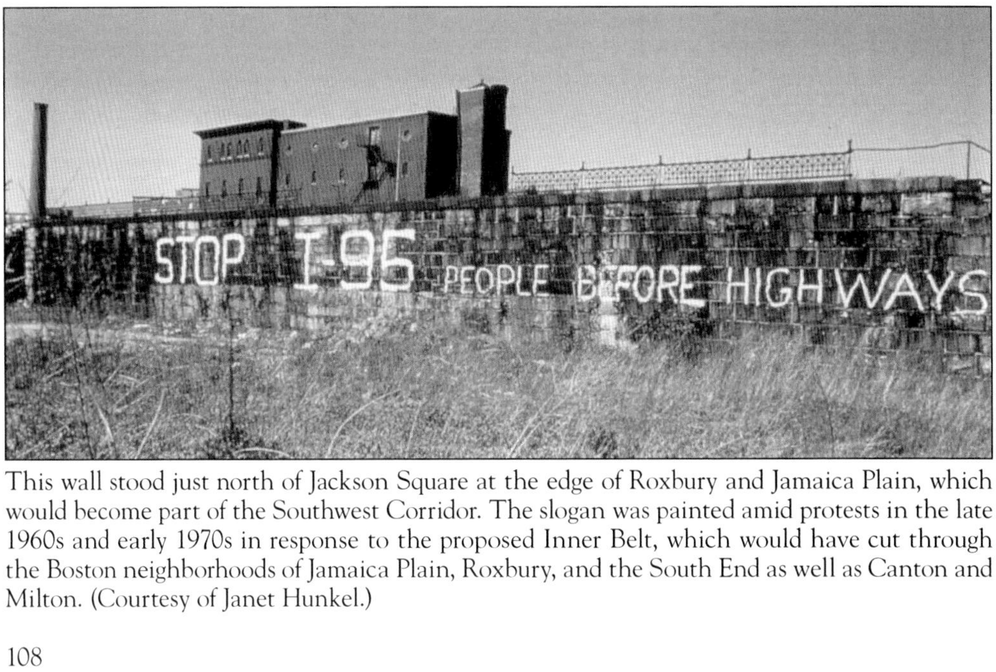

This wall stood just north of Jackson Square at the edge of Roxbury and Jamaica Plain, which would become part of the Southwest Corridor. The slogan was painted amid protests in the late 1960s and early 1970s in response to the proposed Inner Belt, which would have cut through the Boston neighborhoods of Jamaica Plain, Roxbury, and the South End as well as Canton and Milton. (Courtesy of Janet Hunkel.)

This flyer, produced by those opposed to the Inner Belt, shows the proposed highways as dotted lines. Inner Belt discussions started in the 1930s and included the introduction of an eight-lane Interstate 95, which would have cut through Cambridge and Boston. This southern section of I-95 was referred to as the Southwest Expressway. (Courtesy of University Archives & Special Collections, Joseph P. Healey Library, University of Massachusetts Boston: Ann Hershfang Collection.)

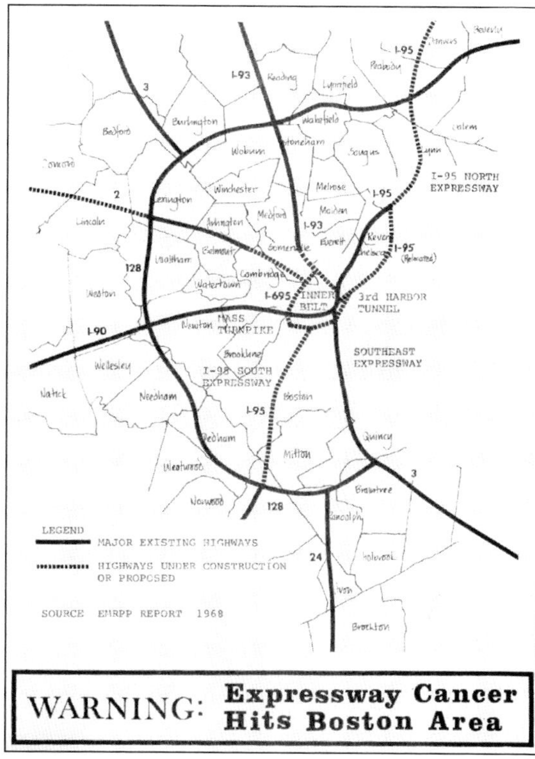

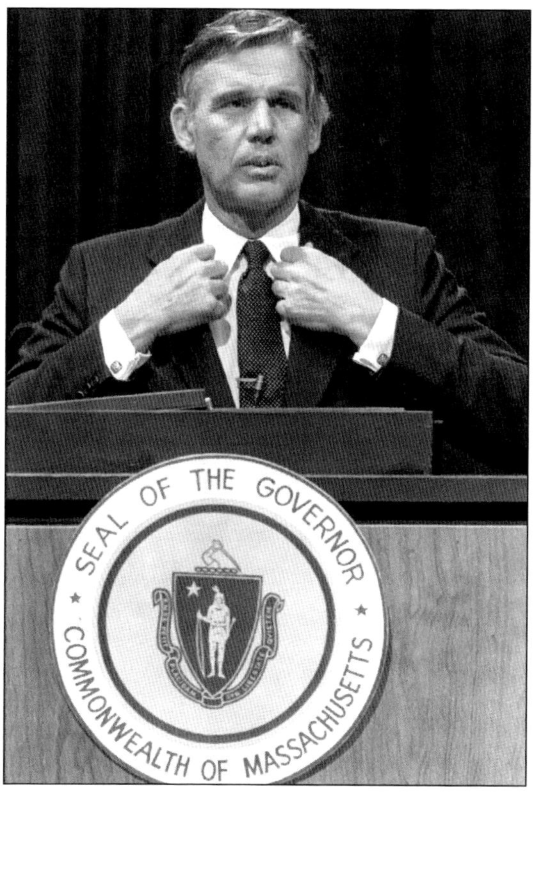

Gov. Francis W. Sargent ultimately abandoned the Inner Belt plan, largely due to community protest, as well as the I-95 proposal. However, while preparations were under way throughout the 1960s, about 150 acres in Roxbury and Jamaica Plain—including homes, businesses, and parkland—were taken through eminent domain and cleared, creating open space eventually used for the Southwest Corridor. (Courtesy of the *Boston Globe*; photograph by Donald C. Preston.)

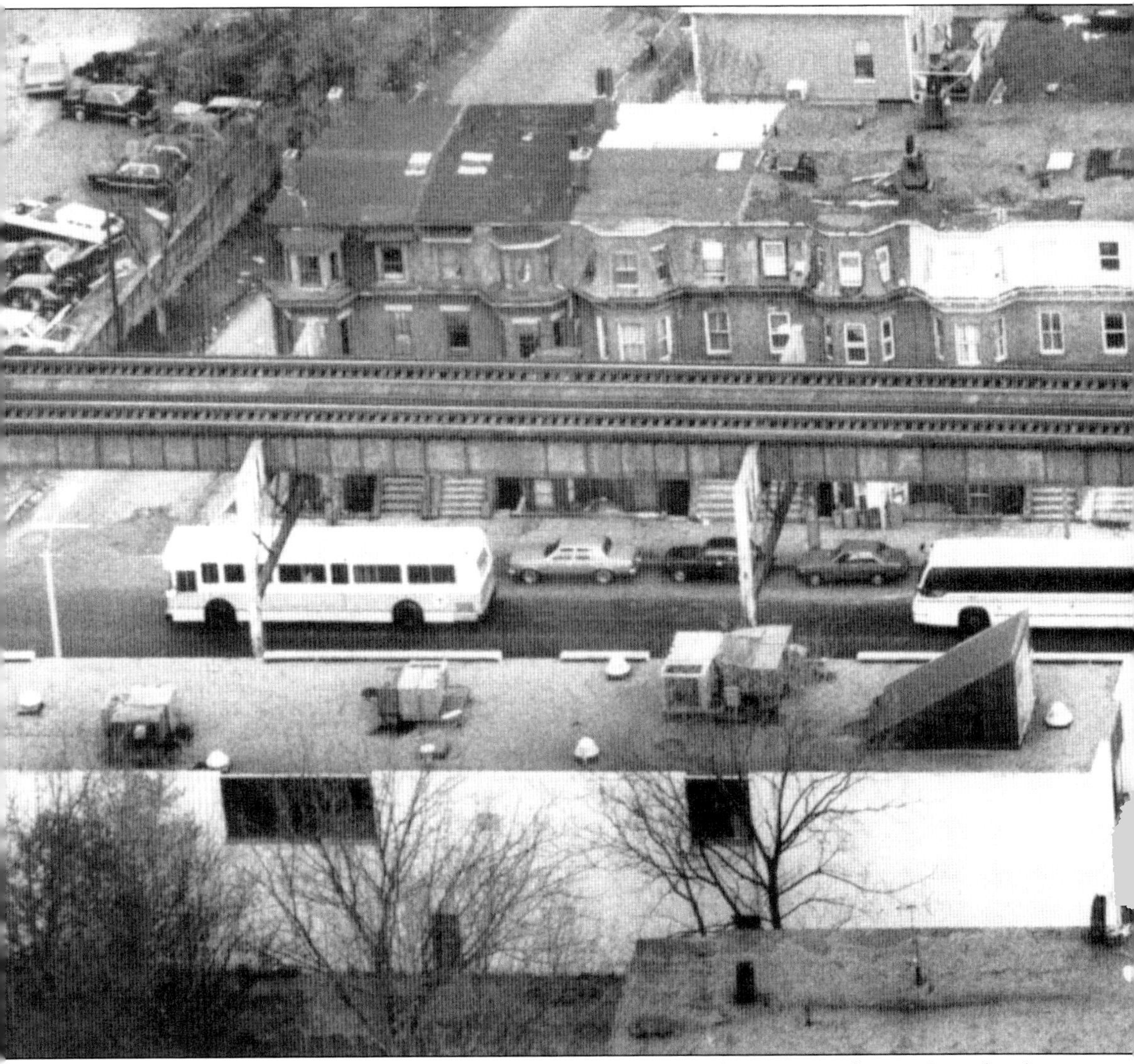

Shortly after the rerouted Orange Line started service on the new Southwest Corridor, buses replaced train service along the Washington Street Elevated, as shown in this May 1987 image of Roxbury. In the years leading up to the scheduled closing of the Washington Street El, the MBTA worked with community members on plans to replace the El with light-rail service. However, light-rail plans were canceled soon after the El ceased operations in 1987, and the MBTA did not

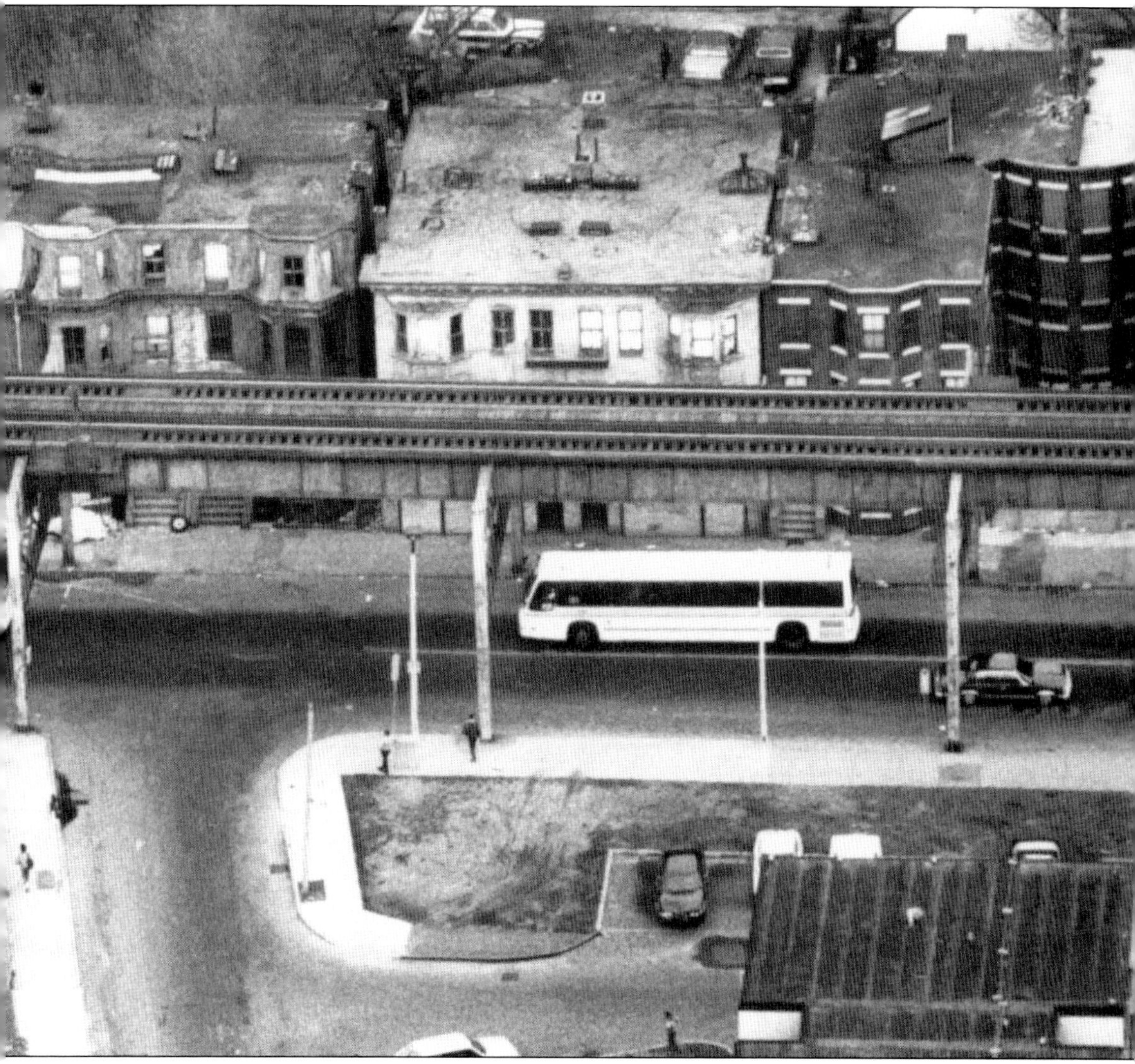

introduce its Silver Line service until 2002. The Silver Line is a high-speed bus line that includes service between downtown Boston and areas formerly serviced by the El, including Dudley Square. Many community members have criticized the line as an inadequate replacement for high-speed train service. (Courtesy of the *Boston Globe*; photograph by Thomas Landers.)

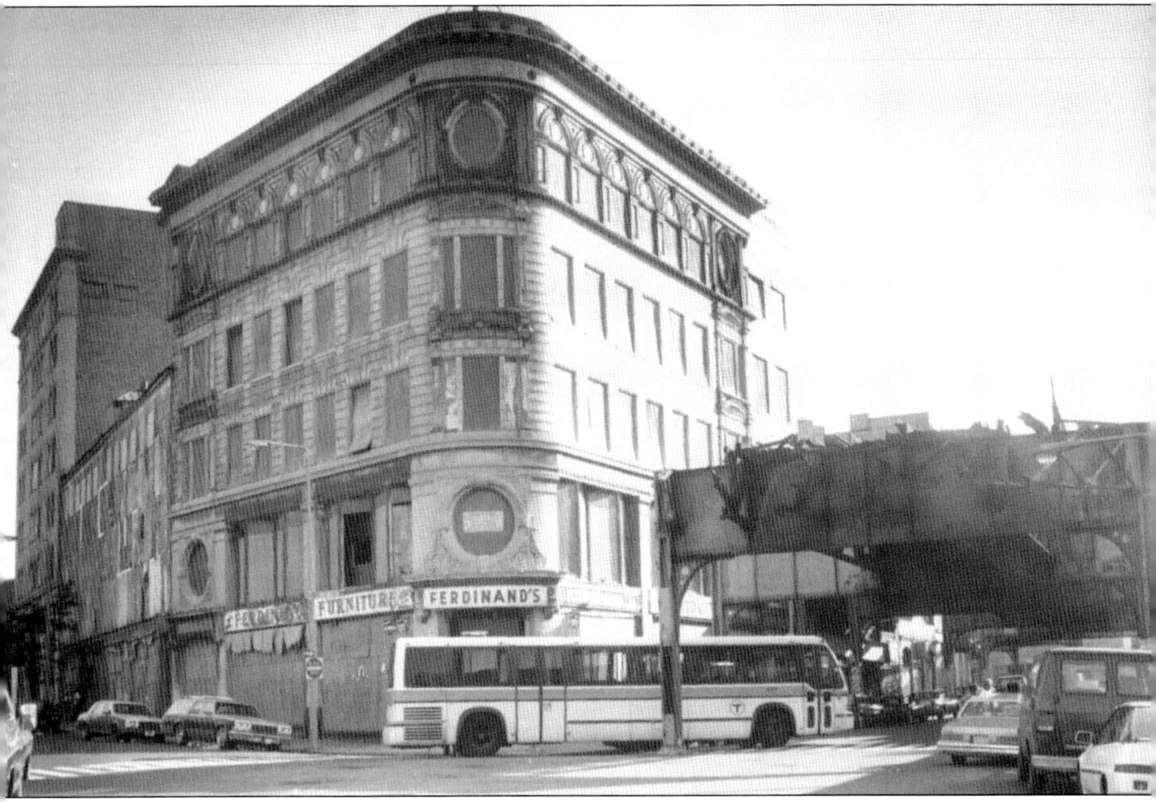

Ferdinand's Blue Store sat vacant in 1988 as the Washington Street Elevated tracks were dismantled in Dudley Square. Built in a Baroque Revival style in 1895 and designed by architect John Lyman Faxon, it became vacant in the 1980s and fell into disrepair. The preserved facade was incorporated into the design of a new municipal building planned for offices for Boston Public Schools. (Courtesy of the *Boston Globe*; photograph by Thomas Landers.)

The shell of New England Medical Center Station, seen here at its Tremont Street entrance, was constructed with the South Cove Tunnel around 1968 as part of the planned Interstate 695 but remained unfinished until the Southwest Corridor route was completed. It opened in 1987 and was renamed Tufts Medical Center in 2010 to reflect the change in the hospital's name. (Photograph by and courtesy of Andrew Lynch.)

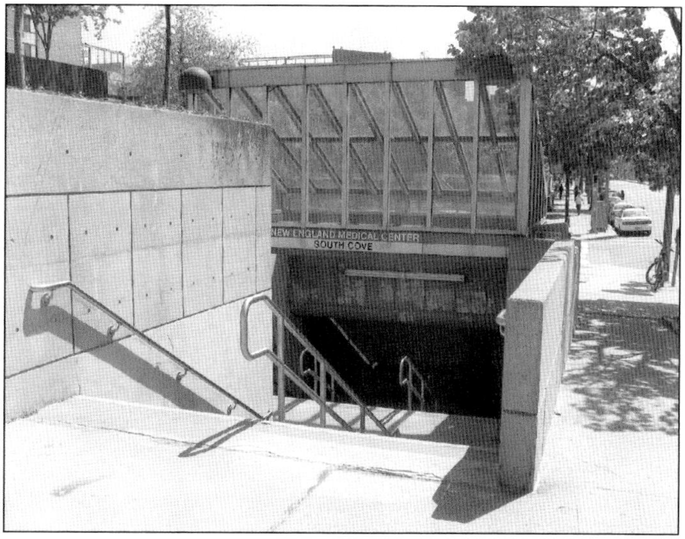

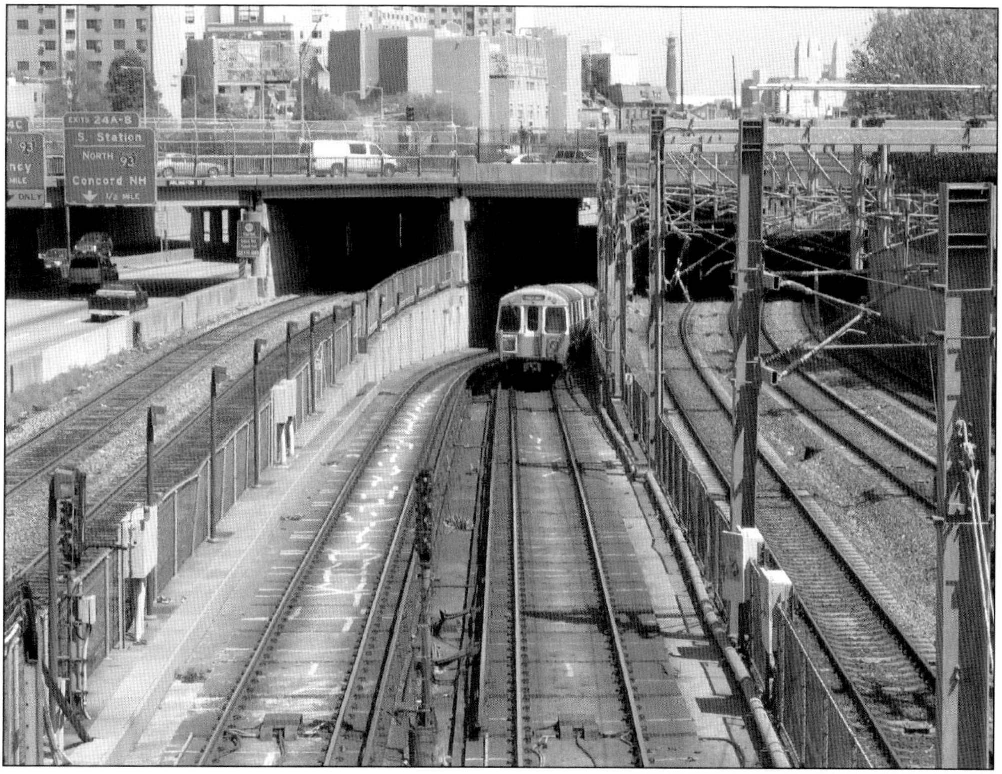

An Orange Line train moves east alongside the Massachusetts Turnpike (at far left) on its way to New England Medical Center. The Arlington Street overpass is above the train, with the Mass Pike Towers at upper left and Josiah Quincy School beyond. To the right of the Orange Line are tracks serving Amtrak and Commuter Rail trains; at left are more Commuter Rail tracks. (Photograph by and courtesy of Andrew Lynch.)

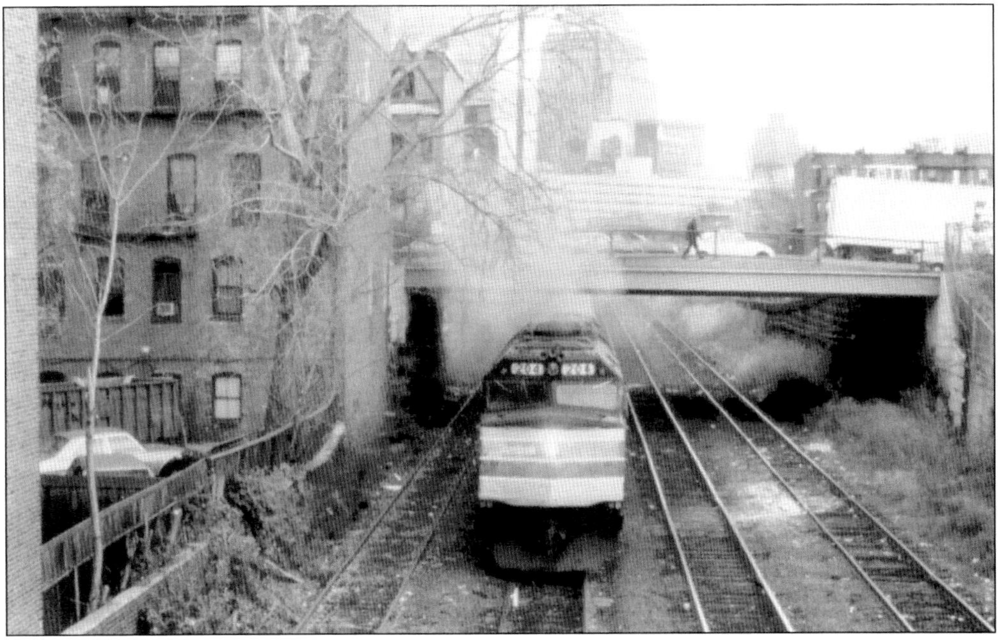

At the end of 1979, Commuter Rail service out of the old Back Bay Station ended to make way for Southwest Corridor Project construction. According to community activist Janet Hunkel, who was active in protests related to the defeated Southwest Expressway, this photograph shows the last train leaving Back Bay Station before construction began on the Southwest Corridor. (Photograph by and courtesy of Janet Hunkel.)

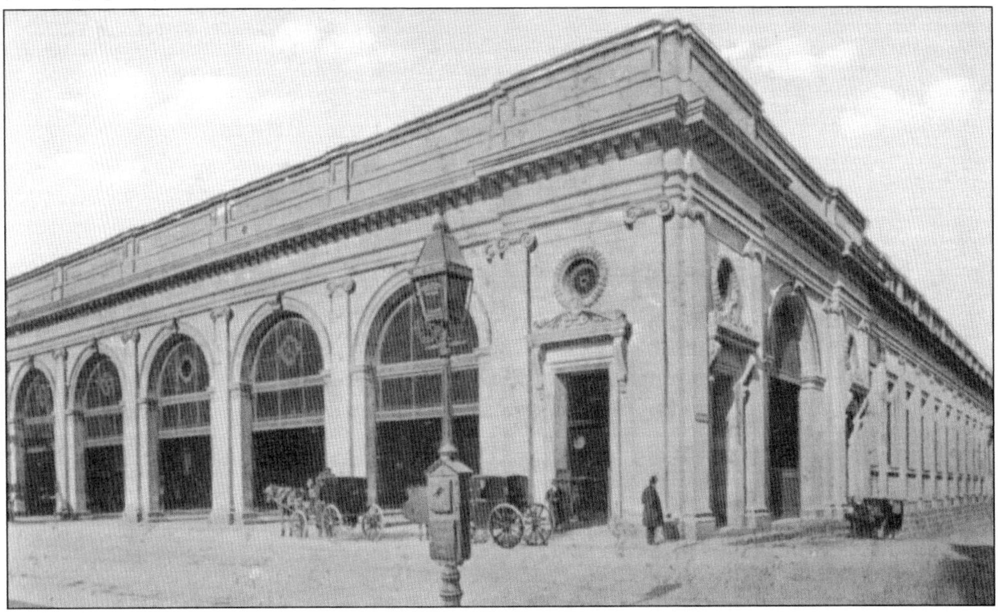

Constructed in 1899, the original Back Bay Station was rebuilt in 1929 after a fire destroyed much of the original structure. The building was demolished to make way for the new Back Bay Station, which opened in 1987 as part of the Orange Line rerouting along the Southwest Corridor. (Courtesy of University Archives & Special Collections, Joseph P. Healey Library, University of Massachusetts Boston: Anthony Mitchell Sammarco Collection.)

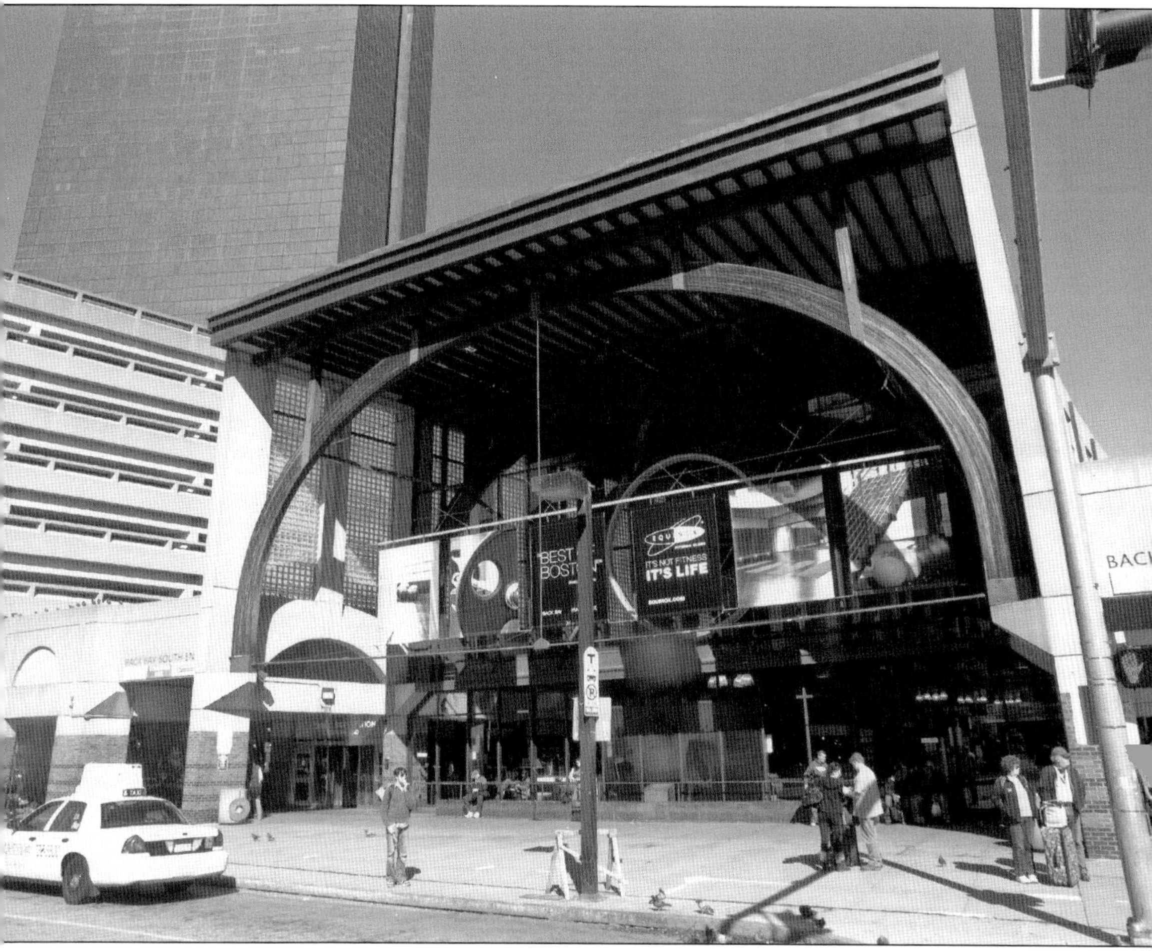

The new Back Bay Station was planned to carry on the monumental tradition of its predecessor. Marianne Abrams, president of the Back Bay Association and a member of the station's site committee, told the *Boston Globe* in 1986: "We wanted to reflect the romanticism of the rail and the importance of the Back Bay station, which has existed in some form for 100 years." (Photograph by and courtesy of Nathaniel Marsh.)

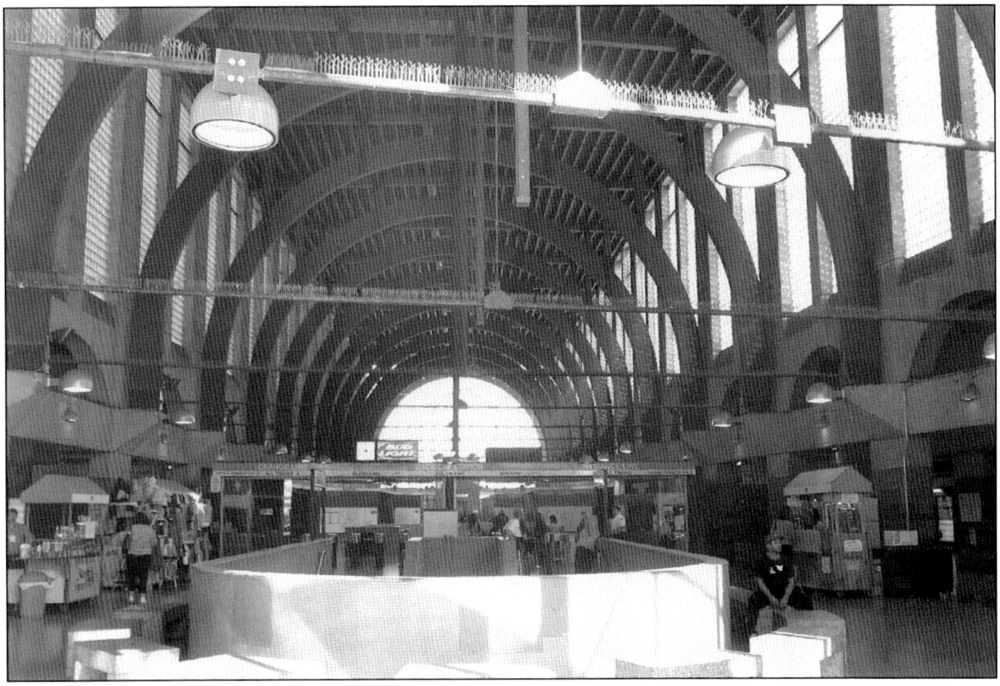

The interior of the Back Bay Station, designed by the architectural firm of Kallmann, McKinnell & Wood, has a dramatic arcade supported by arched ribs. Beneath its high ceiling, more than 500,000 passengers per year use the Orange Line, the Commuter Rail, and Amtrak trains. (Photograph by and courtesy of Andrew Lynch.)

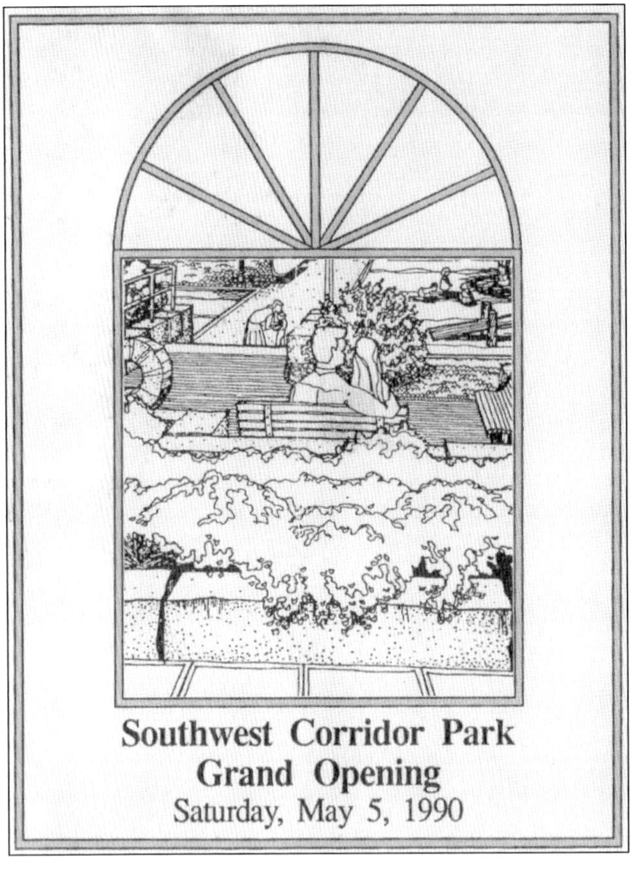

Besides being a transit hub and the second-most trafficked station on the contemporary Orange Line (after Downtown Crossing), Back Bay Station is also the gateway to the Southwest Corridor Park, which officially opened on May 5, 1990, as shown on this opening ceremony program. (Courtesy of University Archives & Special Collections, Joseph P. Healey Library, University of Massachusetts Boston: Ann Hershfang Collection.)

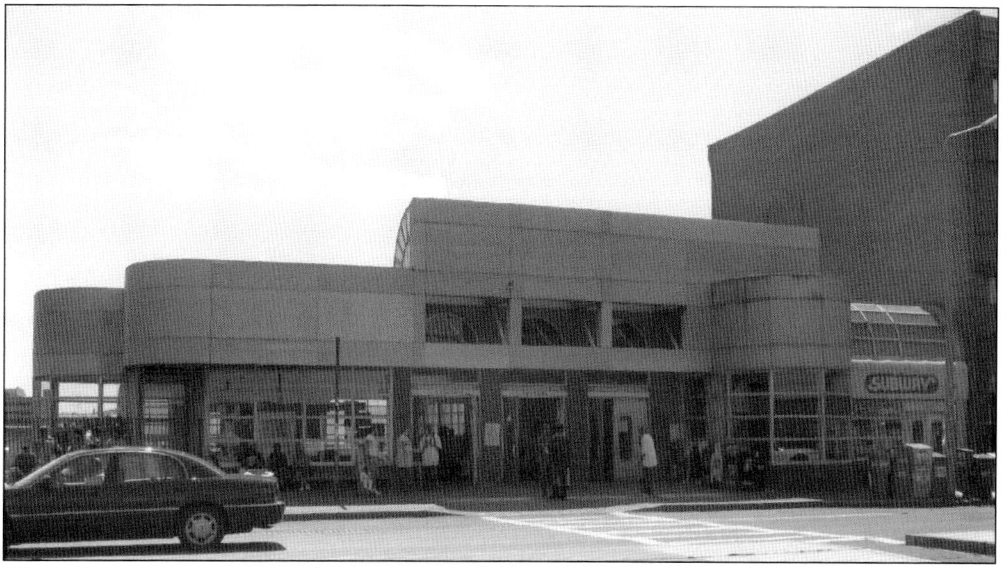

The main entrance to Massachusetts Avenue Station sits on the southwest side of the street. In a nod to the 19th-century architecture surrounding it, the Massachusetts Avenue Station was designed with bowed, windowed elements that refer back to traditional bowfront facades. Along the Southwest Corridor immediately behind this station is the William Carter School, a public school for children with severe disabilities. (Photograph by and courtesy of Andrew Lynch.)

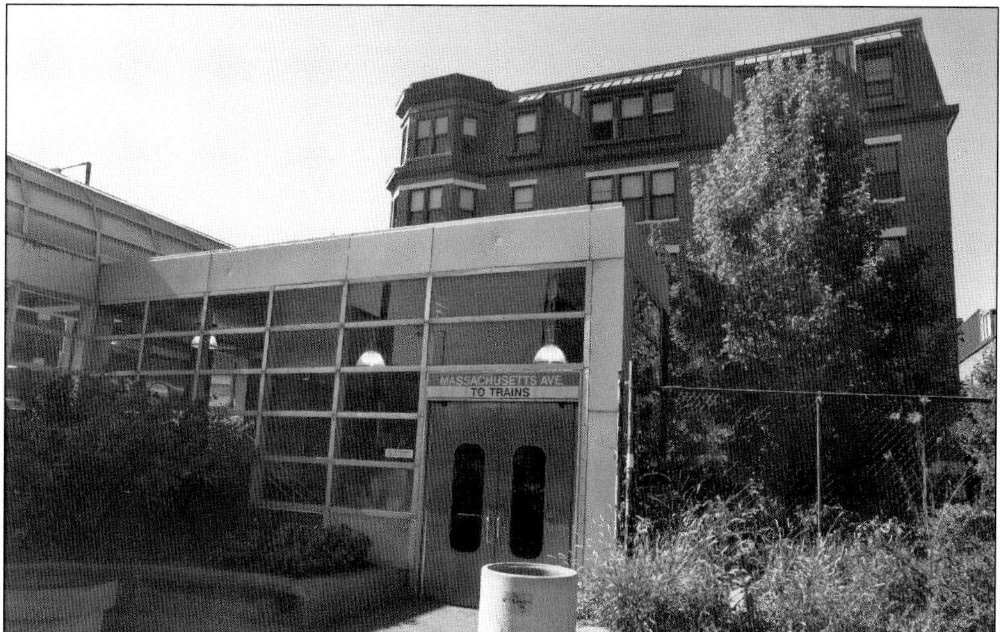

This view shows the smaller entrance to Massachusetts Avenue Station on the northeast side of the street, adjacent to the Southwest Corridor Park, with the Susan S. Bailis Assisted Living Community, located at 352 Massachusetts Avenue, visible behind it. The assisted living community was built in 2003 in a style consistent with surrounding brownstones. (Photograph by and courtesy of Nathaniel Marsh.)

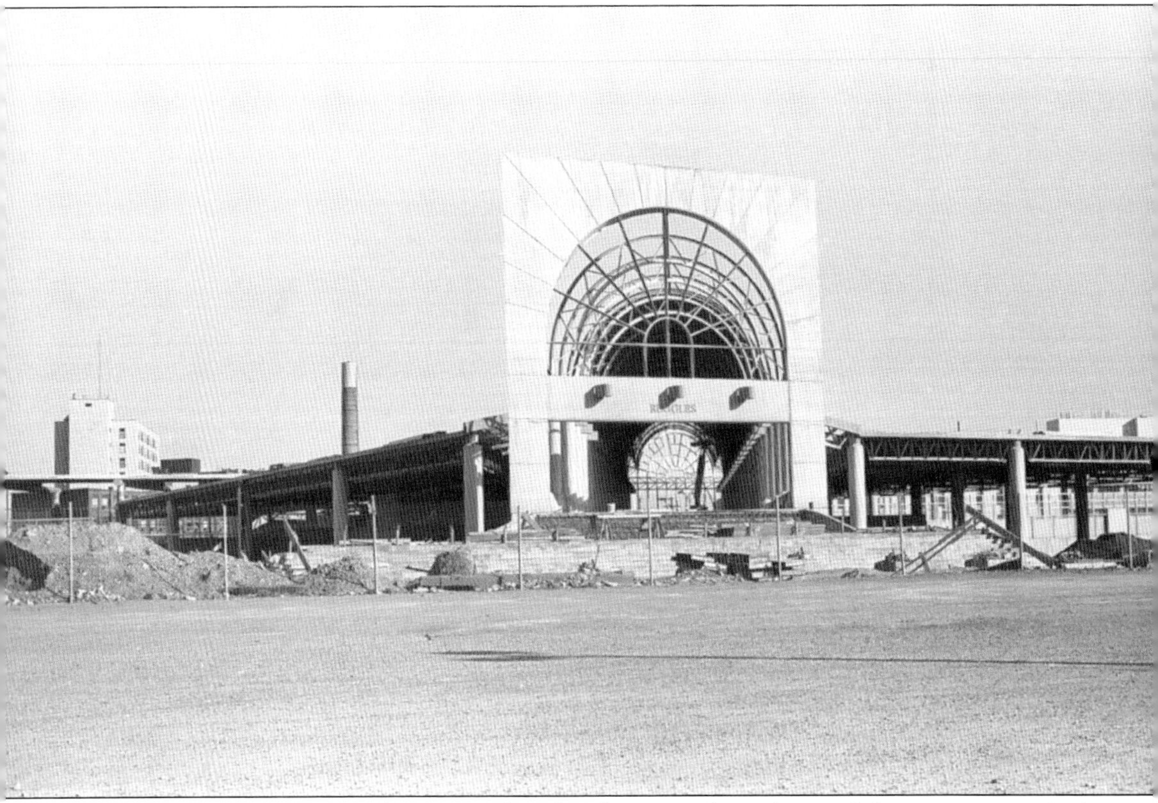

Stull and Lee Incorporated, a Boston-based architecture firm, designed the new stations built along the Southwest Corridor for the rerouted Orange Line, an $800-million project. Stull and Lee also oversaw land use plans and other design plans along the Southwest Corridor. This image from 1986 shows construction of the new Ruggles Station near Columbus Avenue and adjacent to the Northeastern University campus. Each of the new stations on the rerouted Orange Line was designed with considerable community input, as was much of the Southwest Corridor planned in the late 1970s and 1980s. The same community activists and groups who were involved in successfully halting the proposed Southwest Expressway quickly shifted their focus once the Southwest Corridor Project was announced to ensure that community voices, concerns, and needs were addressed in the project's planning and design. In 1989, the National Endowment for the Arts awarded Stull and Lee with the Presidential Design Award for their Southwest Corridor project. (Photograph by and courtesy of Paul W. Locke.)

Community involvement is reflected in the neighborhood- and community-inspired art showcased in stations along the Southwest Corridor. John T. Scott's sculpture depicting movement and African musical tradition was installed under the barrel-vaulted archway (pictured) at Ruggles Station. Adjacent to a stairway is the mural *Geometree* by Paul Goodnight. (Photograph by and courtesy of Nathaniel Marsh.)

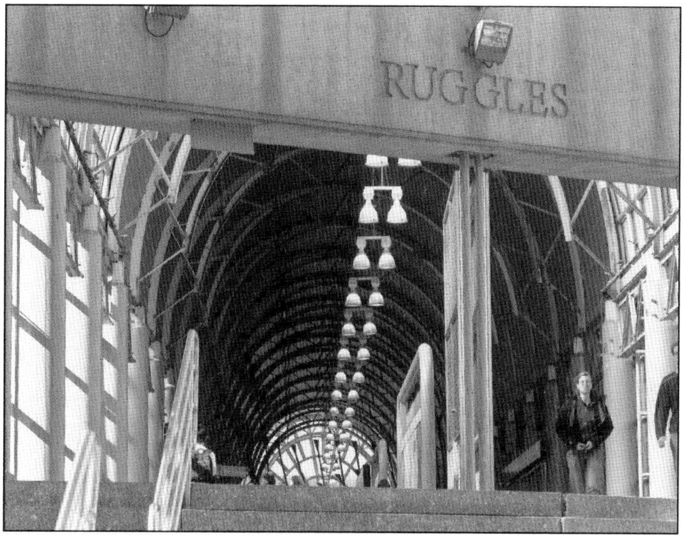

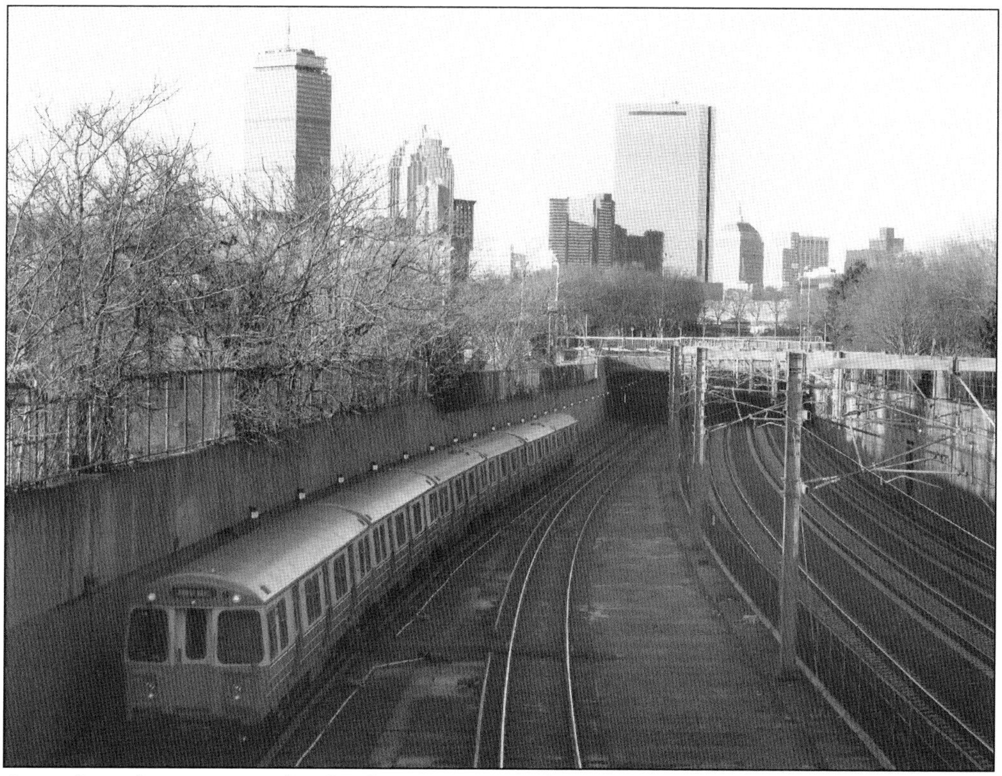

An outbound train approaches Roxbury Crossing at lower left, with the inbound tracks visible at center and Commuter Rail tracks at right. In the distance are the Prudential Tower, completed in 1964; 111 Huntington Avenue, completed in 2002; and Hancock Place, completed in 1976. (Photograph by Jeremy C. Fox.)

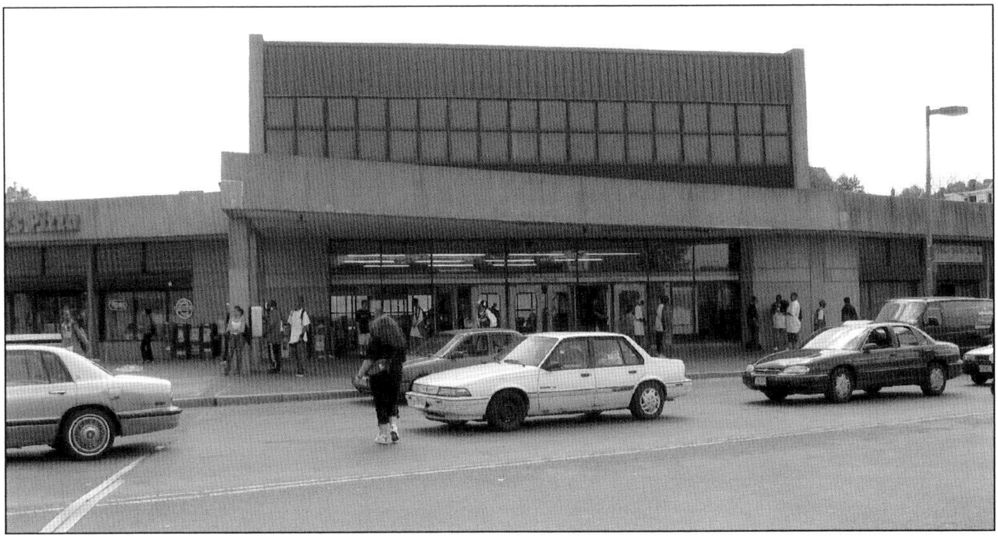

Roxbury Crossing Station sits at the intersection of Tremont Street and Columbus Avenue on the edge of Mission Hill and across Columbus Avenue from Roxbury Community College. This station is just over a half-mile east of the old Dudley Station, while Ruggles Station is about a half-mile to the northeast of Dudley Square. (Photograph by and courtesy of Andrew Lynch.)

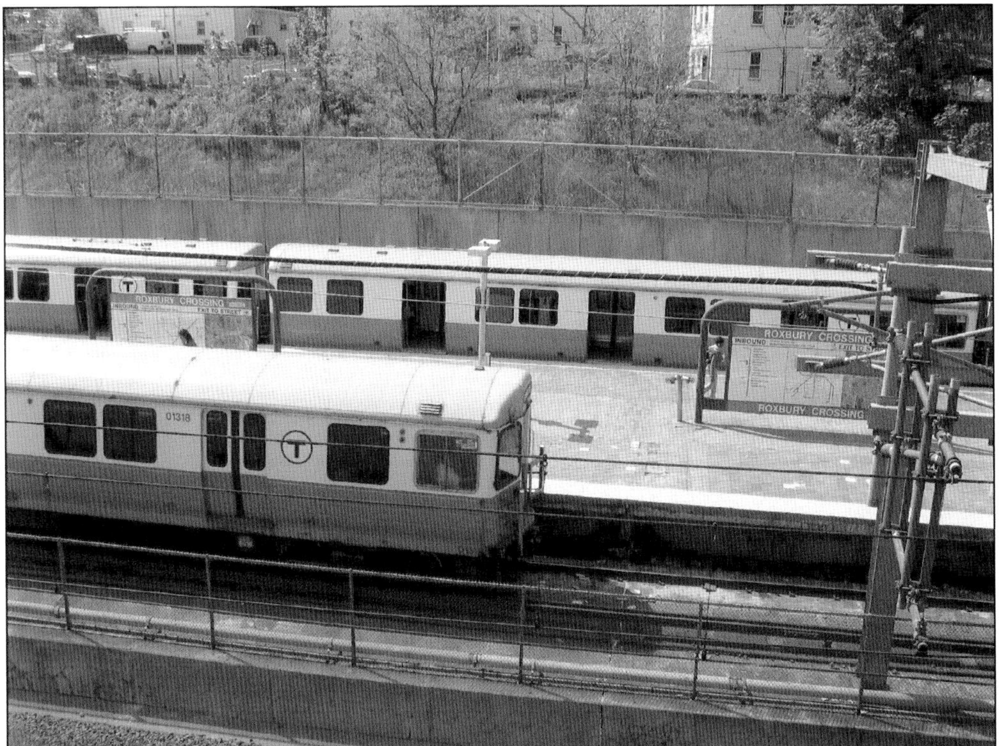

In this image, inbound and outbound trains sit at Roxbury Crossing. Upon the opening of the Southwest Corridor in 1987 and well into the 2000s, the Orange Line has run trains of six 65-foot cars of the 01200 series, built by Hawker Siddeley Canada Car and Foundry between 1980 and 1981. (Photograph by and courtesy of Andrew Lynch.)

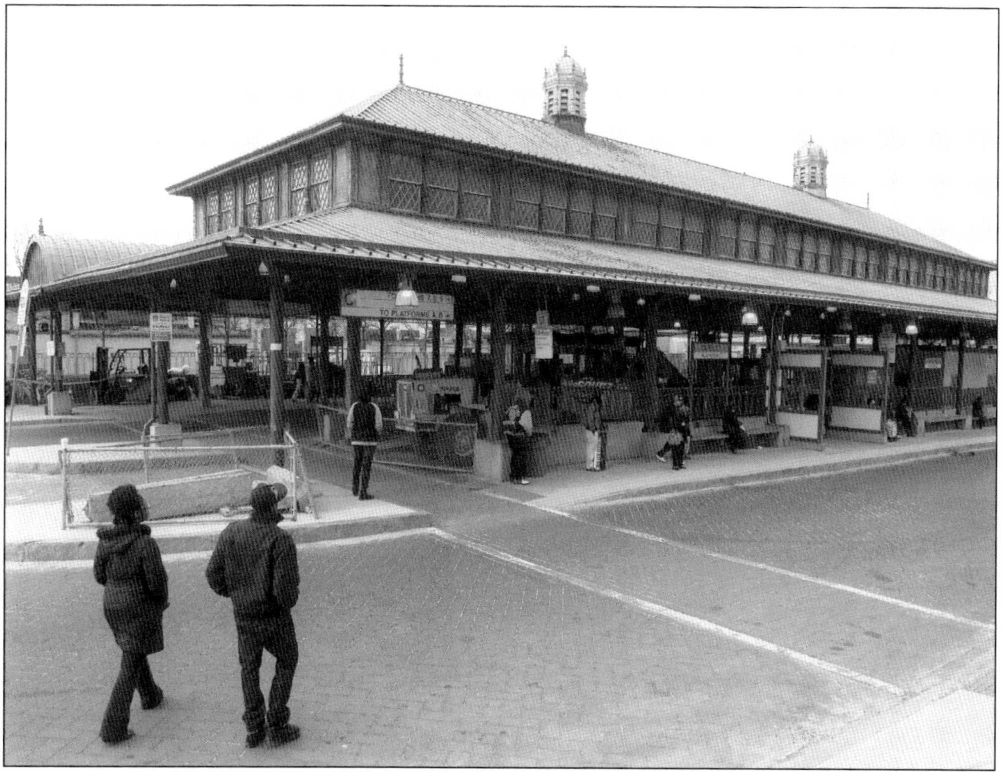

When Dudley Station was taken down, the MBTA recycled the 175-foot-long copper-clad canopy that covered the central area of the station, placing it above a reconstructed bus platform. The neighborhood lost its rapid transit but retained some of the grandeur of Alexander Wadsworth Longfellow Jr.'s Beaux-Arts design. (Photograph by Jeremy C. Fox.)

The canopy appears almost entirely unchanged since 1901, though its surroundings and function are wholly different. In 2002, the MBTA introduced the Silver Line, a bus rapid transit system with two routes from Dudley Square to downtown Boston—one ending at South Station and the other at Bowdoin Station. Silver Line buses operate in reserved lanes on Washington Street, tracing much of the old Elevated route. (Photograph by Jeremy C. Fox.)

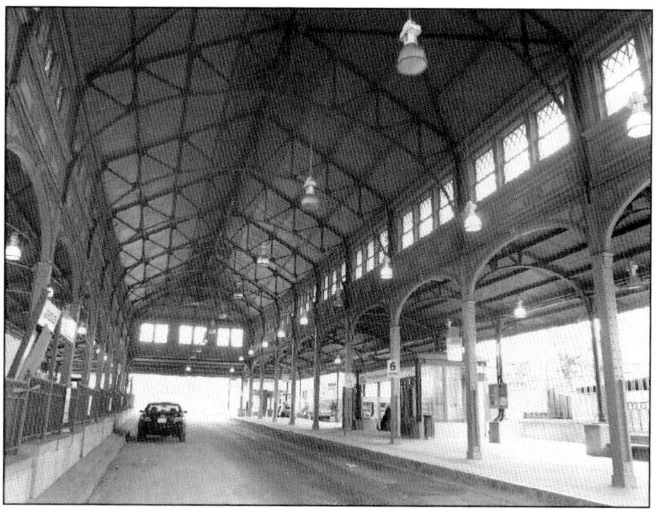

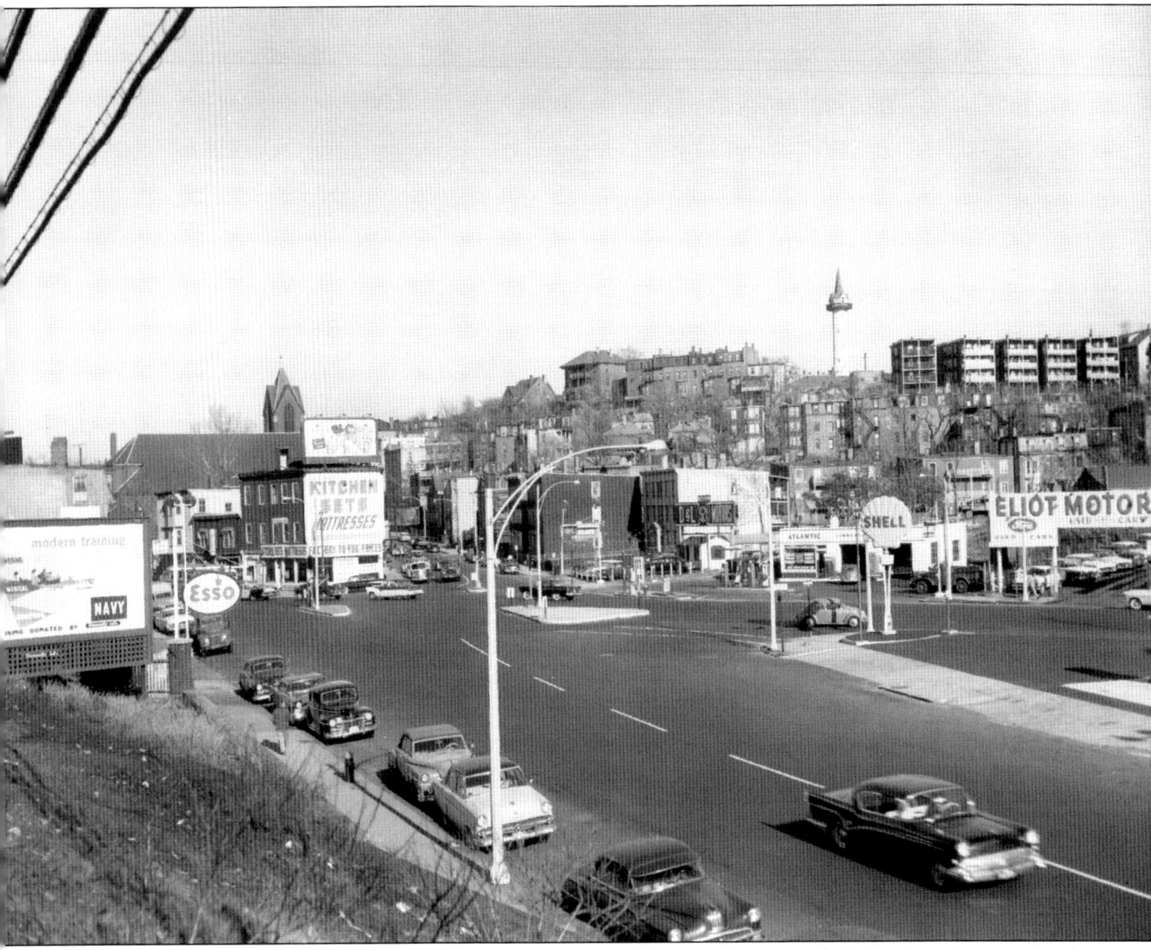

This 1960s image offers a view of the intersection of Centre Street and Columbus Avenue in the old Jackson Square, along the border of Jamaica Plain and Roxbury. Centre Street was completely realigned into two disconnected halves during the neighborhood's redevelopment as part of the Southwest Corridor Project, while Columbus Avenue was simplified, widened, and made more linear. (Courtesy of the Boston Public Library; photograph by FayFoto/Boston.)

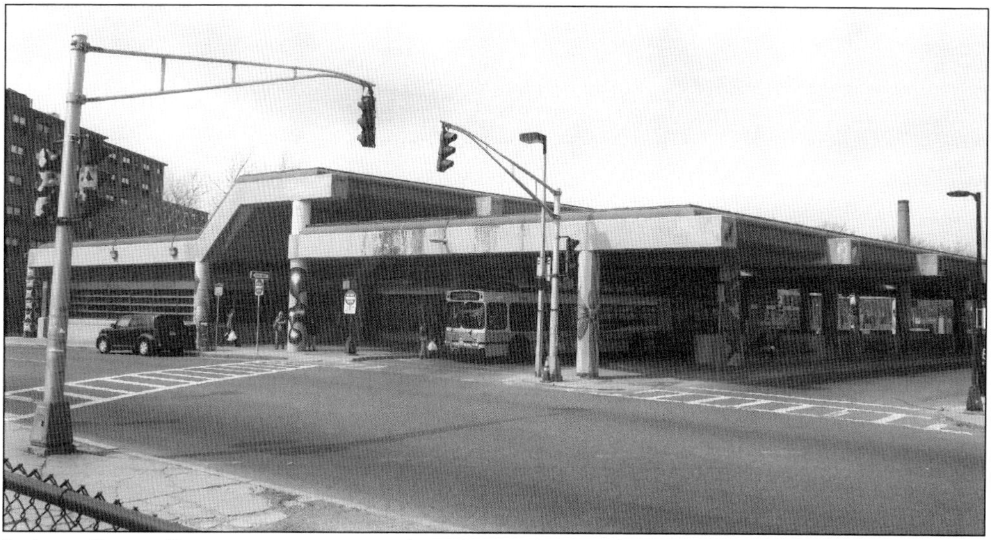

Jackson Square Station was constructed on Centre Street adjacent to the Bromley-Heath public housing project, which is partly visible at far left. In 2004, exterior pillars supporting the station's roof were painted with fanciful designs by local artist Roberto Chao and a group of 10 young people from the Hyde Square Task Force as part of an effort to make the station more welcoming. (Photograph by Jeremy C. Fox.)

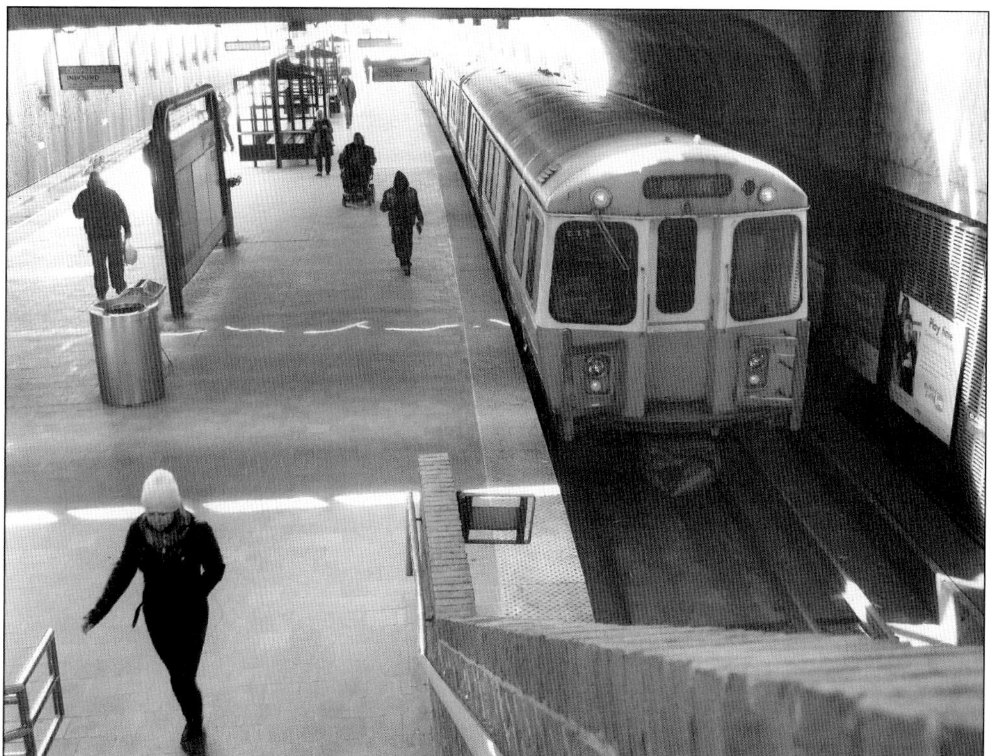

Passengers, including a man in a motorized wheelchair, depart an outbound train at Green Street Station. Like all the new Orange Line stations, and unlike the old Elevated stations, Green Street is fully accessible to people with disabilities. (Photograph by Jeremy C. Fox.)

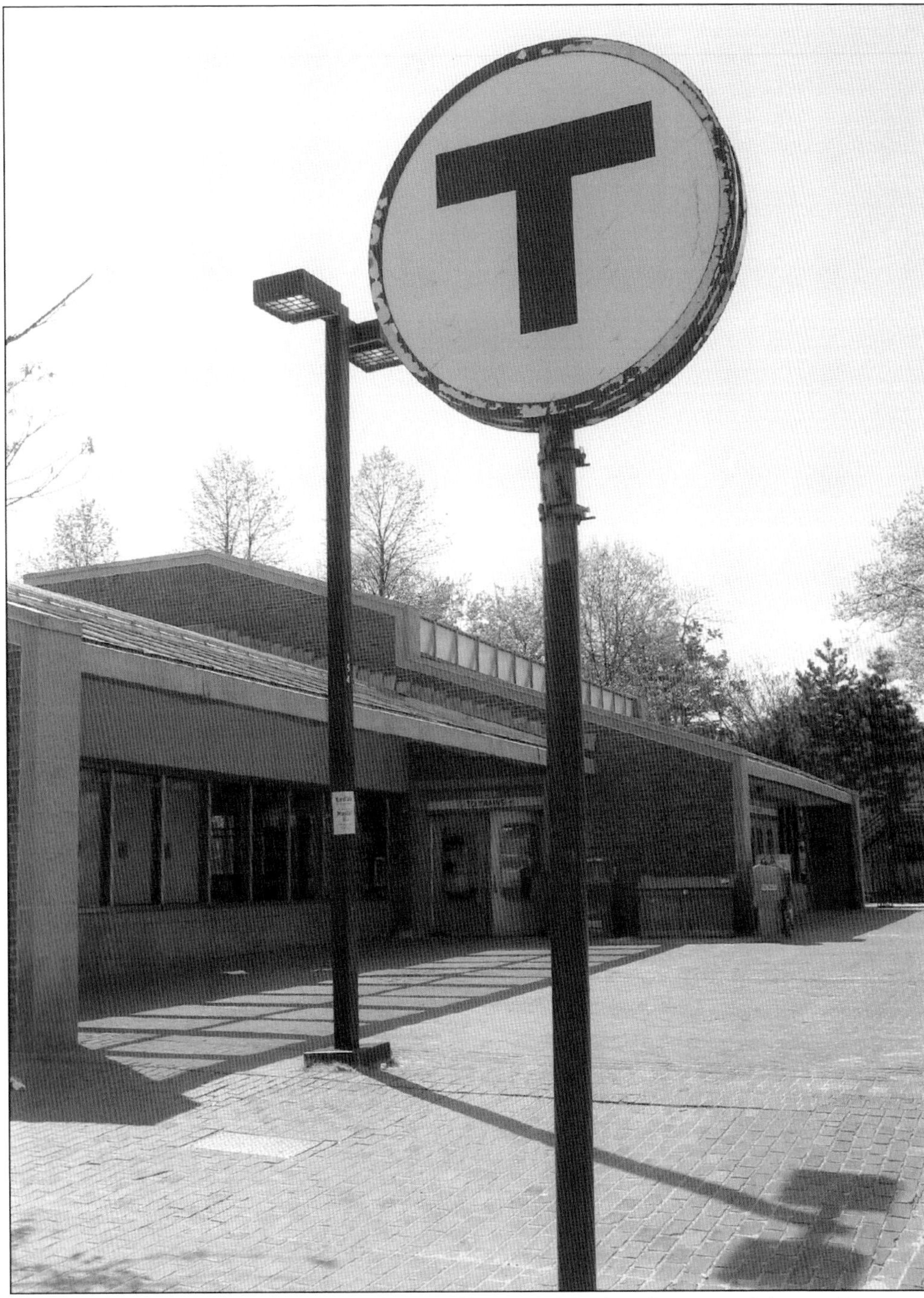

The new Green Street Station was constructed between Woolsey Square and Amory Street in a largely residential area of Jamaica Plain three blocks northwest of the Elevated Green Street stop and about two-fifths of a mile from the neighborhood's main business district on Centre Street. (Photograph by and courtesy of Andrew Lynch.)

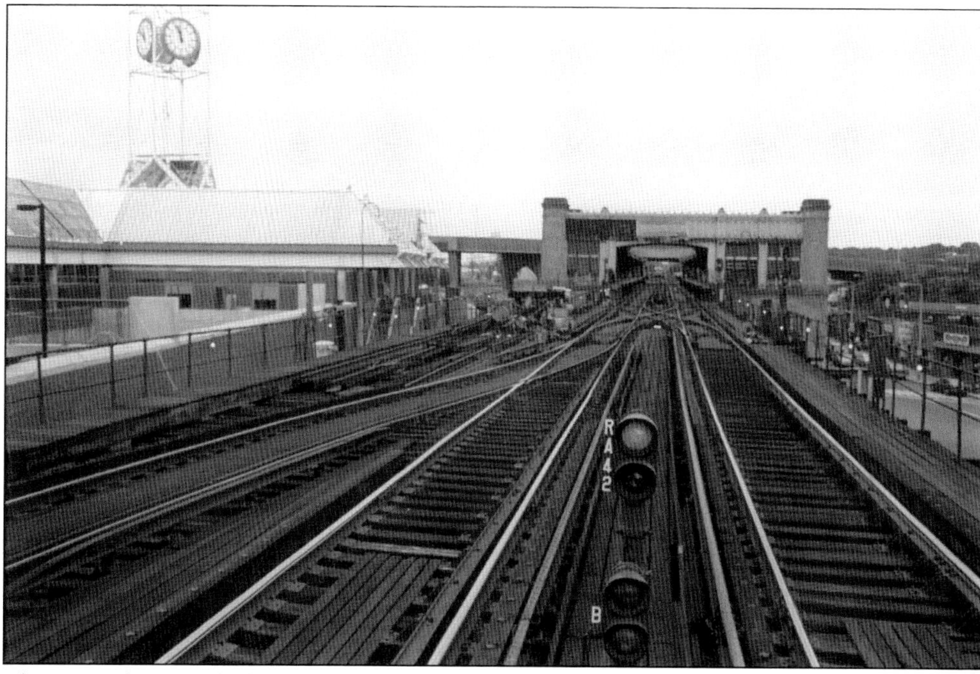

This 1986 photograph shows the newly constructed Forest Hills Station (left), with the station's distinctive clock tower, alongside the original 1909 station and Hyde Park Avenue (right). After the new Orange Line opened along the Southwest Corridor, the old station was torn down, and the space reused as a busway. (Photograph by and courtesy of David Akiba.)

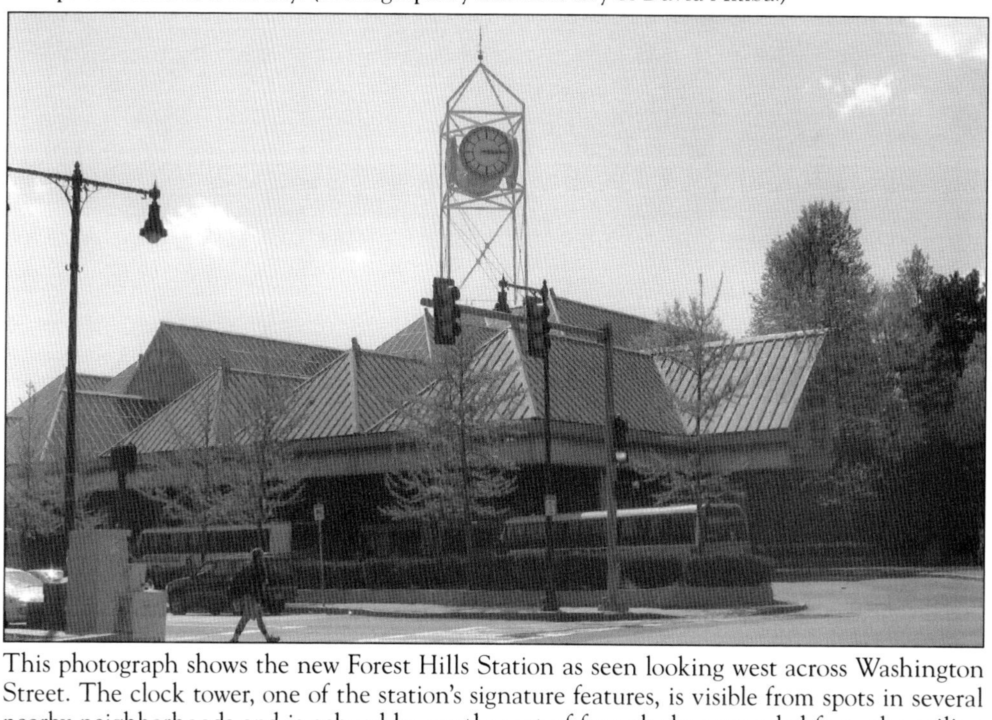

This photograph shows the new Forest Hills Station as seen looking west across Washington Street. The clock tower, one of the station's signature features, is visible from spots in several nearby neighborhoods and is echoed by another set of four clocks suspended from the ceiling inside the station. (Photograph by and courtesy of Andrew Lynch.)

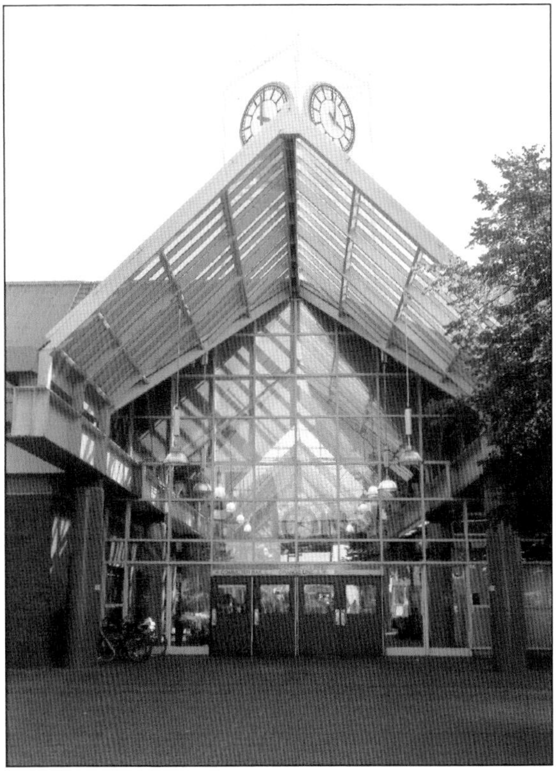

In contrast to the original, monolithic Forest Hills Station, the new station is light and airy, with large sections of glass that flood it with sunlight. Its architects, Cambridge Seven Associates, designed the structure to resemble the greenhouses of surrounding parks. The northern entrance (pictured) leads to a busway and the former Arborway stop on the Green Line, which closed in 1985. (Photograph by and courtesy of Nathaniel Marsh.)

Looking north from Forest Hills, this view shows the Orange Line progressing south along the Southwest Corridor adjacent to Commuter Rail tracks, with the city skyline above, showing some of the areas serviced by the line. Just left of center are the Prudential Tower and 111 Huntington Avenue, both near the Massachusetts Avenue stop, and at right is Hancock Place, near Back Bay Station. (Photograph by Jeremy C. Fox.)

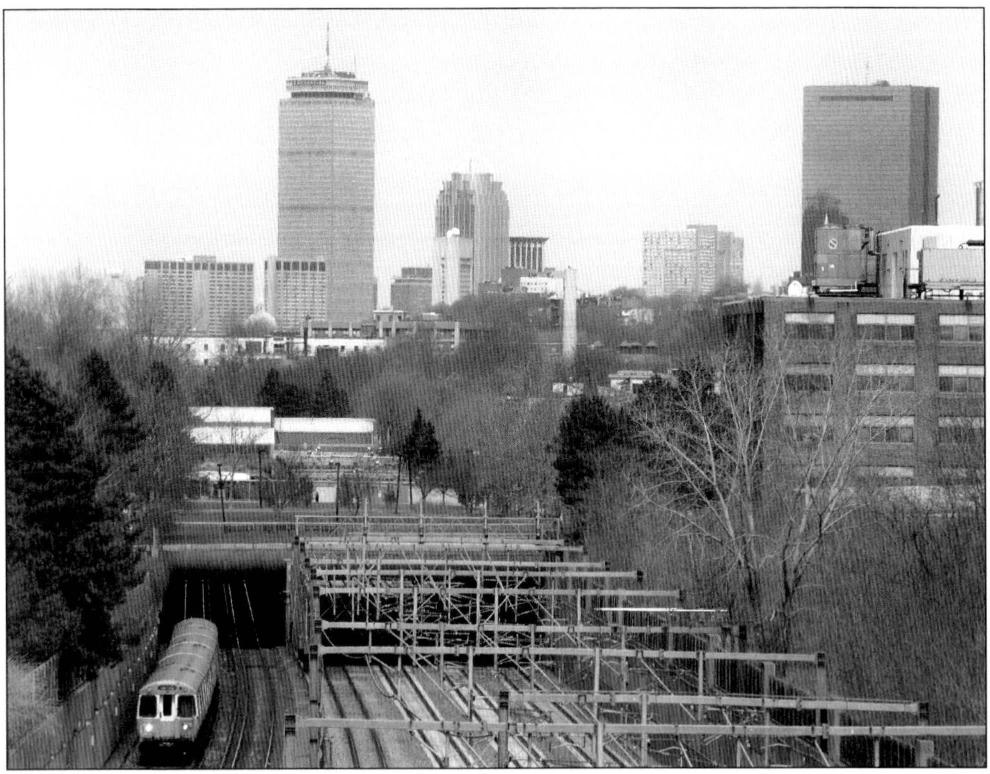

BIBLIOGRAPHY

Annual Report of the Board of Public Trustees of the Boston Elevated Railway Company. Boston: Boston Elevated Railway Company, 1937–1945.

Berchen, William, and Ursula Berchen. *Aspects of Boston*. Boston: Houghton Mifflin Company, 1975.

Boston Elevated Railway Co: Investigation, 1916: Arguments and Exhibits. Boston: Boston Elevated Railway Company, 1916. Internet resource.

Cheney, Frank, and Anthony Mitchell Sammarco. *When Boston Rode the El*. Charleston, SC: Arcadia Publishing, 2000.

Clarke, Bradley H. *The Boston Transit Album*. Cambridge, MA: Boston Street Railway Association, Inc., 1977.

———. *Transit Boston: 1850–1970*. Cambridge, MA: Boston Street Railway Association, Inc., 1970.

Hunnewell, James F. *A Century of Town Life: A History of Charlestown, Massachusetts, 1775–1887*. Boston: Little, Brown, 1888.

Lupo, Alan, Frank Colcord, and Edmund P. Fowler. *Rites of Way: The Politics of Transportation in Boston and the U.S. City*. Boston: Little, Brown and Company, 1971.

Massachusetts Bay Transportation Authority. *Southwest Corridor Project*. Boston: Massachusetts Bay Transportation Authority, October 1982.

Nolan, Martin F. "Tracking History this Week Marks the End of the Line for the El. as the New Orange Line Prepares to Open, One Chapter of the City's Story—Complete with Villians, Heroes and Urban Intrigue—Comes to a Close and an Equally Compelling One Begins." *Boston Globe*, April 26, 1987.

Price, Mike. "Jamaica Plain and I-95." *Urbanaction* (Spring 1970). Cambridge, MA: M.I.T. Urban Action.

Sammarco, Anthony Mitchell. *Boston's South End*. Charleston, SC: Arcadia Publishing: 1998.

Southwest Corridor News: Southwest Corridor Project Newsletter. Boston: Massachusetts Bay Transportation Authority, 1985–1987.

Zaitzevsky, Cynthia. *Historical Documentation: Boston Elevated Railway Company: Washington Street Elevated Mainline Structure (MBTA Orange Line)*. Washington, DC: Historic American Engineering Record, National Park Service, Dept. of the Interior, 1987.

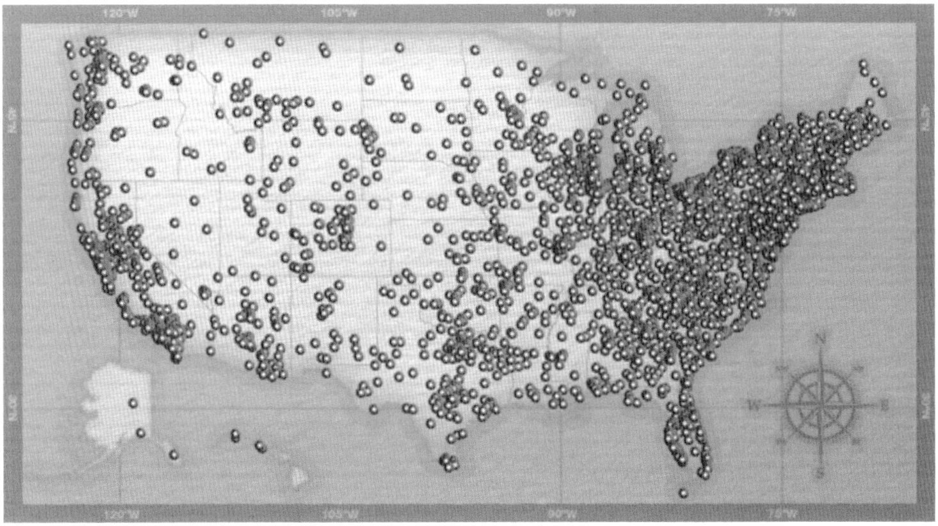